The European Dream

WALTER GERHARD SCHWIMMER

continuum
LONDON • NEW YORK

CONTINUUM
The Tower Building, 11 York Road, London SE1 7NX
15 East 26th Street, New York, NY 10010

www.continuumbooks.com

First published 2004
Reprinted 2004

British Library Cataloguing-in-Publication Data
A catalogue record for this book is available from the British Library.

ISBN: 0-8264-7637-6

Typeset in Adobe Minion by Tony Lansbury, Tonbridge, Kent.
Printed and bound in Great Britain by MPG Books Ltd, Bodmin, Cornwall.

For my wife, Martina, who helps me unfailingly, not just with sound advice and by sharing my European dreams, but also, as a superb hostess, with her own special brand of 'goulash diplomacy'.

For my grandchildren, Julia and Georg, in the hope that the Europe they live in will be broader, peaceful and free of dividing lines.

*'Without dreaming of a better Europe,
we shall never build a better Europe.'*

Vaclav Havel, speaking in the
Council of Europe's Parliamentary
Assembly on 10 May 1990.

Contents

Foreword

As the first, and now the largest, of Europe's institutions, the Council of Europe has played a vital role in realizing the dream of bringing peace and stability to this continent. Created in the aftermath of the Second World War, the Council has worked tirelessly to turn the vision of a united Europe into reality and to enshrine human rights, parliamentary democracy and the rule of law in the psyche of its Member States and citizens. The potency and allure of this vision has not waned. Since the end of the Cold War, countries from eastern and central Europe have also made the necessary reforms in order to be able to share in it. It is, therefore, very appropriate that Dr Schwimmer should have entitled this book 'The European Dream'.

It is also very appropriate that Dr Schwimmer should have weaved so much of his own experiences and family history into this book. In so doing he underlines what is true for all of us as citizens of Member States belonging to, or aspiring to, the Council of Europe – that Europe's history is our history, and its future is ours too. In approaching his chosen subject matter in this way, Dr Schwimmer manages to guide the reader smoothly through the intricacies, twists and turns of European politics and its institutions.

In as much as the *The European Dream* is a retrospective soliloquy from a respected European politician and diplomat, it is also a confident piece of analysis of the challenges and issues facing the continent in the years and decades to come. Dr Schwimmer, as leader of what he refers to as a 'convoy' of Member States travelling along the same road, offers his vision of where this road should lead and alerts his readers to the pitfalls along the way.

As European Commissioner for External Relations, I share many of his views including that this year's historic enlargement of the European Union from 15 to 25 Member States should not create new dividing lines on our continent. While Romania and Bulgaria are already negotiating their accession to the EU, and still others are waiting in the wings, it is clear that the EU will never have as many members as the Council of Europe – not least because some members of the Council of Europe do not want to join the EU. This should not mean that the old lines of 'haves' and 'have nots' are just re-drawn elsewhere. The EU and the Council of Europe are complementary bodies. They dream the same dream. This is why the enlarged EU is so keen to extend its hand to its new neighbours, via the European Neighbourhood Policy. And so the EU together with the Council of Europe will continue to play a vital role in ensuring that in the future there will be what Dr Schwimmer calls 'one Europe'.

Brussels, April 2004

CHRIS PATTEN
European Commissioner
for External Relations

Instead of an Introduction:
the legend of Europa

Europe is a special continent with a special name – the name of an Asian princess whom Zeus, greatest of the gods, carried west to a new world. Poets from Homer on have given us their versions of her story. One of the earliest, Moschos of Syracuse, adds an extra twist by having her dream that the continents are vying for her favours. The myth itself is mysterious, and successive generations of scholars have tried to unravel its meaning. One of them, historian Wolfgang Schmale, seems to feel that this tale of a princess who has given her name to a continent – and possibly a dream – is, quite simply, inadequate. Indeed, he even suggests that a 'myth deficit' may prove fatal to the European project.[1]

It is certainly true that 'eurospeak' lacks poetry, and that today's myths are mainly of the nationalistic, chauvinistic, 'no-to-Europe' type. But my Europe is not the Europe that regulates the curve on bananas, quarrels over subsidies for farmers or fights for places on the Council or Commission. I still believe in dreams, especially the European dream – and, as Zeus loved Europa, so I love Europe. That is why I have taken Vaclav Havel's words, 'Without dreaming of a better Europe, we shall never build a better Europe' as my epigraph. And why I prefer to let Ovid's well-known lines from the *Metamorphoses* do duty for a drier, more conventional introduction:

Gentle he is, yet shrinks she ever from touching,
Till, emboldened, with flowers she ventures his mouth to approach.
Rejoicing, the amorous god, in hope of raptures still sweeter,
Repays with fierce kisses her hand, his shape scarce longer enduring.
He wantons about her, and sports through the neighbouring verdure;
Then stretches his form, white as snow, on the sea's yellow margin.
He sees her fear ebbing, puts forward his breast for caressing
To her maiden hand, then lowers his horns to receive

1

The fresh garlands she offers. Already the maid, little knowing
Who bows to receive her, mounts boldly the back the bull lowers.
Now behold how the god slips subtly away from the seashore,
First his treacherous foot in the next breaking wave slyly dipping;
Then, further advancing and breasting the surge with his booty,
He strikes for the main. She, seized with a doubt, gazes back
At the land left behind. One hand on a horn, one braced on his neck,
She reclines – and the wind makes a curve of her raiment.

Europe is a strange continent. Strictly speaking indeed, it is not a continent at all, but a mere peninsula tacked onto Asia, from where many of its first inhabitants undoubtedly came – from the forests of the North and the once fertile lands of the East – with literatures and religions following the same path. And yet, despite its huge variety – of features, landscape, languages and peoples – this smallest of the continents has achieved an unmistakable cultural identity.

NOTE:

1. Wolfgang Schmale, *Scheitert Europa an seinem Mythendefizit?* (Verlag Dr Dieter Winkler, Bochum), 1997.

CHAPTER ONE

One dream, many lives

Dreams recur: Europe at the turn of the millennium

'Round-number' birthdays, anniversaries and dates always have a special significance and fascination. This is true of centuries, seen either in *fin-de-siècle* or dawn-of-era terms, and even truer of millennia, of which the modern age has seen just two. People's basic attitudes determine whether they see an approaching new millennium as unknown and threatening, or new and challenging, and, the nearer it comes, the faster fears and hopes, apprehensions and expectations, gloomy prophecies and bright promises succeed one another. The connection between this mood and a merely mathematical or astronomical process may well be irrational, but the mood – or rather the many moods – involved do seem to prepare people for real changes, with hopes of a 'golden age' usually outweighing fears of disaster.

Millennium fears, millennium hopes

When I spoke at the opening of the Council of Europe's 27th art exhibition – actually two exhibitions: 'The Centre of Europe around 1000 AD' and 'Otto the Great, Magdeburg and Europe' – I drew a number of parallels between the turn of the first and the second millennia:

> 'A thousand years ago, people and their rulers were trying to achieve the very same things that people and their governments are trying to consolidate at the start of this third millennium. Then, many of them did not even recognise the goal; today, we see it clearly. In the meantime, of course, we have had, not a thousand years of stasis, but a long maturing process, marked by periods of despotism, nationalist upheaval, warfare and conflict – but also by periods of unity and co-operation.
>
> In the early Middle Ages, relations between the peoples already established in the centre of Europe and the successive new arrivals from the East were changing all the time – peaceful interaction one moment, open warfare the next. As

time went on, new life patterns – trade instead of pillage, Christianity instead of paganism – emerged and became the basis of shared cultural and political development. Gradually, acceptance of the new ideas bred a desire for unity. Finally, around the turn of the millennium, that wish took concrete shape, when the Ottonian rulers set out to create a new version of the Roman Empire.

In our own era too, after a prolonged period of conflict unleashed by various totalitarian regimes, the peoples at the centre of Europe[1] can again look to a new vision – a vision rooted in shared values and consolidated by ever-closer co-operation.'

Imperial revival: from Rome to Europe

The efforts made to achieve unity and community in Europe around the year 1000 present a fascinating spectacle. They were fuelled by two great ideas. The first was Charlemagne's vision of a revived Roman Empire, which was realised when he was crowned Emperor on Christmas day in the year 800. This vision underlay his own policy, and that of the Ottonian emperors, particularly Otto III. The second was Christianity – still a novelty both for the Ottonian emperors in Saxony and for their Slav and Hungarian neighbours in the East.

Together, these two ideas brought Mediterranean civilisation to the north and east as something the whole continent could share. This explains Otto the Great's proud boast to 'his' Romans that he had extended the Roman Empire further in both those directions than any of his predecessors.

The ideal of an empire which would bring peace (like the old *pax romana*) and which shared Christian values to the whole of known Europe found ready acceptance at the turn of the millennium, when the Magyar and Avar wars had recently swept over large parts of Europe, sowing havoc and misery, with victors and vanquished switching roles repeatedly.

Paradoxically, the growth of the imperial idea and the spread of Christianity – both powerful centralising forces – went hand-in-hand with the emergence of modern states, based on the peoples of eastern central Europe, who had now entered the European story. In 955, Christians and Magyars had clashed on the Lech. Now, a shared ideal had reconciled the former foes.

And so the year 1000 saw kings crowned in Hungary and Poland, and their peoples, or at least ruling classes, converted to Christianity, or at least baptised. The Emperor and Pope stood joint sponsors at the birth of these states, with Otto crowning the Polish King at Gniezno, and the Pope officiating in Hungary. The inspiration behind the new kingdoms is reflected in the word for king, a new term for a new office: Korol, Kral or Kiral – a straight derivation from Karl or Charlemagne, King of the Francs and Holy Roman Emperor. These new nations, and also the old ones, some of them barely emerging from the inchoate legacy of the old Roman Empire and the great migrations, would – with their eastern neighbours, who took their first step towards nationhood at much the same time – shape the next 1000 years of European history.

In spite of the conflicts, disputes, wars, and relapses into barbarism and genocide that Europe has seen in the last thousand years, the sense of a community – not just cultural, but political too – has somehow survived, inspiring countless Europeans to work for a *pax europeana*, and cultivate values with the power to bring people together.

In fact, none of the great cultural movements has ever been confined within national frontiers: when the Renaissance and Enlightenment burst upon Europe, they burst upon all of it, and toleration and democracy have been pan-European ideals from the outset.

A century of extremes

The century which preceded the dawn of the third millennium was a century which added two world wars, unspeakable atrocities, the wholesale slaughter of Europe's Jews, the liquidation of entire social classes, and the brutal expulsion of millions of people from their homes to humanity's fratricidal legacy. Most of this occurred in the first half of the 20th century, but the second half had its horrors too. The Iron Curtain, the crushing of liberation movements, the Berlin Wall, the gunning-down of fugitives attempting to cross it, and finally the things that no longer seemed possible – the savage wars in the former Yugoslavia and Chechnya – these too were part of the 20th century.

But the 20th century also saw the birth of a movement which looked at the past, and took from it neither doom-laden visions of a world hastening to destruction nor blind belief in a golden age to come. Instead, it took from it the lesson that unity, community and coexistence offered real hopes of a better future, and set out to realise a dream which had in it something of the ideal that people had been chasing at the turn of the first millennium. There is one difference, however: the people of the third millennium have outgrown the need for myths, for visions of a revived Roman Empire and *pax romana*.

What they do need, like their ancestors a thousand years ago, are shared values which allow them to dream a shared dream – and realise it together. European co-operation and unity, and the institutions founded to promote them, are rooted in traditions which developed west of the Iron Curtain, but are also a magnet for the heirs and successors of the fallen communist regimes in the East – and indeed a part of their own true identity. Both

Hitler and Stalin failed in their terrible attempts to substitute despotic ideologies, which treated individuals as worthless, for European principles – division of powers, law-based government – which ultimately derive from the conviction that every human being is unique. Apart from a few political mavericks (the West has them too), no one in the East is now likely – in principle, at least – to question the validity of our shared belief in democracy and human dignity. The old, autocratic communists have been replaced by new-style socialists, social democrats and even liberals, who have actively supported, and sometimes been the driving force behind, their countries' accession to the Council of Europe – once denounced as a capitalist tool of the US imperialists. They, like yesterday's dissidents (today's political rivals), have raised no objection as democratic structures have replaced the old communist machinery. In the former Warsaw Pact countries, there is broad agreement on joining NATO and the EU; indeed three – Poland, the Czech Republic and Hungary – are already in NATO, and the Baltic states, as well as Bulgaria, Romania, Slovakia and Slovenia, will be joining shortly.

We may no longer have a common religion, but the new ideas are still rooted in the old ones – in the Judeo-Christian and humanist traditions, in which human rights, the rule of law, division of powers, and accountable, democratic government are implicit. These new ideas have power to make the dream – the European dream – come true.

The age-old dream – my responsibility

As parallels with the turn of the first millennium show, this dream is an old one – probably older than anyone can estimate. Indeed, visions of a realm of universal peace were already one of the threads in Europe's earliest myths and legends, which reflected a longing to live in harmony with all known peoples near and far, without loss of separate identity. Many generations and many individuals dreamed this dream – usually, alas, briefly and in vain. When disaster struck, they saw it in terms of the mythical catastrophes, the apocalyptic twilight of the gods, that had to come before the golden age could dawn – but the golden age itself never came any closer.

Inevitably, when we think in apocalyptic terms, we think of the millions who died in the Second World War, and of those who caused the slaughter – the dictators who set themselves up as gods or idols, with power to decide who was human or sub-human, worthy or unworthy to live. But it was not higher powers which finally put an end to the horrors and the darkness, and brought the false gods down. It was people themselves – the people who rose against injustice, the people who fought to liberate Europe, and finally the people who not only raised Europe from the ashes, but gave it a new democratic society. In that new dawn, there were also a few visionaries who thought beyond the next day's meal and, amid the post-war ruins, took up the age-old dream of unity and at last breathed life into it.

The first step towards realisation of that dream was taken when the Council of Europe was founded in London on 5 May 1949. Although the Council was not to remain the only embodiment of the ideal of European unity, and although other organisations, established for specific purposes by the same founding fathers, were to develop more vigorously, it remained – and still remains today – the only institution with a clear pan-European mission. No European country, no European people, which shares the dream of a golden realm of peace – or, as today's politicians put it more prosaically – a common area of democratic security and guaranteed human rights, is debarred from joining it. But, just as Europeans had to act themselves to defeat the powers of evil in the Second World War, so today's Europeans – the 800 million people who live in the Council of Europe's member states, and are covered by the European Convention on Human Rights – must not wait for higher powers to make the dream come true, but must do the job themselves.

On 23 June 1999, I was elected for a five-year term as Secretary General of the Council of Europe by its Parliamentary Assembly, i.e. by the elected representatives of the then 41 (now 45 of a potential 47) member states of the first and only pan-European organisation. This gave me the task of leading the Council into the third millennium. For me, this is a political, moral, personal and almost mystical challenge. For five – as I believe, decisive – years, the European dream has become my responsibility.

Dreamland or dungeon: multi-ethnic Austria – a model for a united Europe?

'The three highest elected offices in the Council of Europe are now held by Austrians – why do you think that is?' I am sometimes asked whether Austrians have a special talent for European politics. And it is true that Erhard Busek, Franz Fischler, Wolfgang Petritsch, Peter Schieder, Herwig van Staa[2] and I are all Austrians, and all active on the European political scene – quite a score for a small country like ours. I am sure that this closeness to Europe, this instinct for its needs and problems, does indeed have something to do with our national past. If the experts are right, and it is not political or natural frontiers, but a 'shared destiny', which makes Europe, then this symbiotic relationship with Europe is our special destiny as Austrians.

From the Carolingian *Mark* under the Babenbergs and the first mention of 'Ostarrichi' in 996, from Rudolf of Habsburg to Franz Joseph, and

finally Karl I – the story has been a long one. Between the election of the
first Habsburg as Holy Roman Emperor in 1273 and the resignation of the
last Austrian Emperor in November 1918, vast quantities of water flowed
under the Danube bridges. In the intervening centuries, there were many
successes, but more than a few disasters as well.

The fact that the Habsburgs took power in central Europe in the high
Middle Ages, under Albrecht V (King Albrecht II), and ruled, almost without interruption, until 1806, has left its mark on our continent, and on the
people who live in it. If Austrians really have Europe 'in their blood', this
may have something to do with the fact that the Dual Monarchy was, as a
multi-ethnic state, a partial forerunner of a united Europe. Or was it?

It is hard to answer this question without a little history. I have no wish
to bore my readers with dates – but a few significant ones are still needed
to make the story clear.

From the edge to the centre

Reporting on the opening of the Council of Europe exhibition 'The
Centre of Europe around 1000 AD', a respected German paper pointed out
– with, perhaps, a touch of malice – that Austria around the year 1000 had
been little more than a Bavarian fief. It is certainly true that Austria was
then a peripheral entity, and I shall have more to say about that later.

In the year 800, Charlemagne, a German of Frankish descent, and certainly the first potentate to envisage western unity, was crowned Emperor
by the Pope in Rome. He had palaces at Aachen, Paris and Regensburg,
and none of them took precedence. He was, in other words, a pan-
European ruler (admittedly under the social and political conditions of
his time). Because his heirs were unable to agree, his empire was later
divided into three – the Gallo-Roman west, the Germanic east and the
central kingdom, which went to his eldest son, and was named
Lotharingen or Lorraine after Lothar, his grandson.

Around the year 1000 – when the Ottonians held sway in the Holy Roman
Empire – the first Babenbergs emerged in the *Mark* (march or border-
land), a kind of precursor of modern Austria. The 'Danube marches',
essentially controlled by Bavaria and Franconia to start with, formed only
part of the area covered by Austria today. A small border region on the
eastern edge of the Empire – between Bohemia, Hungary and Carinthia –
they were destined to play a huge part in Europe's future.

The next important development came in 1156, when the *Ostmark* (a
term which acquired a special meaning in the 19th and 20th centuries, but
is never used of the Babenberg territories in medieval sources) was raised
to a duchy at the Imperial Diet in Regensburg under Frederick Barbarossa

– a mighty medieval ruler who, allowing for differences in the general context, almost looks like a prototype pan-European politician.

Barbarossa's son and heir died at the early age of 32, and the Staufen empire crumbled. His grandson, Frederick II, was raised as an orphan in Sicily, and the Kingdom of Sicily later became his chief interest, with Germany – the empire – paling into second place.

The ensuing period of conflict and turmoil lasted until 1273, when the Prince Electors met in Frankfurt and chose Rudolf of Habsburg as their ruler. He was crowned in Aachen shortly afterwards. The curtain had risen on the first act of the epic Habsburg drama – and the play was set for a long run.

The Habsburgs – a dynasty conquers Europe

Rudolf turned the acquisition of power into a family matter for the Habsburgs, embarking on a policy of strategic marital alliances (*'alii belli gerunt, tu felix Austris nube'*). In a word, he laid the foundations of his dynasty's future rise in Europe. But his was not yet an empire on which the sun never set.

Rudolf died in 1291. Nearly 150 years – and a few non-Habsburg emperors – later, the next significant Habsburg ruler came on the scene, in the person of Albrecht II. The 'House of Austria' was first mentioned under Duke Frederick the Fair – showing that something akin to Austrian identity (admittedly only acknowledged by certain social groups) had already emerged by 1350.

In 1452, Frederick III became the first Habsburg to be crowned Emperor in Rome (the last time the ceremony was held in the Eternal City). Historians credit him with no special talents as a ruler, but he still laid the foundations of the future Habsburg state. His vocalic mantra, AEIOU, *'Austria erit in orbe ultima'* (Austria's sway will extend to the ends of the earth) has a triumphal ring, but has also attracted criticism. Literary historian Claudio Magris, for example, sees it as a symbol of the whole Habsburg system's political clumsiness, rigidity and inflexibility. Habsburg and AEIOU – shorthand for incompetence and wisdom combined, but also a survival strategy, a sign of both grandeur and decadence.

In the Middle Ages, at least, the kind of bulldog obstinacy shown by the Habsburgs held the only political key to survival. Frederick's son, Maximilian I (1493–1519), was reputedly the last Emperor to embody the old chivalrous virtues (the 'last knight'). Pursuing an astute marital policy, he sought and won the hand of Maria of Ghent, thus extending his influence to Burgundy. This was a further step towards Austrian dominance – but also a source of permanent conflict with France.

The next step was taken when Maximilian's son, Philip (the Fair), married Joanna (the Mad), heiress to the throne of Spain. Her son, Charles V, thus inherited not only Burgundy, but also Spain (and the Spanish possessions overseas). His was indeed an empire on which the sun never set.

Charles' possessions were immense, but there was still no question of Europe's functioning as a single unit. Although there was one ruler, the territories he ruled were far from united. When the Pope crowned him Emperor in 1530, Charles was, to all appearances, the ultimate embodiment of the great imperial idea. But the real picture was one of savage local conflicts, quarrelling heirs and desperate efforts to quell the rise of Protestantism. Charles was determined to keep his possessions 'whole', and saw the battle for Christian unity as one which demanded 'all my lands, my friends, my body, my blood and my soul'. He set out to hold the Empire together by preserving Christian unity – and failed. In 1556, recognising that his ideal of universal rule in the West was no longer tenable, he renounced his crown.

The Habsburgs lived on and continued to rule – although the emphasis shifted to the East. Charles' brother, Ferdinand I (representing the Austro-German Habsburgs), was chosen King of Bohemia and Hungary in 1526. In essentials, the court-based state he created was to last until 1848.

Let us now leap ahead to the year 1648, when the map of Europe was redrawn, after the Thirty Years War, by the Peace of Westphalia, and the borders shifted. As for 'Felix Austria', the Austrian state now counted for more than the German Empire, although people then – and for many decades afterwards – thought above all of Vienna and the Danube lands when they thought of 'Austria'.

After a period of turbulence, Austria's victory over the Turks (repulsed in 1683, as once before in 1529, at the very gates of Vienna) revived the Habsburgs' fortunes in Europe: with the Turks defeated, and the French no longer dominant, Austria emerged as a mighty power at the heart of the continent.

Admittedly, diversity (of culture, language, and interests), not unity, was the hallmark of this power. Maria Theresa made uniting the Habsburgs' hereditary lands the main aim of her policy. Although history remembers her as 'Empress', it was actually her husband, Franz Stephan von Lothringen, who was elected and bore the imperial title (1745–1765). While she reigned, and in spite of all her efforts, the Habsburg Empire remained a conglomerate of over 12 nations, covering Germans, Italians, Czechs, Croats, Slovenes, Slovaks, Hungarians, Poles, Ukrainians, Serbs, Romanians, Ruthenians and numerous other minorities – and the differences between these peoples were immense.

A major power – with many faces

Joseph II, Maria Theresa's son, reigned from 1765 to 1790, and was probably the first Habsburg to try to gain a face-to-face knowledge of 'his' peoples, when – as Count Falkenstein – he travelled incognito through his hereditary lands.

One of those peoples, the Poles, fell victim to the power-hungry machinations of their neighbours in 1772. Joseph realised that Austria alone was too weak to hinder the plan hatched by the Prussians (who had replaced the French as the Habsburgs' main enemy) and the Russians to carve up the Kingdom of Poland – and so claimed his share of the spoils instead. This first, tripartite division of Poland added the 'Kingdom of Galicia and Lodomeria', with Lemberg as its capital, to his royal possessions.

In 1795 – Franz II had now succeeded Leopold II as Emperor – Poland was wiped off the map. The Polish people re-emerged partly only in 1867, when some of their nobles started to participate in Austrian politics – as parliamentarians.

Under Maria Theresa, the Czechs, who had lost most of their ruling nobility in the Thirty Years War, were absorbed into Austria. Czech itself was looked down on as a peasant language. To unify the realm in practice, however, the laws also had to be published in that peasant language – and so Czech identity survived and national consciousness was able to develop (the fact that Bohemia became the monarchy's main industrial centre also helped the process).

All historians agree that the most important phase in the formation of the Austrian nation under the Habsburgs began in 1790.

A new constitution – and what it might have led to

In the revolutionary year of 1848, the Czechs demanded the Bohemian Constitution, i.e. their own state structure, comprising Bohemia, Moravia and Silesia, within the Habsburg monarchy. When the Imperial Parliament met in the small Moravian town of Kremsier (fear of the populace, who had sided with the rebellious Magyars, had driven the court from Vienna), a first attempt was made to envisage the monarchy as a *congeries* of separate nations. This idea, however, was allowed to drop.

This parliament was in fact the broadest ever elected, and held that record for another 50 years – in fact, the representative character which electoral reform had given it (all economically independent men, including labourers, but not servants, were entitled to vote) was not equalled until 1907. For the Czechs, however, even 1848 ultimately brought little change. The last phase in the emergence of the Czech nation came after

1867, when Hungary achieved the status of an independent kingdom, with its own constitution and government.

Joseph II's determination to make German the official language in Hungary had already caused unrest. The real problem was not the decision itself – the Hungarians already used various languages and many of them knew German – but the growing dominance of the German civil service, which probably made the Hungarian nobles fear for their privileges. Hungarian was accordingly promoted as the country's official language, ousting Latin, which was still in use. 1848, when the Austrians ostensibly triumphed, but the Hungarians claimed the moral victory, marked the high watermark of Hungarian national consciousness. In 1867, Hungary was finally recognised as a state and given its own government, albeit answerable to the Austrian Emperor as King of Hungary.

This was a constitutional monarchy, its only flaw being the fact that the strong emphasis on all things Hungarian was resented by non-Hungarians, who inevitably felt disadvantaged. Ultimately, the changes created a situation in which two minority groups within the monarchy – the Germans and the Hungarians – dominated the majority. When the monarchy's Slav peoples – Czechs, Slovaks, Slovenes, Croats and Rutherians – demanded the same rights as the Hungarians, the latter thought themselves imperilled, and the Emperor hastily withdrew the planned concessions.

And yet, the Constitution adopted on 21 December 1867, after the settlement with Hungary, might well have allowed the various nationalities to live together on an equal-rights basis under one roof, providing – as it did – solid guarantees of equality before the law, freedom of belief and conscience, inviolability of property and other basic rights for all citizens. Above all, Article 19, which declared that 'All peoples within the state shall have equal rights, and every people shall have an inviolable right to maintenance and preservation of its nationality and language', potentially held the key to peaceful, equal coexistence of the various nations.

This was at least true on paper – 130 years before the Council of Europe's Framework Convention for the Protection of National Minorities and its Charter for Regional or Minority Languages.

Importing the Balkan problem

But Europe was in turmoil once again. The Congress of Berlin, held in 1878, set out to create a new political order in the Balkans. Austria-Hungary was to occupy and administer the provinces of Bosnia and Herzegovina. The people in those territories all shared a language (Serbo-Croat), but not a religion – which was where the problems started. The Muslims in Bosnia would have liked to remain within the Ottoman

Empire, while the Serbs favoured annexation by Serbia. Only the Catholic Croats were willing to accept Austrian rule.

Bosnia and Herzegovina is a relatively new member of the Council of Europe, and my visits there have repeatedly shown me that there is still a general awareness – and indeed a certain appreciation – of the things achieved by the old Austrian administration (the same applies in other former Habsburg lands). At a time when other territories had been lost, acquiring Bosnia and Herzegovina was certainly a gain for the monarchy, but nationalist demands threatened trouble for the future. In fact, annexation in 1908 ultimately led to the First World War and to the collapse of the Dual Monarchy, seen by some as a refuge (by others – not necessarily rightly – as a dungeon). The Emperor Franz Joseph's heir, Franz Ferdinand, was initially bent on achieving good relations with Russia and Serbia. He had also been working out plans for reform of the Habsburg monarchy. 'Try it and see' was his motto. To the old double structure (the Austro-Hungarian monarchy), he intended to add a third element, comprising the monarchy's southern Slav territories (with special status for Bosnia and Herzegovina). He also envisaged a new federal structure, which would respect national identities and aspirations, and so help to counter 'Greater Serbian' ambitions.

But the old Emperor was opposed to all of this. And everything came to an abrupt end on 28 June 1914, when Franz Ferdinand and his wife were murdered in Sarajevo by the young Bosnian Serb, Gavrilo Princip. Austria reacted by declaring war on Serbia, and the federal plans already worked out for the monarchy went back into the drawer. An example of the projected changes was the language decree passed by Count Edward Taaffe's government, authorising the use of Czech as an official language, even in the German Sudetenland – which would have helped Czechs who knew both languages to make good careers in the civil service.

Federal Austria – plenty of theory, but no practice

These various attempts to re-emphasise non-German elements within the monarchy, and so achieve greater equality, were usually wrecked by local German opposition. And the German nation within the monarchy came up with its own demands as well.

Towards the end of the 19th century, Georg von Schönerer emerged as the leader of a radical German nationalist movement. He wanted to see Austria's German territories incorporated into the German Empire, which had come into being in 1871 (the old Empire had already been dissolved under Napoleon: in 1805–1806, the Treaty of Bratislava had recognised the full sovereignty of the German princes; on 6 August 1806, Franz II –

who, as Franz I, had been Austrian Emperor since 1804 – renounced his crown as Holy Roman Emperor of the German nation; in 1815, following Napoleon's defeat, the Congress of Vienna redrew Europe's national frontiers, with a view to achieving a balance between the five great continental powers – Prussia, Austria, Russia, the Netherlands and Spain).

Starting in the mid-1880s, Schönerer's followers added a radically anti-Semitic note to the programme. The Christian Socialist Party was founded around the same time. Led by Karl Lueger, it proclaimed its loyalty to Austria, but a basic anti-Semitism was again unmistakable.

Universal, equal, direct and secret suffrage was introduced in 1907, in the face of powerful opposition from the old feudal nobility, who saw it as a threat to their political influence. The Emperor is said to have hoped that the reform would weaken the conservative nationalists – and so temper disputes between the various national groups within the monarchy – but this hope was not realised. True, the mass parties came to power, but the German National Association succeeded in rallying numerous parliamentarians to its cause.

The social democrats (Karl Renner, Otto Bauer) also came forward with proposals on setting up an association of states with equal rights. Theory, but no practice. And the idea of a 'United States of Greater Austria' – a close friend of Franz Ferdinand's had canvassed this in a book – was no more successful. It was this clinging to old principles – principles which had suited the 17th and 18th centuries, and, even before that, had served the Habsburgs well – this failure to move with the times, which ultimately brought the monarchy down. The traditional governing class in the Habsburg state, thinking in supranational terms and representing nearly every population group, was not quick enough to sympathise with peoples who clung to their identities and wanted political freedom. The Hungarian settlement certainly worked well enough between 'Austrians' and Magyars, but was otherwise a political mistake, merely fuelling the jealousies of other groups.

The Danube Monarchy – was it really a dreamland, in which equal rights and national identities were promoted? Alas, it was nothing of the kind, even if – as I have said – there is still a definite and perceptible nostalgia for the old Austria, not just in Bosnia and Heřzegovina, but also in Krakow, Lemberg and Transylvania. Perhaps that old Austria might really have developed into a community of equal states, but it did not have (or no longer had) the energy to change. With nationalism gaining ground, the idea of giving the smaller peoples undue independence was already too frightening.

The Danube Monarchy – was it really a dungeon, in which repression and injustice were the norm? Here too, the answer is a categorical 'no'. In fact, as we have seen, the privileged position of the 'German' element, and the implementation of Habsburg administrative principles, did not really interfere with national development. A lack of administrative rigour – one might even (affectionately) say, the right dose of Austrian sloppiness – left countries ruled by the double-headed eagle room to cultivate their own identities.

Was the Danube Monarchy an early version of united Europe? Obviously not in the Council of Europe sense, since the necessary voluntary element was missing, but perhaps to the extent that – 1848 apart – this strange supranational entity did enjoy a kind of internal peace, however flawed. Despite the rise of nationalism, it helped to keep the dream of everlasting peace, in an 'empire' covering the whole of Europe, alive.

When the last German King and Roman Emperor accepted the Austrian imperial crown as Francis I in 1804, the implication was that – alongside the usurper Napoleon, and in spite of him – the Empire still existed, even if it had been 'shifted'.

Missed opportunities, obstinate emotions

The theoretical and organisational precursors of an association of equal states which existed sporadically under the Danube Monarchy were stifled at birth by contemporary developments. And, with their eyes fixed on national independence and identity, the peoples united within the common Habsburg home were essentially struggling to escape it. The undoubted opportunities inherent in the Habsburg brand of coexistence went unrecognised and unexploited.

We are left not with nostalgia, and certainly not with imperial ambitions, but with a sense of the ties that still bind us to peoples with whom we once shared so many joys and sorrows. I obviously love Rome, Paris and London, but in Prague and Budapest, in Agram/Zagreb, Laibach/Ljubljana and Bratislava/Pressburg, I feel doubly at home – as a European and as an Austrian.

Being 'on the edge of the centre of Europe' has its rational side – and its emotional side too. But perhaps it may also fit the people of this small country with a great past to accept responsibility for Greater Europe.

Realists and dreamers: the path to the common European home

At the turn of the first millennium, one thing certainly made life easier for people who were trying to realise the dream of unity: the existence of just one model – the Roman Empire, as revised by Charlemagne. Of course, belonging to the Empire carried certain obligations, above all (at least ostensibly) renouncing paganism and accepting Christianity. This has parallels in the criteria governing European enlargement, in both the Council of Europe and the EU, i.e. 'acceptance' of certain basic values, including pluralist democracy, the rule of law and human rights. Above all, belonging to the Empire brought security, enshrined in the *Pax Romana*. Looking at countries' reasons – above all, their emotional reasons – for wanting to join the EU today, the parallels are again striking. Many of the applicants are chiefly looking for security, anchored in a new *Pax Europeana*, itself partly overlaid by a *Pax Transatlantica*. Under the Empire, patchy acceptance of the new religion was certainly matched, for quite different reasons, by the patchy nature of the peace which followed. Let us hope that the parallels stop short of that.

Pax Europeana

And what about parallels when it comes to citizen involvement? The mass-baptised Hungarians, Poles and Czechs probably knew little or nothing about the Holy Roman Empire, for whose sake they were being forced to abandon the old gods. They could sense only dimly, if at all, why their rulers were adopting a new religion. Things are very different in today's mass-media age. Thanks to TV, radio and the press, we know what the EU Commission, Council, Presidency and Commissioners are saying, and get all the information we need on Maastricht, Amsterdam, Nice and Schengen. Of course, Schengen and the others are no longer mere place-names. For those in the know, 'Schengen' now denotes an EU treaty and the issues it covers. Only those who are not in the know are likely to be confused when they find that this treaty does not apply to all the EU states, but does apply to Norway (which has twice voted against joining the EU). The picture is complicated even further by the presence of the Western European Union, and finally the Council of Europe, which has been around for years, but whose links with the rest are not totally clear. (This probably explains why one European leader, whose country was occupying the EU Presidency, and so the Presidency of the European Council, proudly told his parliament that he was now President of the Council of Europe.) What, in heaven's name, is the difference? We also get huge amounts of information (is that really the word?) on the EU's plans to expand, adding 10 – and later 12 or 13 – new members to its previous 15. Just a moment! Surely the Council of Europe (we've heard of it somewhere) has far more members already – something like 40? It certainly does! In fact, since Armenia and Azerbaijan joined in January 2001, Bosnia and Herzegovina in April 2002 and Serbia and Montenegro in April 2003, it has 45. Armenia and Azerbaijan! And Russia's in too! So what's all this about enlargement to the East? Surely our ancestors, back in the year 1000, must have had a clearer picture of what was going on?

The European home – too many architects?

The structure of the common European home is indeed confusing. When he coined the image, Mikhail Gorbachev was probably thinking more of the roof than of all the things which the architects, builders, experts and occasional botchers, who are beavering away on the plans today, would try to put under it. At least the building has one flag – and one anthem too. Like Beethoven's *Ode to Joy*, which is the European Anthem, the blue flag with its 12 gold stars was originally a Council of Europe emblem, and is now universally used by the EU as well (it even appears on the European Central Bank's euro notes). If we want a clue to guide us through this labyrinthine structure, we at least have the flag and the anthem to remind us of the founding dream – the dream of a united Europe. But a dream as a blueprint? Dreamers as architects? No wonder the house seems so confusing when new designers keep turning up with new visions, with new and conflicting ideas on converting or extending it. No wonder the managers at the project meetings (or 'summits') cannot agree on what to do next – complete the interior or extend the building first?

Does this mean that the sceptics are right – the ones who come flocking to warn us that our architects are sleepwalkers, charlatans or even pied pipers, that the building itself will become a Tower-of-Babel nightmare, and leave Europeans with a dungeon, not a dream home?

From the very beginning, this debate between 'realists' and 'dreamers', sceptics and visionaries, nationalists and federalists, isolationists and Europeans, has dogged the dream of European unity. Both the idealists, like Richard Coudenhove-Kalergi, founder of the Pan-European Movement, who preached European union immediately after the First World War, and the hard-headed realists, like Gustav Stresemann and Aristide Briand who, not content with trying to reconcile their countries, actually produced a memorandum on the 'United States of Europe' (Churchill's Zurich phrase in 1949), were derided. The same fate overtook the 16 'Christian' parties which, at the prompting of Don Sturzo, the Italian Christian Democrats' great leader and Alcide de Gasperi's mentor, met at Bierville (Normandy) under Marc Sangnier, founder of the French *Parti Démocratique Populaire*, and adopted a programme entitled 'Mercato comune/Common market'. In the nationalistic climate of the inter-war years, their message went unheard – both by those still basking in an arrogant (but deceptive) sense of having won, and by those among the losers who had either despaired or were thirsting for revenge. Europe – and the world – had to pass through an even worse catastrophe before the dreamers got their chance. But the dreamers were there already: Alcide de

Gasperi as Secretary General of the Italian People's Party, Don Sturzo in exile, Robert Schuman as Marc Sangnier's ally, and Konrad Adenauer who, as Mayor of Cologne, hosted the 16 'common market' parties' last meeting in 1932, just before the Nazis seized power and sent everything hurtling in the opposite direction. In fact, Adenauer and Schuman had already met and discussed prospects for a united Europe in 1926.

Progress and regression

Even after the inferno of the Second World War, not everyone was convinced by the European idea – let alone inspired by it. The story of the founding of the various European institutions (and sometimes of the failure to found them, e.g. the aborted European Defence Community) is highly instructive here. National hesitations and national caution also stopped the first of those institutions, the Council of Europe, from moving faster and playing the bigger role actually intended for it. To that extent, being 'the first' was not necessarily an advantage.

The idea of founding a 'European Institution for Coal and Steel', for example, was first raised in August/September 1949 in the Council of Europe's Parliamentary Assembly – at the time the only (and thus central) forum for European union. The initial project was effectively talked out of existence, largely thanks to one member state – a state which later stayed out of the six-member Coal and Steel Community founded under the Schuman Plan, which only brought itself much later to join the EEC, continues to have major problems with EU enlargement (above all, the bogey of federalism), and which still holds back from European Monetary Union, i.e. the euro. Embryonic supranationalism was present in the Council of Europe's Assembly, but was totally alien to its Committee of Ministers, since the Organisation was intergovernmental (not supra-governmental), and national sovereignty was still paramount. At the Council, where the projected Coal and Steel Community and its supranational 'supreme authority' had slipped away and simply been implemented by Robert Schuman, European restrictions on national sovereignty were imposed indirectly, through basic conventions, like the European Convention on Human Rights and the European Convention against Torture. The European Cultural Convention (1954) and the European Social Charter (1961) were also trail-blazers in their day.

The fact that, with the one great exception of the European Convention on Human Rights, the Council of Europe was effectively kept on the back burner for the first 40 years of its existence (unlike the Coal and Steel Community, which evolved at breakneck speed into the EEC, the EC and finally the EU) is largely due to this lack of a supranational element in the political (non-human rights) sphere, but also to the fact that there were no tangible internal-market, i.e. economic, interests to help shield the Council from the braking effects of Euroscepticism.

Putting on the brakes: the Eurosceptics

Those effects were, and are, relatively powerful. They are the product of highly diverse motives, interests, emotions, fears and, all too often, imagined short-term political gains. Hardly surprising, then, that they also come in diverse guises – occasionally even slipping on an ostensibly pro-European mask. Sometimes they can be overcome or changed by argument. Sometimes they are reflected, more or less distinctly, in compromise solutions. But sometimes they also block progress. For example, clear acceptance of the Schuman Plan at the Council of Europe and its implementation in Strasbourg would have spelt acceptance of a uniform blueprint for European unity, making yesterday's, today's and tomorrow's Europe a very different one.

The abortive tug-of-war over a 'European Political Community' in the early 1950s, the controversy over Britain's (largely informal) Eden plan for an 'Atlantic Community' with very limited powers and the rival Pleven plan for a European Defence Community with supranational authority, and the unexpected vetoing of the latter by the French National Assembly, are other early examples of these effects at work. Part of the battle was fought out in the Council of Europe's Consultative (now Parliamentary) Assembly in the autumn of 1952 between the British Foreign Secretary, Anthony Eden, and the Italian Prime Minister and Foreign Minister, Alcide de Gasperi. The fact that members of the Assembly of the Western European Union – founded as a substitute for the European Defence Community – were required to be members of their national delegations to the Council of Europe shows that the various European projects were closely connected to start with, and at least intended to converge on the Council.

When the Council itself was founded, its own Statute was fiercely debated in the French National Assembly and also, for different reasons, in the German *Bundestag*. Unlike the European Defence Community five years later, however, it got a clear majority.

But opponents and sceptics could do nothing to hinder the further progress of European union: neither the unspectacular, but useful work done by the Council in many different areas – the Convention on Human Rights, the Bern Convention (one of the world's first environmental instruments) and the European Cultural Convention being just three examples – nor its integration of the new democracies into the 'family' after 1989. What opponents and sceptics did manage to do was to under-mine the unity of these endeavours, adding kinks and detours to the European path.

Change – and opportunity

The one great exception, at a time when Europe was trying to find its way (fortunately without straying too far off its course), was certainly the period immediately following the historic changes of 1989–1990. When the un-believable showed signs of happening, and then happened, Europe opened its eyes – not just to new members of its democratic family, but also to a clearer vision of its old objectives. The Council of Europe opened its doors (wide) to the East, and the other institutions also shifted their sights to 'geo-graphical Europe', instead of the old 'political Europe', which had stopped at the Iron Curtain. NATO and EU enlargement to the East suddenly became realistic goals. But unrealistic promises, disappointed hopes and new disputes over deepening or expanding, moving fast or more slowly, soon revived memories of the old zigzag Europe.

A final plan for the common European home had still to be adopted.

The baroness and the count: peace and Pan-Europa

The publication of Count Richard Coudenhove-Kalergi's book, *Pan-Europa*, in October 1923 and the parallel founding of the Pan-Europa Union are commonly seen as the start of the European movement. Of course, there were other associations and precursors, and the 'European idea' – the idea of uniting all the lands of Europe, more or less closely – was already centuries old.

As early as 1464, King Georg Podiebrad of Bohemia reacted to the fall of Constantinople (1453) by proposing that a community (*universitas*) of Christian Europe be founded – with an assembly of permanent represen-tatives, a council, its own staff and funding, and power to pass laws and give judgment. Better known is the utopian *Treatise on Everlasting Peace*, published by the Abbé Saint-Pierre (Charles Castel) in 1713, which pro-posed permanent institutions of 'European union' on Dutch, Swiss or German lines. That was the year of the Peace of Utrecht, which – like so many peace treaties before it – proved a mere staging post on the path to further wars. In other words, the project was at odds with its time: it was simply too good to be realised, as Jean-Jacques Rousseau remarked in dis-cussing it many years later, when he spoke of its author as a 'child'.

Equally at odds with their time, and so equally unrealistic, were various 19th-century projects, particularly the detailed constitutional arrange-ments which Claude Henri de Saint-Simon worked out (clearly with help from the historian, Augustin Thierry) in his book, *De la nouvelle organisa-tion de la société européenne* (1814). This was expressly aimed at the Congress of Vienna, from which he expected the worst: 'Everything you do will serve merely to provoke new wars – you will not put an end to them.' Indeed, at a time when 'concert of powers' and 'balance of power' were the dominant concepts, when nation-states were emerging and nationalism was rising, the European idea stood no chance of succeeding. Even Europe-minded geniuses like Giuseppe Mazzini and Victor Hugo could do no more than add 'United States of Europe' to their century's conceptual vocabulary.

'My fellow Europeans' – these were Victor Hugo's opening words in a message containing a lyrical vision of a 'European Republic', which he sent to the Lugano Peace Congress in 1872. These congresses (Hugo him-self had chaired the first in 1849) had become platforms for propagation of the European idea and milestones on the path to peace and disarma-ment. Ultimately, they anticipated the Pan-European Movement, which made working for a lasting peace in Europe its main task.

Ground arms!

A leading role was played in the movement by Baroness Bertha von Suttner who, as a young woman, had experienced the horrors of the 1866 war between Prussia and Austria in Bohemia at first hand. Her family was one of the oldest in Austria, but, shunning high society, she devoted her whole life to working to prevent further wars. Her book *Ground Arms* (1888) became a world bestseller. It was she who persuaded the inventor of dynamite, Alfred Nobel, to found the Nobel Peace Prize, which she her-self was awarded in 1905. In *The World of Yesterday*, Stefan Zweig describes meeting her in 1913: the old lady was deeply distressed – she had seen the writing on the wall and knew that war was coming.

The First World War was followed, like the Second, by a concerted effort to secure international peace through a global organisation – Woodrow Wilson's 'general and common family of the League of Nations', of which Immanuel Kant, in his epoch-making book, *Eternal Peace* (1795), had been one of the main intellectual forerunners. During the war and imme-diately afterwards, writers like Barbusse, Genevoix and Dorgelès described their experiences at the front with almost unbearable realism. 'No more war' was the message – and national peace associations drew up plans for an international peace-keeping organisation.

The League of Nations

The decisive impetus came from US President Woodrow Wilson's speech of 8 January 1918, in which he set out his 'Fourteen Points'. In 1919, he succeeded in having the statute of a 'League of Nations' approved and written into the various peace treaties, thus ensuring that the defeated countries would be bound by the League, even if they did not belong to it. The central element was a highly complex war-prevention or peace-keeping system, with sanctions (primarily economic, but military too, when necessary) as the chief means of enforcement.

The pacifist Richard Coudenhove-Kalergi was one of the Europeans who gave Wilson's plan and the action taken to realise it a whole-hearted welcome: the League of Nations, he wrote, embodied a 'great hope for the ideals of peace, freedom and human progress'. But these great hopes were disappointed. True, the League of Nations did produce some interesting ideas on economic co-operation, particularly in Europe (ideas which again became topical in 1945), but it soon proved a paper tiger in terms of its central mission. Only once did it manage to apply sanctions – against Italy at the time of the Abyssinian crisis in the 1930s – but by then its peace-keeping role had been discredited.

Also important was the fact that the League (unlike the later United Nations) never became universal. The USA itself rejected it from the outset, since Congress refused to ratify the founding treaty and thus the peace treaties as well. In other words, the country whose troops had ultimately decided the war stayed aloof from the organisation which she herself had inspired, looking on from the sidelines while it drowned in rhetoric. After the Second World War, Congress was wiser – but was also deeply aware that a new superpower, capable of threatening even the USA, had arrived on the scene.

Destination Pan-Europa

Disappointment over America's withdrawal in 1919 helped to fuel discussion of a regional peace-keeping system for Europe. This was Coudenhove-Kalergi's great moment. He was a notable, indeed impressive, figure. He was, Thomas Mann noted, 'the Eurasian embodiment of a noble cosmopolitanism, and unusually fascinating'. Born in Tokyo in 1894 to a Japanese mother and a multilingual father descended from a long line of north Brabantine and Greek nobles, he grew up in Bohemia. As he himself put it, he thought 'not in nations, but in continents'. Parliamentary democracy, however, meant nothing to him. Some of his ideas (an 'intellectual aristocracy', a 'social aristocracy of the intellect', an 'inter-social race of nobles') were undeniably strange. Turning first to elites, he always sought out the leading figures (including Mussolini).

At least in the 1920s, he distrusted the USA and Russia equally (he was, to use a Cold-War term, non-aligned).

'Neither the West nor the East will save Europe. Russia wants to conquer it, America to buy it. The path between the Scylla of Russian military dictatorship and the Charybdis of American financial dictatorship is a narrow one. This path is called Pan-Europa and it means: Europe's helping itself by uniting to form a political and economic interest association.'

This is what Pan-Europa is about, and, however alien Coudenhove-Kalergi's terminology may seem (it certainly helped to isolate him later), the profound effect of this manifesto in book form cannot be doubted.

Why did he choose the purely descriptive term 'Pan-Europa'? Even then, more expressive, more politically meaningful terms were in use: 'union', 'Federation of Europe' and, of course, 'United States of Europe'. Ultimately, 'Pan-Europa' denoted the final aim of the process he was proposing. But he wanted another label for the actual stage-by-stage process, fearing that an off-putting name might handicap it from the start. The endless and futile federation/superstate, yes/no discussions of the late 1990s and early 21st century show that, on this point at least, he was a realist and knew his politicians.

What's in a name?

The discussion, of course, still drags on today – and remains as bewildering as ever. In fact, the name an institution carries provides no real clue as to whether it is a federal state, an association of states or an ordinary international organisation. The term 'United States of America' was used in the Declaration of Independence (1776), at a time when there was still no question of a federal union of 13 colonies or states. The name 'United Nations' has never misled anyone into taking the UN for anything more than an international organisation. The Swiss Constitution still calls Switzerland a confederation (think of the CH plate on cars), although it has been a federal state since 1848. Finally, the European Council is an EC/EU body, but the Council of Europe (often confused with it, alas) is an independent international organisation, covering nearly all the countries of Europe.

Coudenhove-Kalergi identified various stages on the path to Pan-Europa. The first was to be a Pan-European conference, meeting at regular intervals, with its own secretariat and specialised committees on such issues as arbitration, guarantees, disarmament, minorities, transport, customs, currency, debts, and culture – but not border issues. The second stage was to be a general agreement on compulsory arbitration. Part of the plan was that states would guarantee one another's frontiers. Coudenhove-Kalergi was convinced that a clearly beneficial peace-keeping association of this kind would gradually attract all the countries of Europe. He wanted, however, to exclude the British Empire, fearing that its presence might embroil continental Pan-Europa in Asian and Pacific conflicts. He presumably felt that France's possessions in three continents were less likely to cause trouble – quite a mistake, when one thinks of the Moroccan and Lebanese risings in 1925, let alone the conflicts in Indo-China and Algeria, the effects of which still rumble on today. Only democratic states would be allowed to join – and so Russia, too, was excluded.

The third step was to be the gradual establishment of a customs union and uniform economic area, possibly accompanied by monetary union within a tighter circle of states ('enhanced co-operation' in modern EU terms). The whole project was to culminate in the founding of the 'United States of Europe', patterned on the USA, which would allow Europe to present a united front in its dealings with other continents and global powers.

The longing for peace

Here again, as so often in earlier centuries, the desire – indeed longing – for lasting peace in Europe was the prime driving force behind a plan for unity. Coudenhove-Kalergi himself declared that protection against further wars in Europe was the chief benefit that his proposed federation had to offer. He argued that current policies, if pursued, would inevitably lead to another calamitous European conflict. His programme was promising, but the opposition was still formidable. He knew who his adversaries were, and he named them – the nationalists and chauvinists, the communists, the militarists and the industries that owed their profits to protectionism. There were also the internationalists or world federalists, still under the League of Nations' spell – one type of Eurosceptic we no longer have today.

Nonetheless, with the help of the Pan-Europa Union, which he founded to promote his ideas (and of which he stayed President until the end of his life), he attracted considerable support. Aristide Briand became Honorary President in 1927 and held that office until 1932. His failed attempt in 1929–1930 to persuade the League of Nations to establish a European association (or community or union – Briand never committed himself to a title), with a conference, secretariat and political committee, was certainly part-inspired by discussions with Coudenhove-Kalergi. His scheme was well-meant, and made full allowance for national sensitivities, but most national leaderships failed to see that the old approach – League of Nations plus intergovernmental relations – was no longer enough. In any case, Briand was himself too wedded to the League of Nations to give the European idea the charismatic punch it needed.

Winston Churchill (who had himself produced a newspaper article on 'The United States of Europe' in 1930) referred to Aristide Briand in his

Zurich speech of 1946 – a fitting tribute to a man of good will who had tried, at a critical stage in what turned out to be a pause between wars, to show Europeans a way of averting fresh disaster.

After Austria's annexation by Nazi Germany (the *Anschluss*), Coudenhove-Kalergi went into exile in the USA. Returning to Europe in 1947, he found himself surrounded by new associations, founded in his absence and without his knowledge. Unwilling to accept a subordinate role, the elitist cosmopolitan became an increasingly marginal figure. He did, however, attend the celebrated Hague Congress in 1948 – he was not, in other words, entirely absent when the new 'united' (if far from 'one') Europe started to take shape. He died in 1972. His refounded Pan-Europa Movement still exists, and is led today by the son of the last Austrian Emperor, Dr Otto Habsburg who – paradoxically, or logically enough in European terms – for years represented, not his own country, but the Federal Republic of Germany in the European Parliament.

What do Europeans dream of? Is there a European consciousness?

The Council of Europe's 1949 Statute speaks of 'ideals and principles' which are 'the common heritage' of the European nations. The Maastricht Treaty speaks of 'European awareness'. And the EU Treaty itself uses the term 'European identity'. These are big, portentous words. But what really lies behind them? What does Europe mean to Europeans in practice?

By comparison with objective factors, consciousness is the subjective element in collective identity, which rests, as the famous French historian, Fernand Braudel, has put it, on 'residues, amalgams, additions and dilutions'. Europe's 'residues' are easily identified. They are the classical (Athens and Rome) and Judeo-Christian legacy. Byzantium (certainly a concept in all the languages of Europe), the imperial idea and the longing for a golden age were added later. Humanism and enlightenment, romanticism and pragmatism, are certainly part of the picture as well, as is, to a greater or lesser degree, Islam – from Moorish Spain through the Balkans to the Caucasus.

Nor must we forget Europe's seafarers, discoverers and empire-builders. It made no difference to the natives whether the strangers wading ashore on their coasts were Britons, Frenchmen, Dutchmen, Spaniards or Portuguese – they were all 'white men' from a faraway continent. Ever since, Europe has remained open to the rest of the world and brought a substantial dose of natural curiosity to all its undertakings – and openness has long ceased to be a mere synonym for conquest.

But have all these elements fused to an 'amalgam', forming the basis of a European identity? What we are considering here is in fact European

consciousness – a subjective state of being, which is also extensively influenced by the subconscious.

There are also, however, countless dark pages in Europe's history – wars of conquest and religion, repeated abuses of state sovereignty, and regular outbreaks of rabid nationalism. All totally negative, one might suppose. But these things can be seen in another light too: as shared traumas, offering a firm foundation for the building of a better, stronger edifice, and as perverted forms of a basically healthy patriotism.

Do a shared past and culture guarantee a shared future?

Only those who love themselves can really love others ('Love thy neighbour as thyself'!). This is why it has been said – not unreasonably – that people who love their own countries are likely to make the best job of building Europe. This is clearly true of the 'fathers' of European unity – founders and master-builders like Jean Monnet and Robert Schuman, Winston Churchill and Paul-Henri Spaak, Alcide de Gasperi and Konrad Adenauer, Walter Hallstein and Jacques Delors, François Mitterrand and Helmut Kohl. All of them have undoubtedly entered the European consciousness, as figures in the founding myth which Europe needs and actually possesses, and which is also rooted in the experience and effects of the two world wars.

However, we have to dig deeper to plumb European consciousness. The first thing that strikes us when we do is how many of the emblematic figures – Odysseus and Helen, Antigone and Electra, Oedipus and Narcissus, Ariadne and Dionysus, Joan of Arc and Don Juan, Faust and Hamlet – belong to all of Europe, and have found their way into the literature, music (and sometimes everyday language) of many different countries. Of course, 'national literatures' do exist, but surely Homer and Virgil, Thucydides and Tacitus, Dante and Petrarch, Shakespeare and Goethe, Cervantes and Swift, Tolstoy and Dostoyevsky, Proust and Joyce are part of the heritage all Europeans share? And this shared heritage is matched by a longing to be at home, not just in a state, but in a wider community.

Even more than in literature, the transfrontier colouring of European consciousness is apparent in philosophy, music and art. Is Picasso limited to Spain or France, Bach to Germany, Kandinsky to Russia, Mozart to Austria? In art and architecture, it is clearly reflected in transnational styles (from Romanesque to abstract), and peripatetic builders (St Petersburg was primarily the work of Italian architects).

In the same way, the British national anthem was once the German imperial anthem, while the German anthem was composed by an Austrian, Joseph Haydn, and was for many years his own country's imperial anthem.

The philosophers, too, have always thought and spoken in European terms. Indeed, wanderers between worlds have always been part of the European scene. Heinrich Heine was one example in the 19th century, Jorge Semprun is another today. And the man who gave Britain parliamentary government, Simon de Montfort, came from the south of France. In Russia, Peter the Great owed at least part of his renown to the breadth of vision and experience his travels in western Europe had given him. Carlos Primero, Charles I of Spain, was also Charles V, the German Emperor, an Austrian Habsburg, who had grown up in Flanders, then part of Burgundy.

Nor must we forget the many women, famous and less famous, who made dynastic marriages in other countries, thus helping to stimulate cultural exchange. Catherine the Great was just one of many.

Regardless of language and national frontiers, all of this adds up to a shared foundation, of which all Europeans – and not just the elites – are conscious. There are many things in which all Europeans can recognise themselves. But is this enough to justify the claim that there is, today, a pan-European sense of belonging together, indeed a desire to be together?

At national level, myths and legends, emblems and symbols are all sources of cohesion. At national level too, there are numerous buildings with which people identify proudly: the Houses of Parliament in London, the Louvre in Paris, the Kremlin in Moscow, the Winter Palace in St Petersburg, the Escorial outside Madrid, the Scala in Milan, the Coliseum in Rome, the Brandenburg Gate in Berlin, the Acropolis in Athens. Europe as a whole has, however, no building with which it can identify.

Pan-European myths and legends are equally rare (apart from 'national sovereignty' – if that counts as a European myth – and perhaps the Greek myths, including the mysterious tale of Zeus and Europa). This is certainly a weak point. Another is a dearth of public debate at European level, which is an essential precondition of a democratic European civil society.

The power of symbols

Thanks to the Council of Europe, which chose and adopted them in the 1950s, Europe has an anthem and a flag. These were later taken over and popularised by the EU (in 1971 and 1986 respectively). For some time, EU governments have been flying the European flag beside their own. This practice is a good one, and has been adopted, not only by candidates for EU membership, but by other Council of Europe countries as well. I would be pleased if it helped to bring the flag 'home' to the Council of Europe and thus to 'one' Europe.

The importance of the role played by such symbols in forging consciousness cannot be over-estimated. Wherever it flies, the flag means: we belong to Europe, we are Europe! If all European countries systematically flew it with their own, this would send a strong emotional message: we are all Europe – one Europe! Similarly, always playing the European and national anthems together, with people standing for both, would undoubtedly help to create a European consciousness.

Although only 12 states use it at present,[3] the euro is already helping too. Not only have people in those 12 states accepted it remarkably quickly, it holds a clear attraction for people in other countries too. The euro is another symbol of identity, and its significance is bound to increase. Indeed, it would not surprise me to see it adopted, officially or unofficially, by more states outside the EU.

All of these things express cultural unity in the midst of diversity, and they help Europeans to look beyond their local, regional and national roots, and think of Europe itself as a kind of greater homeland – one where frontiers are becoming less divisive, and freedom to travel, plentiful goods, prices brought down by competition, and a noticeable growth in prosperity are no longer mere dreams.

Keeping the peace – quintessence of the European project

Even that is not all. Also vital is the fact that lasting peace in Europe – one of the quintessential aims of the European project, as it took shape during and after the Second World War – has largely been achieved. For Europeans, that, and international human rights protection, are certainly the main points of European union.

It is true that Europe has had its tragic conflicts since 1945 – in Greece, Hungary, Czechoslovakia, Northern Ireland, the Basque country, Chechnya, Nagorno-Karabakh and the Balkans – and that some of them, alas, are still unsettled. But war between Turkey and Greece was averted, and disputes concerning Gibraltar, the South Tyrol's German-speaking minority, and minorities in the Carpathians were resolved in a civilised manner. The balance of terror also ensured that the Cold War did not turn, catastrophically, into a hot one. And some of the conflicts which did erupt into violence, e.g. in Cyprus, Moldova and the South Caucasus, were 'frozen' relatively quickly.

Since the Cold War ended, the 1945 ideal of a pan-European peace-keeping system, based on democracy, the rule of law and human rights, has again become relevant. Those shared values are central to the identity which Europe – like every collective entity – undeniably possesses.

The one thing we need to remember is that European identity is not fixed, but is constantly evolving. The Europe we know took centuries, even millennia, to become what it is today – centuries and millennia during which people did not always coexist peacefully, but often teetered on the brink of conflict, and indeed plunged over into it. But the civilisational and cultural bridges were never completely destroyed. The German philosophers were still studied outside Germany between 1933 and 1945, and even Stalinism could not stop people outside the Soviet empire from enjoying Russian literature and music.

Today, 800 million Europeans are protected by the European Convention on Human Rights, and usually its Protocols too (particularly that concerning abolition of the death penalty), and by the Anti-Torture Convention. This is precious – and they know it. The cry, 'Back to Europe!', showed how much it meant to people east of the Iron Curtain in the miracle-years of 1989–1990. Since they and their countries had never ceased to be part of Europe, they were obviously thinking of freedom, democracy, the rule of law and human rights – of sharing in a heritage which, though truly European, had been temporarily restricted to just part of the continent.

Of course, they soon started wanting to join the EC/EU too, and economic considerations clearly played a major part in this. The strong feeling that some of the new democracies would, if forced to choose, have opted for NATO membership first, showed that security and peace were their primary concerns (most of them did, in fact, join NATO before the EU). Intellectually and emotionally, however, one of their chief reasons for seeking EU membership was surely the urge to enter the innermost circle of a family where people and nations were respected and respected one another, and where old and varied traditions were cherished, not suppressed.

Shared Europe – for the head and the heart

Many people today are certainly afraid of seeing everything homogenised and forced into a single mould. The 'Brussels Moloch' and even the Strasbourg vision of law may leave them uneasy, making them feel that too many decisions are being taken over their heads, that their lives are being run for them. Many may feel, too, that national traditions are insufficiently understood and respected. Of course, these anxieties must be allayed, and Europeans taken even more seriously as people. But these concerns are often voiced by hypocritical politicians, whose only real fear is for their own authority. Intelligent Europeans have long since realised that Europe's shared ideals and principles are those of a free, developing society. For them, European unification is not just a matter of interest and the intellect, but a matter of the heart as well.

There can be no doubt – and surveys bear this out – that most people give Europe their vote in a kind of ongoing plebiscite. Of course, there may well be national variations, particularly on 'feeling European', sovereignty, and trusting the European institutions. I am obviously pleased that there is, especially in the new democracies of central, east and south-eastern Europe, widespread confidence in the Council of Europe (particularly in the Parliamentary Assembly and the European Court of Human Rights, but also in the Committee of Ministers), and that its Secretary General is seen as a moral – not just bureaucratic – authority.

Europe is distinguished from other continents by its culture, and by its economic, social and political structures. All of these elements help Europeans to see themselves as having a shared destiny, and thus a shared political purpose, which does not depend on uniformity, but can accommodate internal disagreements. To preserve Europe's distinctive features and special identity, it is necessary, as the Council of Europe Statute puts it, 'to achieve a greater unity between the nations[4] for the purpose of safeguarding and realising the ideals and principles which are their common heritage and facilitating their economic and social progress'.

Never before in our continent's history have the wishes and dreams of Europeans been so close to the aims which their leaders are actually committed to pursuing. I am convinced, in fact, that Europe's 800 million people are dreaming of unity, that they want to leave their children and grandchildren a Europe which is not content to proclaim ideals and principles, but really puts them into practice – a Europe of freedom, peace, social justice and prosperity for all. And, for the first time, these dreams stand a genuine chance of coming true for everyone!

Dreams have their price

'Thoughts are free' is the favourite song of my good friend Tomi Ungerer, the Alsatian artist and committed European, who is working actively to give Europeans – and particularly children – a better future (which is why I decided to appoint him the Council of Europe's Goodwill Ambassador for Children and Education). The German proverb, 'There's no tax on thought,' goes a step further – you can think what you like, and it won't cost you anything. But is this also true of dreams, and especially the European dream? Can we really get it for nothing?

I am not talking here about the huge sums which our taxpayers contribute to the EU budget, or about the net contributors and net beneficiaries we hear so much about from Brussels. And I am certainly not talking about the modest sums required by the Council of Europe, which manages, on a fraction of the EU budget (less than 200 million euros), to get things done in 45 states in a wide range of areas (human rights, treaty supervision, cultural heritage, and social cohesion in Europe, to name just a few).

Nor am I talking about the discipline (or lack of discipline) shown by states in respecting the Maastricht criteria in their budgetary policies, although all these monetary aspects are obviously important too.

Basically, I am simply asking: What does Europe demand of Europeans? What sacrifices are necessary, and who must make them? Is Europe worth it? And what does Europe offer Europeans in return?

My own answer here has to be a plain one. We will not get Europe for nothing. This is not the ancients' longed-for golden age, not the land of cockayne and not the earthly paradise. Dreams are not enough – hard work is needed too.

We're not getting Europe for nothing

The first thing we must do is learn to respect other people, their traditions, culture and language. We must learn to be open, not nationalistic, to be tolerant, not xenophobic. That, hopefully, is a price we will gladly pay for Europe.

Another thing Europe needs is genuine partnership, i.e. a willingness to share the problems and interests of others. In the long run, this kind of commitment and investment pays better than selfishness, and benefits everyone – as we soon find out when we need the help of others.

And Europe is not for the lazy, the people who sit back and leave the work to others – to 'the ones at the top', whether this means the Downing Street, Elysée, Kanzleramt or Kremlin leaders, or the Brussels and Strasbourg authorities. The people Europe needs are the lively ones, the ones who are alert, watchful and ready to take responsible decisions.

But being a European is also a matter of keeping informed, of staying in touch with the game. Only people who do that can react in time if totalitarianism or militarism ever threaten freedom again.

So what do Europe's 800 million people get in return for their efforts? The first thing they get is unprecedented protection for their basic rights and freedoms, which are, in effect, insured on a continental scale. Only Europe has (for the first time in its history) a supranational court to ensure that basic rights are respected by national governments, courts and authorities. That Court – the European Court of Human Rights – can be activated when rights guaranteed in the European Convention have been violated, and national remedies exhausted. Its judgments are binding, and states must respect them. It is, in effect, Europe's human rights conscience, personally embodied in its 45 judges (one for each member state), who are secretly elected by the Parliamentary Assembly from three-name lists submitted by governments.

Also important is the 'European Committee for the Prevention of Torture and Inhuman or Degrading Treatment or Punishment', which works to ensure that the human rights of people in police custody and prison are respected. It is authorised to visit prisons and police stations without warning, and interview prisoners in private. A third independent authority, the 'European Commission against Racism and Intolerance', monitors disturbing developments in this area in all the member states. It makes recommendations and publishes national reports, which obviously receive considerable media attention in the countries they cover. There are other, similar bodies to protect minorities, ensure that courts function properly, etc.

A European Commissioner for Human Rights has the task of promoting human rights education and respect for human rights in member states, working closely for that purpose with national ombudsmen or similar officials.

The second return that Europeans get on their efforts is, as I see it, ongoing promotion and protection of pluralist democracy and the freedoms that go with it. The Council of Europe helps its members to establish, develop and reform democratic institutions, for example through the guidance on constitutions provided by its 'Venice Commission' (European Commission for Democracy through Law). Even this is not all, since the Parliamentary Assembly and the Committee of Ministers both have monitoring systems to ensure that Council members live up to its standards. When necessary, the Council itself makes recommendations or sets up special programmes to help them do this. Elections are observed in countries which are being monitored, or request this (the Parliamentary Assembly sends observers for parliamentary elections, the Congress of Local and Regional Authorities of Europe for local or regional elections).

Observer missions of this kind are backed by useful institutional co-operation with the European Parliament and the Parliamentary Assembly of the OSCE (the 'parliamentary troika'), as well as the OSCE's Office for Democracy and Human Rights (ODIHR).

The third return I would mention is the Council of Europe's many inter-state activities, whose effects – far from being limited to governments – are felt directly by ordinary people in their own countries. The questions ranged all the way from action to stop corruption, organised crime, money laundering and trafficking in human beings, to measures to protect national or religious minorities against discrimination.

Finally, Europeans also benefit directly from the Council's work on culture, education, youth affairs and sport. Leading activities include the European Art Exhibitions (27 so far, seen by millions of people), heritage conservation, and help with rebuilding after natural disasters (e.g. the historic centre of Tbilissi, damaged by earthquake). Other projects cover the methodology of modern language teaching, and the working-out of a shared vision of the past as a basis for history teaching. Also important are action to promote mutual recognition of school certificates and university degrees, the training provided for youth leaders at two European Youth Centres (in Strasbourg and Budapest) and anti-doping measures in sport.

Give and take – governments too

Obviously, the governments of the 45 member states are also expected to do something in return for membership of the European democratic family. For example, their traditional insistence on national sovereignty has to be relaxed when they accept the jurisdiction of the European Court of Human Rights, and the same applies to the sweeping rights which they grant other Council of Europe institutions, e.g. the Anti-Torture Committee, or the Secretary General under Article 52 of the European Convention on Human Rights.[5]

Basically, by renouncing sovereignty in certain areas, states are serving, not a supranational organisation, but values and principles which they all recognise. Nonetheless, in their dealings with the Council, they sometimes find it hard to put the obsolete principle of 'non-interference in domestic affairs' behind them. But experience shows that the Court's judgments are always enforced in the end, that the Anti-Torture Committee's recommendations are accepted, and that information requested by the Secretary General under Article 52 of the Convention is provided.

Obviously, monitoring by the Parliamentary Assembly and the Committee of Ministers is another example of deliberate interference, but interference of a special kind, since it sets out to benefit the monitored country and its people. The attitudes of countries and governments are correspondingly ambivalent. On the one hand, governments (usually) welcome the assistance programmes which develop from the monitoring procedure. On the other, they are nearly always anxious to see the procedure concluded, since 'being monitored' is felt (even if this is not admitted) to be a 'black mark' internationally. Conclusion of the procedure is seen, at any rate, as a sign that things are (back) on track.

I myself had first-hand experience of this ambivalence, first as the Parliamentary Assembly's Rapporteur in three monitoring procedures (Romania, Slovakia and Turkey) and later as Secretary General. The Romanian procedure was concluded while I was still involved, the Slovak procedure some time afterwards. As for Turkey, the procedure lasted until April 2004, which made it no surprise that, on my official visit to Ankara in April 2003, all the people I met – from the President down – raised the question of concluding it.

A few weeks later, I was in Athens for the ceremony to mark the signing of the EU enlargement treaty. There, I met a whole series of delegations from the states accepted for membership, and all of them – without exception – told me that the Council of Europe's dogged insistence on compliance with its standards had helped them to satisfy the EU's criteria too. At the same time, it would be a total mistake to associate the obligations and benefits I have mentioned only with 'new' Council members, i.e. those which have joined since 1989. Turkey, one of our 'old' member states, has been under review since 1995, and the Parliamentary Assembly in 2003 considered opening a monitoring procedure for Liechtenstein (the purpose here was to verify that a constitution approved by plebiscite on the Prince's initiative is – in theory and practice – compatible with our basic principles).

Similarly, the Anti-Torture Committee was recently investigating conditions in British prisons, following the introduction of special anti-terrorist legislation, while the Committee of Ministers' monitoring procedure may be extended to cover public and private media monopolies in Italy.

The fact of the matter is: democracy, the rule of law and human rights are indivisible, and the Council of Europe must not apply double standards. Full, unqualified compliance with its rules, total acceptance of its values and implementation of those values in practice are the price of realising the dream of 'one Europe'.

NOTES:

1. This obviously applies to the whole of Europe too.
2. Erhard Busek, Special Co-ordinator of the Stability Pact for South-Eastern Europe; Franz Fischler, EU Commissioner for Agriculture; Wolfgang Petritsch, EU Special Envoy for Kosovo 1998–1999 and, until 2002, High Representative in Bosnia and Herzegovina; Peter Schieder, President of the Parliamentary Assembly of the Council of Europe since January 2002; Herwig van Staa, President of the Congress of Local and Regional Authorities of the Council of Europe since May 2002.
3. In addition to the EU states within the EMU, Montenegro, one of the entities in the Union of Serbia and Montenegro, and Kosovo, have already made the euro their official currency.
4. The Statute actually speaks of 'member states' (of the Council of Europe).
5. Any member state requested to do so by the Secretary General must supply information on the action it takes to implement the Convention effectively in practice.

CHAPTER TWO

The dream, my life

No dream journey: Alsace to Austria via Russia

Schwimmer is a relatively unusual name, and originates in the southern-most part of Alsace, the Sundgau, which (coincidence?) was once a Habsburg possession. To be exact, it comes from Hochstatt, a small village some seven kilometres south-west of Mulhouse. When Hochstatt itself was sacked and burned by the Swedes in the Thirty Years War, the parish records were unfortunately lost. And so the village's first recorded Schwimmer is the father of Georg Schwimmer, whose name appears in the baptismal register for 1685, and from whom all the Schwimmers in upper Alsace, the Haut-Rhin *département*, are probably descended.

The only reference before that is to a Schwimmer 'from the Burgundian lands', who served as a juror in a court case. The name possibly comes from the German 'schwemmen' (to water), which would suggest that one of my ancestors may have kept a stable, where horses were rested and watered. As I say, the name is unusual in German-speaking regions, although it does turn up in the Nuremberg area and Saxony, and also in the Hartberg district in Steiermark (Austria).

My 'European' origins

The name is, however, relatively common among Jews from pre-Trianon Hungary. From there, emigrants took it abroad, chiefly to Israel and the USA. Their name probably has nothing to do with the German 'schwimmen' or 'schwemmen', but is simply transcribed from the Hebrew. In its written form, of course, Hebrew has no vowels. But the character 'ו' is used both for the consonant 'w' and for the vowels 'o' and 'u'. This means that two derivations are possible: *schomer* and *schumer*. *Schomer* means 'watchman', and may be the origin of the name I share with various Hungarian Jews, probably Sephardim, who emigrated from the Ottoman

Empire to Hungary. More interesting is the word *schumer*, used of Jews who originally came from the Jewish communities in the Rhineland, the Palatinate and Hessen. Apart from the fact that Alsace always had large Jewish communities, who were constantly in touch with fellow communities in the Rhineland, it is quite conceivable that a Schumer who had turned Christian might have settled in the Sundgau after the Thirty Years War, and been entered as Schwimmer in the parish register.

For something like two centuries, the Schwimmers led ordinary lives in the Sundgau, which the Peace of Westphalia had transferred to France, married girls from Hochstatt (in one case, the daughter of a mayor called Fochler) or neighbouring villages, survived the upheavals of the French Revolution and Napoleonic Wars, and were respected members of their community.

They spoke their own Alemannic-German-Alsatian dialect, but thought of themselves as loyal sons of France. For them, as for many Alsatians, the incorporation of Alsace-Lorraine into Bismarck's German Empire after the war of 1870 came as a profound political and cultural shock. Many Alsatians preferred to stay French and remain in France – which meant leaving their home region. This number included various Schwimmers, some of them with married daughters in France, in nearby Belfort or faraway Nantes. My great-grandfather, Jacob or Jacques Schwimmer, stayed in Hochstatt to start with and worked as a calico printer in a textile firm in Mulhouse.

Paris, Russia, Bohemia

The family was still in Hochstatt when my grandfather, Johann or Jean-Baptiste, was born in 1879. However, three years later – possibly for political *and* economic reasons – Jacques took his family to Paris. His stay there was obviously brief and, over a hundred years before Schengen, he set out – without needing a visa or work permit – for Russia, where he hoped to practise his trade in St Petersburg and Moscow. His wife, Barbara, his daughter, Rosa (known in the family by the French name Julie), and his son, Jean-Baptiste, accompanied him on this truly European odyssey. Their next stop after Russia was Friedland in Bohemia, now Frydlant v Cechách in the Czech Republic. Two children died along the way: we do not know whether they were buried in France, Russia or Bohemia – we only know that they lie in European soil. Wherever they went, the Schwimmers remained true to their Alsatian past. From a porcelain-maker in Friedland, they commissioned the typically Alsatian Christmas plates (we have one for 1888) as well as a special coffee service, marked 'Amitiés' for their wedding anniversary.

1889 found the family within 200 kilometres of their starting point, at Hard am Bodensee, in the Austrian Vorarlberg, which had important textile manufactures and spoke a low Allemanic dialect very close to Alsatian. Jean-Baptiste was just 10 when they settled in Hard. They never forgot their old home in the Sundgau, and stayed in touch for many years with relatives still in the region: from that point on, however, the Schwimmers were Austrian.

From Slovakia to Vienna

Around the same time, in the far north-western corner of the Hungarian half of the Dual Monarchy – at Moravski Svete Ján (Slovak), Sankt Johann an der March (German) or, to use the official Hungarian name, Szent Janos – another man with a wife and children, Stefan Mracsna, decided, like so many others, to seek his fortune, and above all a living for his family, in Vienna, the imperial capital. In addition to Slovak, which they spoke with neighbours, and Hungarian, which they used with the authorities, his family also spoke German. According to family tradition, ancestors, originally named von Wolken, had moved from Hesse to the Marches under the Empress Maria Theresa. At that time, no one really cared about language or group affiliations, although the first nationality-based conflicts had already broken out, and blinkered politicians and rabble-rousing nation-alists saw an all-German, all-Hungarian or all-Czech state as their panacea. My mother's father, Anton, was born in Vienna in 1880.

My paternal great-grandfather, Jakob, had brought his wife, Barbe or Barbara (née Neff), from Alsace to the Vorarlberg. My maternal great-grandfather, Stefan, found his Bohemian wife, Theresia Kratschmann (probably written differently to start with, perhaps as Kračman, but parish priests often used phonetic spelling in their records), in Vienna. My two grandmothers, Maria (née Walter) and Stefanie (née Buchwinkler), had their family roots in the Vorarlberg and Tyrol, and in Salzburg and German Bohemia respectively. My great-grandfather, Theodor Walter, who came from a mining family in Häring, had worked as an engineer on the Arlberg tunnel, before settling in Dornbirn or, more precisely, Hatlerdorf (originally an independent commune, now part of the town) and marrying into an old local family, the Fusseneggers, thus acquiring links with Dornbirn's leading patrician families. As I have already said, my grandfather, Jean-Baptiste Schwimmer, moved to the Vorarlberg with his parents at the age of 10. His pious Catholic parents had sent him to the Cistercian school at Mehrerau, which he left at the age of 14 to work, like his father, in the textile trade. Having joined the Catholic Workers' Association in Hohenems, and the Christian trade unions which dominated the labour scene in the Vorarlberg, he temporarily entered politics, becoming secretary of the Vorarlberg Workers' League and the Christian Socialist Party, and editor of the *Vorarlberger Volksblatt.* In 1912, he married Maria Walter and his son – my father, Walter Schwimmer (whose first name, like my own, preserved his mother's family name) – was born just before he left for the Italian front in 1914.

My mother Johanna was born in Vienna in 1920. Her father, Anton, son of the Slovak immigrant Stefan and a butcher by trade, had married Stefanie, whose family (also butchers) came originally from the Salzburg area and had settled in a village west of Vienna. Before my mother was born, he had set up a modest carter's business in Vienna, but soon sold it and settled down as an innkeeper and butcher in a village north-east of the city. In February 1934, during the violent civil disturbances in Vienna, he got caught between the two sides while delivering meat to a hospital, and lost the whole, large, consignment. This left him a ruined man, and he was eventually forced to give up his business and take a job in a factory.

War story

Once again – as it had at the time of the Thirty Years War, and later, when the Franco-Prussian war brought Alsace into the German Empire – European history entered my family's story. On 12 March 1938, my father – then serving in the Austrian army – was preparing to defend his country on the German frontier near Bregenz. But the national leadership caved in, and the orders never came. Without being consulted, Walter Schwimmer senior was drafted into the German *Wehrmacht* and posted to Vienna shortly afterwards. Feeling at a loss in his new surroundings, where no one understood his dialect, he used his free time to study commerce at evening classes, which were also attended by Johanna (Hansi) Mracsna. Johanna's position was complicated by the fact that, somewhere along the way, perhaps when the family moved from Moravski Svete Ján to Vienna, or when the Monarchy collapsed and the March became a frontier, someone had overlooked one minor formality. As a result, Anton Mracsna and his daughter somehow fell between nations and were suddenly neither Austrian (officially, Austrians had ceased to exist in 1938), nor German, nor Hungarian nor Slovak (Czechoslovak was not an option either, since Hitler had crushed the country). The German bureaucrats marked them down as 'stateless' – typical products of a time when the great ones of the earth shifted frontiers as they pleased, destroying and creating states, and leaving ordinary people, sometimes deprived of a country overnight, to sort themselves out as best they could. Eventually, however, there was a happy ending, and two Austrians with archetypal

European backgrounds were given official leave to marry – as a German national and a stateless person – in 1941, shortly before my father was sent to the Russian front. I was born on 16 June 1942 at 11.30 in the morning and was named Walter Gerhard Schwimmer – Walter for my father and his mother's family, Gerhard for a boyhood friend of my father's, who was killed in the early days of the war, when Hitler invaded Poland; one of the first of the countless senseless deaths that were to follow.

There is nothing unusual about my family's story, nothing dramatic, nothing special, nothing that did not happen to millions of others. It is the story of a very ordinary, very typical European and Austrian family. Stories very like it lie behind all the Czech, Hungarian, Croatian, Italian, German and countless other names listed in the Vienna phone-book. *Austriacus ergo Europaeus sum.*

Dream career and political reality

When I was 12 or 13 years old, I decided that I wanted to teach history and geography – always my favourite subjects – when I grew up. Against the wishes of my father, who wanted me to go into business, I stayed on at grammar school after the age of 14, instead of going to a commercial college, and took my school certificate at 18. When I was still at school, friends in the Young Christian Workers (KAJ) introduced me to the Austrian branch of *Jeunesse ouvrière chrétienne* (JOC), founded by the Belgian worker priest, Joseph Cardijn, which I joined. The KAJ gave me its basic motto: 'See – judge – act', but it also taught me what solidarity – practical and, above all, international – and responsibility meant. Working on social problems also gave my interest in politics a keener, more practical edge.

See – judge – act

In the meantime, my thinking on future careers had also changed. I was still interested in history, and in other peoples and countries, and the diplomatic life was starting to look tempting. Wanting this was one thing, but I knew that paying for ordinary studies was already a strain on my parents' resources, and that I should be trying to contribute myself. That was why, when it came to the choice which would-be diplomats in Austria have to make between three qualifying subjects, I opted for legal and political science, instead of history or economics. I also felt that this would leave me with other interesting career options, if my diplomatic ambitions came to nothing.

My work in the KAJ had also given me an interest in home politics, including social policy in the broad sense. And so when I found that I could, at the age of 19, get involved in politics myself, I went along with two like-minded friends and joined the Austrian Manual and Office Workers' Association (ÖAAB), which was affiliated to the Austrian People's Party (ÖVP). The values I had absorbed at home and as a committed Catholic made me feel closest to the (Christian Democrat) ÖVP, although I disagreed with it on many issues – and particularly social policy, where I sided far more often with the Socialists. At the same time, the ÖVP provided an umbrella for various vocational groups, not just the Farmers' Association and the Economic League of Businessmen and Self-Employed Workers, but also the ÖAAB itself, which had a powerful sense of social commitment, was linked to the Christian trade unions and – on social issues – was certainly on the party's left. Indeed, inside and outside the ÖVP, it was often accused of 'overtaking the Socialists on the left'. This was the very reason it appealed to me – and it gave me an immediate, open-arms welcome.

Politics and trade unionism – first steps

In Vienna, and particularly working-class areas like my own, the ÖVP was mainly run by the ÖAAB, and I soon got involved at local level, becoming Chairman of the ÖAAB's branch (which had around 3,500 members) in the second district of Vienna at the age of 28. Neither working to help finance my studies, nor being active in the KAJ and politics, stopped me from taking my law degree in minimum time – although some projects, such as improving my languages and specialising in international law, had to be shelved. Another interesting job, which tied in well with my political interests, had come up in the meantime. The KAJ's national Chairman had become Central Secretary of the Union of Private Office Employees and, shortly before I graduated, he recruited me to the Union's legal department. In 1969, I was elected for the ÖAAB to the General Assembly of Viennese Workers' Associations, a public-law body founded to represent the interests of workers – my first political office, which I held for a total of 30 years.

My trade union activity and increased concentration on labour and social law questions had attracted the ÖAAB Central Office's attention and, from 1966 to 1970, when the ÖVP was alone in government, I played an important advisory role in shaping policy. I also acted as adviser to the country's first female Social Affairs Minister, the Christian trade unionist, Grete Rehor. The ÖVP lost the 1970 elections and Bruno Kreisky, who had taken over as leader of the Socialist Party after its defeat in 1966, formed a minority government with the tacit acquiescence of the FPÖ (Freedom Party of Austria), which was led by Friedrich Peter, an SS veteran. To win back the ground it had lost, the ÖVP needed new policies and new faces. When early elections to the National Assembly were called in 1971, I found myself included – to my own surprise – on the ÖVP's list of candidates for Vienna. On 4 November, I was duly elected to the Assembly, entering as its youngest member, and leaving (as one of its longest-serving) only when I was elected Secretary General of the Council of Europe 28 years later. Anyway, I kept my youngest MP status until 1976.

New boy, old house

My grasp of social policy had earned me my place on the ÖVP's ticket, and so foreign policy – my first love – had to wait. Nonetheless, I took to Parliament like a duck to water, finding it as varied and eventful as my own political career was to prove. With the one exception of the Agricultural Committee, I must have served on nearly all the Assembly's committees. For many years, too, I was Chairman or Deputy Chairman of the Social Affairs Committee (my original field) and simultaneously my party's spokesman on social affairs. When the party projected a radical shift in pension reform policy which I felt unable to support, I turned my back on social policy *per se* and took over as Chairman of the Health Committee. For a year, I was also Chairman of the prestigious Justice Committee, but then – having to make a choice, and facing heavy demands on my time from the Council of Europe's Parliamentary Assembly (I shall be saying more about this later) – I opted for the Chairmanship of the Buildings Committee, since housing and rent questions had been one of my main concerns in recent years. In short, I never found Parliament boring. In the first eight years of the SPÖ/ÖVP coalition, which was formed in 1987, I was also my party's Deputy Chairman.

But the political longing for faraway places, which had made diplomacy alluring, was still there. As so often in my life, all I needed was the right opportunity – this time, to get involved in foreign policy – and I seized it when it came. In 1972, the ÖVP's youth organisation had invited me, as the National Assembly's youngest member, to join a multi-party delegation on a visit to Israel. I had never been there before, and that one week brought all the things I had merely heard and read to total, pulsing life. I had grown up in a formerly Jewish part of Vienna, later 'cleansed' of Jews by the Nazis, and here I suddenly found myself talking to Austrians driven from my country before I was even born, meeting Holocaust survivors, and seeing the incredible things these people had achieved. In an instant, theoretical knowledge became personal experience, became emotion – became a clear political vocation. I realised that, as one of the countries where Jews had suffered unspeakable atrocities and been brutally driven from their homes, Austria had special obligations to Israel. This was something deeper than the admiration I had naturally felt for the Israelis in 1967, when they fought back bravely and turned the tide against their enemies. Seeing and experiencing Israel for myself gave 'Never again' – the words chosen as their motto by the founders of the Council of Europe, of which I then knew relatively little – a deeply personal meaning.

I talked to friends about the deep impression the visit had made on me. One of them – a journalist, who edited the Austria-Israel Association's journal – told me about the Association and its work, and its Secretary, a Socialist MP (and so one of my 'adversaries'), invited me to join its committee. Some friendship associations may provide interesting or diverting opportunities to visit other countries and meet their people, and may bring a touch of colour into the humdrum lives of politicians, but this one proved a real challenge, demanding hard work and testing my convictions. Whatever the context – the Yom Kippur War in 1973, when oil was used to blackmail many of Israel's supporters, or Kreisky's attacks on Golda Meir or Menachim Begin – friendship with Israel was something that had to be proved. But it also led to personal friendships, in both Israel and Austria. In spite of our home political differences, Heinz Nittel, the Association's Secretary, and I soon became fast friends. In fact, when he took over as its President in 1977, I became his deputy. And so I was deeply shocked by the news a phone-call brought me at home on 1 May 1981 – a public holiday, when I had stayed in bed longer than usual and had not bothered to turn on the radio or TV. The caller was another good friend, Josef ('Joschi') Leitner, the Association's treasurer and a practising Jew. Doubly endangered – as a Jew and as a member of the Fatherland Front, the then governing party – he had been forced to flee Austria in 1938, had joined the British army and had spent the war in Palestine, later becoming one of the few to return to Austria after 1945. I barely recognised his voice: 'Haven't you heard the radio? – Heinz has been shot!'. Palestinian extremists had gunned him down on his own doorstep, just two months after he had called in Israel for reconciliation with their people, as he was getting into the official car (he was now on the City Council) which had come to take him to the Social Democrats' traditional May Day celebrations. Traffic had been his portfolio on the Council, and he is now commemorated in Jerusalem by a road safety practice circuit for children, funded by the Austria-Israel Association, run by the Jerusalem Foundation and named after him. Both Jewish and Arab children use it.

As Deputy President, I automatically took over the day-to-day running of the Association. Later, as its elected President – an office I held until I became Secretary General of the Council of Europe – I steered it through the years which saw the Lebanon campaign and the Intifada, and also through the serious tensions with Israel which resulted when the former UN Secretary General, Kurt Waldheim, was elected President of Austria – a time when it was particularly important to keep the bridges intact. In fact, just a week after the second, decisive ballot, I talked in Israel to President Chaim Herzog, Foreign Minister Yitzak Shamir and my old friend, Teddy Kollek, Mayor of Jerusalem.

Inter-parliamentary experience

Because of my involvement with Israel, I also took an interest in the work of the Inter-parliamentary Union (IPU), and attended several of its general assemblies. The so-called 'non-aligned' and communist countries had an automatic majority, making attacks on Israel predictable. I have particularly vivid memories of one IPU meeting in Pyongyang (North Korea). On the last day, when the voting takes place, these meetings are traditionally chaired by the president of the host country's parliament. One of the resolutions covered the Middle East conflict, and the Political Committee had given it a one-sided, anti-Israeli slant. Opinions in the Austrian delegation were divided, and it was my task, not simply to record the votes of those who opposed the resolution, but to ask for a 'roll-call vote', with each delegation indicating votes for, votes against and abstentions. This had been agreed beforehand by a few western representatives who, like myself, were against the resolution. When the President of the North Korean 'Parliament' took the vote, he simply announced (probably standard procedure in his country) that the resolution had been unanimously adopted, without even going through the motions of asking for a show of hands. I raised a point of order. The President ignored me, and my microphone stayed dead. The hall was enormous, and the luck of the draw had put the Austrians right at the back. Dealing with hecklers in my home Parliament had helped to develop my voice, and I needed all of it now to make my objection – which was totally legitimate – heard. At this point, the President was starting to lose his temper, but the IPU Secretariat explained the procedure, and he had no choice but to take a roll-call vote, which still resulted in the resolution's being adopted – but not 'unanimously'.

Another episode, which extended my political horizons and helped me to understand people behind the Iron Curtain better, was my relatively brief involvement with the Austria-GDR Association. Unlike the Austria-Israel Association, this was not an association of individuals voluntarily committed to working for better relations with a country and its people, but a kind of 'spear-head' organisation, set up and run by the German Democratic

Republic itself, with the help of its political allies, i.e. communists. However, the opening of diplomatic relations and the growth of trade had prompted various groups and institutions, including the political parties, to appoint representatives to the Association as a sign of goodwill. The ÖVP was due to provide a vice-president and, on the strength of my experience with another (for very different reasons) 'difficult' association, the Party Chairman chose me. This gave me an opportunity to visit the so-called workers' and peasants' state several times between 1978 and 1980, and take a close look at the absurd, authoritarian regime which Prussian militarism and 'international' communism had combined to produce. I particularly remember a lecture tour arranged for me in 1980, to mark the 25th anniversary of the Austrian State Treaty. Wherever I went, the questions I got were – word for word – the same. Clearly, they had been circulated in advance, and even prominent members of the East German CDU and the People's Friendship League, professors of international law and other high-ranking participants were content to parrot them. Moreover, none of my hosts' efforts could conceal the fact that the CDU (and certainly all the other 'parties' which eked out a kind of shadow existence alongside the SED) toed the official line slavishly. 'The fact is', the CDU's District Chairman in Dresden assured me, speaking more to my 'minders' than to me, 'since 1949, it has acknowledged the leading role of the party of the working class.' The GDR leadership's hypocrisy and phrase-making were interesting in their own way, but eventually exhausted my patience. Partly for this reason, and partly because the Association's really committed members, i.e. the communists, could not help misusing it for propaganda purposes, I resigned in 1980. For all their interest in political and trade relations, the ÖVP leadership also came to see that this was no place for an active politician, and asked a friendly industrialist with business connections in the GDR to take over. The episode had at least given me a close-up look at life behind the Wall, at the 'people' who were to take their destiny into their own hands ten years later, and at the party officials, great and small, whom they then – deservedly – chased out of office.

The Iron Curtain goes

My own experience made *glasnost* and *perestroika* seem logical, indeed inevitable, developments. In spite of their apparent military strength and rigid police control, GDR-type systems were sure to fall victim to their own inherent weaknesses. Even now, looking back, I can hardly find words for what I felt when Alois Mock, our Foreign Minister, and Gyula Horn, his Hungarian counterpart, symbolically cut the barbed wire on the Austro-Hungarian frontier, when the GDR citizens, who had massed and were waiting in Hungary, were suddenly allowed to travel on through Austria to the Federal Republic, when the Berlin Wall came down, and when the Eastern-bloc countries turned, one after another, to democracy – some quietly, like Czechoslovakia with its Velvet Revolution, others, alas, like Romania in a last surge of violence provoked by falling leaders. I am not ashamed to say that, more than once, I found myself moved to tears.

The first priority now was to help our newly free neighbours. On 1 May 1990, I travelled by special train to Bratislava with 1000 members of the Vienna ÖAAB to join Jan Cernogursky and his Slovak Christian Democrats for the first free May Day celebrations – intended as a deliberate contrast to the earlier state-organised parades. When elections were held in Hungary, I was, like other Austrian politicians, a welcome guest at events organised by our sister parties. Even more important was the passing-on of know-how at seminars held in Vienna and in the reform countries themselves. I was also aware, however, of the foreign policy and European challenges involved, and wanted to play a more than episodic part in helping to shape a better future. My reputation, experience, seniority and undiminished interest in foreign affairs had at last earned me a place in the Assembly's Foreign Policy Committee some years before – and the time had now come to get permanently involved at European level. Free Europe was no longer an unfinished canvas or impossible dream for 50% of Europeans, but had become a historic opportunity. I realised that a new and (not just in area) Greater Europe, with democracy and freedom for all, had always been my political dream, although – or perhaps because – my country's good fortune had allowed me to grow up just 60 kilometres from the Iron Curtain, but on the right side of it.

Milestones and stumbling blocks: my life as Secretary General

On 1 September 1999, Daniel Tarschys, a Swede, handed over as Secretary General of the Council of Europe to Walter Schwimmer, an Austrian – and by chance an Austrian with family roots in an Alsatian village which the Swedes had burned in the Thirty Years War. In a sense, therefore, taking office in Strasbourg was coming back to the land of my forefathers. The dream had become reality, the kind of reality that catches up with most idealists fairly quickly. The road to greater unity between European nations, as the Council of Europe's Statute puts it so solemnly, is not paved only with ideals and dreams – as I soon found out, it has plenty of stumbling blocks too. Thank God, it also has milestones, which help us to see how far we have come and measure our progress.

Things started well. My first official visit, within a week of taking office, was to Iceland, which was then chairing the Council's Committee of

Ministers with exemplary commitment. As a boy, I had devoured the stories about Nonni and his brother Nanni, in which the Icelandic writer Jon Svensson evoked his own childhood – and the lonely northern island had fascinated me ever since. Now I could see it at last. My second official journey, which followed at once, was highly symbolic. It took me to Bucharest, where I joined President Constantinesco in opening the campaign, 'Europe, a common heritage'. This combination of 'new' democracy and 'ancient' culture, shared values and shared heritage, effectively foreshadowed my future activity as head of the oldest European and only pan-European organisation.

'Greater European unity' had still to be achieved (and will probably, alas, remain to be achieved at the end of my five years in office). Forty-one states had already, as it were, joined the convoy, the latest being Georgia, in the April preceding my election. Today, the convoy is still a loose one: it has difficulty maintaining to the same speed and is often very strung out, while members occasionally go off the road and have to be hauled back again. After scratching my head to find an image for my role as Secretary General of the Council, I decided that the convoy leader, who makes sure that the others stay together and keeps them heading in the right direction, was a better analogy than the (possibly more impressive) pilot on the flight-deck or captain on the bridge.

By April 2003, just under four years later, there were more new members. One a year: the pace had slowed since the decade which began in 1990, and which brought the Council 18 new members in breakneck succession, but it still topped the growth rate for the 40-year period from 1949 to 1989, with its total of 13 accessions. Nonetheless, the process was nearing its natural conclusion – and the arrivals of Armenia, Azerbaijan, Bosnia and Herzegovina, and finally Serbia and Montenegro, were undoubtedly milestones on the way.

Unresolved conflicts

None of this had seemed likely in September 1999. The conflict in Kosovo had just been provisionally settled by the arrival of the Kosovo Force (KFOR) and the establishment of the UN administration (UNMIK), and the Council of Europe's first special representative had started work in Pristina a bare two weeks before I took office. In Belgrade, however, Slobodan Milosevic was still firmly in the saddle. In Bosnia and Herzegovina, the nationalists, who had already dominated the political scene in the terrible days of the armed conflict, had stood Clauswitz's theory on its head and were continuing to make war by other means, sharing out the country's pitiful resources among themselves – seemingly undisturbed by the fact that only the international community's presence kept it limping along as a kind of semi-protectorate. Armenia and Azerbaijan were still officially at war, although a *de facto* truce was almost totally observed, leaving Armenia in possession of various parts of Azerbaijan, from which the populace had been forced to flee. At home, both countries were still licking the wounds inflicted by the war over Nagorno-Karabakh, now occupied by Armenia, which had started under the Soviets and been fought out – sometimes with unbridled savagery – between the newly independent republics.

The two Caucasian states were the first of the four to join the Council, and they did so together. Previously, doubts had been expressed concerning the maturity of their democratic institutions, and their ability to protect basic rights and freedoms. The shooting in the Armenian Parliament (never fully explained), in which a number of leading parliamentarians died, and sharp international criticism of the elections in Azerbaijan, made many people wonder whether either country satisfied the Council's membership criteria. The Parliamentary Assembly had itself insisted that the cases of hundreds of alleged political prisoners, chiefly in Azerbaijan, must be investigated, and the prisoners themselves released. This was a matter of principle and of deep humanitarian concern, and it became my business when both states joined the Council in January 2001. With the help of internationally recognised experts, we have so far succeeded in finding solutions – release, amnesty or reopening of proceedings – in 700 cases. More work is needed on 80 others – very diverse and 11 of them, alas, particularly important – in which proceedings have been reopened.

One disappointment is the fact that, in spite of unequivocal assurances – given to me by, among others, President Kocharian of Armenia and President Aliyev of Azerbaijan, when I talked to them privately at the time of the accession ceremony – and of the efforts made by the OSCE's Minsk Group, which is chaired by France, Russia and the USA, no progress has been made on Nagorno-Karabakh, and no official peace has been concluded. Nonetheless, Council membership has paved the way for contacts which would not have been possible before – from ministerial meetings to participation by both countries in courses at the 'school for political studies', a Council-sponsored forcing-house for young political talents, which operates in nearby Tbilissi (Georgia).

There is also work for the Council in Georgia itself, where democracy, the rule of law and human rights have still to be genuinely consolidated. In addition, Georgia has unresolved separatist problems in Abkhazia and South Ossetia, and is, like the two other Caucasian states, facing a refugee crisis.

Nonetheless – progress!

Even under Milosevic, the Council of Europe had been preparing the ground for democracy in Yugoslavia, with help from civil society and democratic allies in local government, such as Zoran Zivkovic, Mayor of Nis, who later succeeded the murdered Zoran Dzindzic as Prime Minister of Serbia. I had had a long talk with Dzindzic himself at the OSCE Summit in Istanbul in December 1999. Other names too, which came to prominence in democratic, post-Milosevic Yugoslavia – Kostunica, Svilanovic and Micunovic – were not unknown in Strasbourg. In Podgorica, capital of Montenegro, I was able to open a Council of Europe office to promote democratic reform, even before Milosevic had fallen.

The Dayton Agreement had already tied Bosnia and Herzegovina firmly to the Council of Europe standards embodied in the European Convention on Human Rights, and I regarded the country as a priority target for assistance. A non-nationalist coalition eventually put through the reforms needed for Council membership – though a long list of post-accession commitments was attached to it.

Milestones and stumbling blocks lay as close to one another with new arrivals as they had with older members. Our assistance programmes for democratisation and reform had been constantly expanded, producing powerful effects in many countries. New civil and criminal codes, and the necessary constitutional legislation, were drafted, discussed and adopted with the help of Council of Europe experts. Courts, once blatantly used by the state to keep citizens compliant, needed to be made independent, so that they could administer justice impartially. Police and security services, previously run on military lines, needed – like prisons – to be 'civilised'. Even democratically elected and legitimate parliaments and governments were sometimes tempted to manipulate public opinion via state-controlled media, and to deny opponents a hearing. The fact that, today, the Copenhagen criteria are satisfied, not only by the eight ex-communist countries which signed the EU accession treaty in Athens on 16 April 2003, but also by a number of other central, south-eastern and eastern European states, is – as even the EU Commission admits – chiefly due to Council of Europe membership and the Council's active help.

Convince and persuade

Some countries, however, took a lot of persuading to fully accept the Council's help and put through the reforms this implied. When I took over, Ukraine, for example – partly because Parliament was locked in a kind of ongoing crisis and hopelessly at odds with the President – was badly in arrear with the promised reforms. We have since succeeded in breaking the stalemate on most of the legal reforms, including abolition of the death penalty, but media independence and freedom of speech still require long-term guarantees. Successfully investigating violence against journalists, and above all the notorious case of the murdered Heorhiy Gongadze, is a vital part of this.

Effectively protecting free speech and independence of the media (including public television and radio services) is still – like action to protect and promote ethnic and religious minorities and integrate the Roma – on my list of tasks not yet completed. Things have improved for some national minorities, but the Hungarian 'status law' has recently brought problems concerning the Hungarian minorities in Slovakia and Romania back to the boil. Similarly, although some progress has been made, the Russian minorities in the Baltic states are still a cause for concern.

One member state, whose turn to chair the Council's Committee of Ministers was due to come round in May 2003, plunged into a full-scale political crisis early in 2002. The kidnapping of a prominent member of the Christian Democrat opposition, himself a member of the Council's Parliamentary Assembly, massive demonstrations, opposition boycotting of Parliament, where free elections had given the communists an absolute majority, and limited experience of political dialogue – the mixture seemed explosive and likely to threaten something even more important than the country's chairing of a major European body. Personal talks with the country's parliamentary leaders, and the building up of a relationship of trust, particularly with the President, helped to launch important democratic and rule-of-law reforms, and bring all the country's parliamentary and extra-parliamentary political forces together at a round-table meeting.

In the Russian Federation, alongside intensive co-operation programmes focused on legal reform and federalism, the Chechen crisis has been my main concern throughout my term in office. So much so indeed, that the 'special case of Chechnya' deserves a chapter to itself. Even before I took office, bomb attacks in Moscow and other Russian cities, for which Chechen terrorists were blamed, and military-style raids from Chechnya on the neighbouring Republic of Daghestan, had added to the tensions. Vladimir Putin, then Yeltsin's Prime Minister, decided that a military attack on the Chechen separatists was justified. Without questioning Russia's right to protect its citizens against terrorism or defend its territorial integrity, considerable doubts were voiced concerning the scale of the response and the action taken to protect civilians. I myself felt obliged to react when the remaining inhabitants of Grozny were given a military ultimatum in December 1999 (anyone failing to leave the city was to be treated as a terrorist). For the first time in the near 50-year history of the European Convention on Human Rights, I decided to invoke the Secretary General's right to demand explanations from a member state concerning its compliance with the Convention in a particular situation. I shall say more about this, and about what followed, in Chapter 5.

King-pin achievement: the Human Rights Convention

The 50th birthday of the European Convention on Human Rights (ECHR) in November 2000 was marked by a ministerial conference in Rome, a private audience with the Pope and a reception, hosted by the Italian President, for the Council of Europe representatives. In my speech on that occasion, I quoted Pierre-Henri Teitgen, a French member of the Parliamentary Assembly and one of the driving forces behind the Convention, whose words in 1950 struck me as equally valid today:

> 'Democracies do not become Nazi countries in one day. Evil progresses cunningly, with a minority operating, as it were, to remove the levers of control. One by one freedoms are suppressed, in one sphere after another. Public opinion and the entire national conscience are asphyxiated. And then, when everything is in order, the "Führer" is installed and the evolution continues even to the oven of the crematorium.'

Alertness to dangers to democracy and human rights is something I have made an unshakeable guiding principle in my work. Without it, progress towards the kind of European unity I envisage would be seriously compromised.

With this need for vigilance in mind, we were not content to celebrate and commemorate in Rome. A twelfth Protocol to the Convention, containing a general prohibition on discrimination, was also opened for signature – certainly another genuine milestone. The thirteenth Protocol, which has followed in the meantime, completes one of the Council's most important undertakings: abolition of the death penalty throughout Europe. The sixth Protocol had banned it in peacetime, and the thirteenth extends that ban to wartime. The sixth Protocol has been ratified by 44 of the Council's member states, and signed by the Russian Federation (which are therefore bound, too, not to violate the substance and purpose of this international agreement). This means that no Council of Europe country may now enforce the death penalty in peacetime.

Observers – and more problems

The Council of Europe has members, and it has observers too. These are non-European countries with a basic interest in forming a community of culture and values with Europe: Japan, Canada, Mexico and the USA (the

Holy See, which is party to the European Cultural Convention, has had similar status since the 1970s, and Israel's Knesset or Parliament has been an observer ever since 1957). I am the first Secretary General to have visited all the non-European observer states, not just to trade compliments, but to discuss closer co-operation – and the thorny problem of the death penalty came up in both Tokyo and Washington.

Long before the war in Iraq drove a wedge between the USA and much of Europe, the death penalty and its blatantly discriminatory enforcement in most of the US states had been a serious strain on our relationship. Here too, US observer status gave us at least a chance to air the question. Of course, I am not forgetting courageous politicians like former Governor Ryan of Illinois, who commuted the sentences on all death-row prisoners in his state (I congratulated him publicly on this, and later received him in my Strasbourg office). In Japan, where the number of death sentences and executions is far lower, but enforcement practices raise serious problems, I got, in some respects, a better hearing than in Washington – chiefly, of course, from the sizeable non-party group which is campaigning for abolition in the Japanese Parliament.

Onslaught on civilisation

But the whole of Europe rallied behind America again, when terrorists carried out their still inconceivable attacks on the World Trade Centre in New York and the Pentagon in Washington. Our values, too, had been the target, and all Europe joined in mourning, when I spontaneously passed on the EU's call for a three-minute silence to the 800 million people in our 43 member and two applicant countries. As I said at an interdenominational memorial service, held shortly after the tragedy in Strasbourg Cathedral, we must work together to resist this threat to the things we believe in. The best way of doing that is to strengthen our values – instead, perhaps, of weakening or undermining them, on the pretext of combating terrorism. The Council of Europe itself has responded by, among other things, devising new conventions and forms of co-operation, intensifying intercultural and inter-religious dialogue and, above all, producing guidelines on protecting human rights in the fight against terrorism, which have attracted wide attention.

For many years, the Council has been following the Middle East conflict closely, and not simply because of the Israeli observers in its Assembly. Obviously, having worked for many years for friendship between Israel and Austria, and reconciliation between Israelis and Palestinians, I am deeply involved. We are in constant touch with the Israeli and Palestinian authorities, and I made it my business to visit both, meeting President Katzav, Foreign Minister Peres (my old acquaintance), Chairman Arafat and many others. In spite – and indeed because – of the endless spiral of violence, I remain convinced that there is no alternative to the peace process, to unconditional mutual recognition by the State of Israel and an independent Palestinian state (as soon as an agreement is reached, and not at some point in the future). As the champion, not of economic and military interests, but of a community of values, the Council of Europe has the potential to play an even bigger part in such a process.

Europe and the world

If Europe wants to present a more united front on issues like these, then all it has to do is use the Council of Europe more extensively. The Council, for its part, must speak out more effectively on behalf of 'one Europe'. To some extent, we managed to do that at the UN Summits in Durban and Johannesburg, even if the problems which overshadowed both largely prevented the public from realising it. Nonetheless, it was the Council which took the initiative in organising the European Anti-Racism Conference (Strasbourg, October 2000) in the run-up to the Durban Summit, at which I reported its conclusions. And it was also the Council which formulated a joint European position for the Johannesburg Summit on sustainable development.

This is why one of my concerns has consistently been to develop co-operation with the United Nations, in whose General Assembly we have observer status, and which I addressed – becoming the first Council of Europe Secretary General to do so – on 20 October 2000. I later had the pleasure of welcoming Kofi Annan, who had also invited me to the meeting of heads of 'regional organisations', in Strasbourg. On the principle that doing the right thing gets you the right enemies, the trouble which arose in the General Assembly in 2002 over the resolution on UN co-operation with the Council constituted a backhanded tribute to our work. Suddenly, people stood up and started objecting to those parts of the resolution which dealt with abolition of the death penalty, the International Criminal Court and our guidelines on respecting human rights in the fight against terrorism. Encouragingly, the majority eventually came down on our side. Disappointingly, one of our own observer countries – the USA – was among those which did not, and which voted against all or part of the text.

Council of Europe and European Union: one flag, one anthem

One question which is steadily becoming more important is that of the relationship between the Council of Europe and the European Union – two products of the same vision, which have developed and grown in different ways, but cannot be separated. In my election programme, I made it clear that I saw partnership with the EU as natural, but felt that it must be equal. There is only one Europe (which is why the Council of Europe and the EU have only one flag and one anthem), and its aim is greater unity. This is why I attach importance, not only to practical co-operation, based on running joint programmes and on co-ordinating goals at regular 'quadripartite' meetings (high-level representatives of the EU Council and Commission, the Chairman of the Committee of Ministers and the Secretary General of the Council of Europe), but also to visionary planning for the future. This is also why I insisted, in the proposals I submitted to the Convention on the Future of the European Union, chaired by former French President Valéry Giscard d'Estaing, that the (enlarged) EU should avail itself fully of the possibilities and pan-European political forum offered by the Council of Europe. It is only logical, too, that the EU, which uses our symbols (flag and anthem), should also accept our standards, particularly those embodied in the European Convention on Human Rights, the European Cultural Convention and the European Social Charter. Ultimately, the EU should have a firm place within the Council's pan-European framework, possibly as an associate member.

Are these mere daydreams, or do we really have a chance to promote Europe more effectively today than at any time in the past?

Profession – optimist

I believe we do, just as I still believe, particularly after visiting Cyprus early in 2003 and talking to representatives of the Turkish community (and in spite of the Annan plan's failure), that we can solve the Cyprus problem. I believe this because Cypriots themselves – both Greek and Turkish – want a solution and are confident that they can find one. Indeed, I like to describe myself as a professional optimist, since being optimistic is a basic and necessary part of my job.

And I have stayed optimistic, in spite of all the problems, great and small, I have encountered. I have stayed optimistic, when large (and wealthy) member states have tried to trim their contributions to peace-keeping and reconciliation missions, costing less than a million euros in total. Not to mention the annual battle over the Council's budget which, at 175 million euros in 2003, was exactly – and merely – the cost of shifting the European Parliament's personnel and equipment to Strasbourg for its monthly sessions. And the sums many states are happy to spend on their armed forces are right off the scale by comparison.

In spite of all this haggling and battling over cents, I have managed, not only to give the Council an effective presence in Chechnya, Moldova,

Armenia, Azerbaijan, Georgia, Serbia and Montenegro, and 'the former Yugoslav Republic of Macedonia', and consolidate its presence in Albania and in Bosnia and Herzegovina, but also to implement successful administrative and financial reforms within the Organisation. These have included taking approximately one-third of the Council's staff off recurrent short-term contracts and putting them on permanent or clearer fixed-term contracts instead, and setting up an affordable pension fund. That, too, is part of a Secretary General's job – if not necessarily dreams.

After four years, after many milestones and some stumbling blocks too, the Council of Europe is still, for me, the 'dream road' to Europe. Progress is sometimes faster, sometimes slower, and sometimes the road seems to fork, but it always leads on to greater unity between the peoples of Europe – and that is the Council's historic mission and political goal.

CHAPTER THREE

The idea of Europe – and who does what with it

Borderline childhood

Thinking of its many tragic repetitions, the Austrian poet Ingeborg Bachmann once wrote: 'History is always teaching lessons, but it never finds anyone to learn them'. Without doubting the sad wisdom of her maxim, I still feel that the history of the epoch into which I was born, experiencing it first as a child with no real notion of what was going on, and then later ever more consciously (politically too), did teach me a great deal about what being European means.

On 13 March 1938, under threat of invasion by the German army, Austria was incorporated into Nazi Germany. The country's leadership, under President Miklas and Chancellor Schuschnigg, was bullied into compliance. The pressures were simply too great, and the state – in which no one had really believed since the Dual Monarchy's demise – gave way under them. The threat from its northern neighbour was compounded by the deep political rift between the conservatives and the working-class socialists (which had triggered civil war and toppled democracy just four years previously), economic depression with massive unemployment and – doubtless encouraged by all of this – growing support for the outlawed National Socialists, who were busy undermining the state from within. And so, on Vienna's Heldenplatz, before the Imperial Palace, Hitler was welcomed by some 200,000 Viennese, probably part-curious and part-enthusiastic, while 'political undesirables' were already being hunted down, and the first attacks launched on the city's 180,000 or so Jews. In Vienna, victims and oppressors lived side by side. At the end of March, the first convoy of prisoners left for Dachau – mainly Christian socialist supporters of the corporative state, but also social democrats, communists and monarchists.

Nazism and the war made countless victims in Austria. Some 247,000 young conscripts were killed fighting for the *Wehrmacht*, 120,000 Jews

55

were stripped of their possessions and driven out, 65,459 died in concentration camps, 24,300 civilians died in air raids, 16,500 non-Jewish anti-
Nazis were murdered in the camps, 16,100 died at the hands of the Gestapo,
and a further 2,700 were executed for political crimes.[1] Resistance was
crushed as soon as it appeared.

Birth sign swastika

And so the Vienna into which I was born in 1942 was a wartime city,
under German occupation. My birth certificate is stamped with the
swastika, symbol of such unspeakable suffering throughout the continent.
My grandmother, with whom my mother, having no flat of her own,
continued to live after her marriage (in any case, her husband was with
the army at the front), was concierge in a house which, before being
'Aryanised', had belonged to a Jewish soda-water manufacturer. A few
Jewish families still lived in it – if waiting fearfully for the worst can be
called living. She herself had grown up in the Leopoldstadt district,
known half-affectionately, half-ironically as the 'Mazzesinsel', because of
its 50% Jewish population and location between the Danube and the
Danube Canal (actually the river's main channel in the Middle Ages). She
had gone to school with Jewish children, and the Nazis' hounding of the
Jews left her bewildered, but still with an instinct to help where she could.
My grandfather and (until I was born) my mother worked in a large meat
and sausage factory, and something was always put aside from their
workers' rations and my pregnant mother's milk ration for the Jewish
children in the house – obviously in defiance of the regulations. Because
of the war, food rationing was general, and the Nazis had cut Jews' rations
to a minimum.

My father was also brought sharply face to face with the tragic fate of
the city's Jews. He was looking for a home for his family and, as a soldier,
was obliged to go through the army's housing office. The first flat he was
sent to inspect was a fine one, but he was shocked to find it still occupied
– by a Jewish family, who were clearly terrified when they saw his uniform,
and had no idea they were leaving. When my father returned to the housing office and reported the 'mistake', he was laughed at. If he liked the flat,
then the Jews would have to leave. In any case, they were all down for
labour service in the east. My father's refusal to put 'someone' out of his
flat was greeted with incredulity – Jews were 'no one'. The obstinate
Vorarlberger refused to accept this, and was eventually given a flat – not
nearly as good, but empty – in the Leopoldstadt, where the Goldsteins
(the original tenants) and three other families had had to survive as best
they could until they were moved out, i.e. taken to the camps.

Before the war, the whole house had belonged to another Jew called Hungerleider, a well-known 'Gansljude' or poultry dealer. Years later, when the Nazis had gone and the war was over, older people in the district still knew it as the 'Hungerleider House'. Hungerleider was married to a non-Jew, and this – at least to start with – gave him some protection. However, his 'Aryan' wife divorced him and took over the house and the business. Hungerleider killed himself, and his ungrieving widow married his Aryan head clerk and carried on the business undisturbed, even after the liberation.

Friends in need

This was the world in which I grew up. In an air raid on a nearby strategic target (the north and north-west railway stations, which were 'carpet bombed', because of the anti-aircraft guns mounted on two towers in the adjacent Augarten park), the Hungerleider House took a hit, which destroyed the rear of the building and collapsed half the cellar where my mother and I had been sheltering. One of my mother's sisters, who was married to a farmer near Vienna, took us in. From there, at the very last moment, my mother managed, by hitching lifts on army trucks and squeezing into jam-packed trains, to escape with me to her parents-in-law in the Vorarlberg, where we were duly liberated – very peacefully – by the French army. While Vienna and its surrounding area suffered heavy fighting and the later exactions of the Red Army, the French in western Austria treated us as friends, whom they were setting free. It was there, at the age of three, that I picked up my first scraps of French. Moroccan troops were quartered in a school across the road from my grandparents' ground-floor flat in the Belruptstrasse, and used the schoolyard for drilling. I used to sit at the window and repeat the words of command, bawling them out at the top of my voice (the amused French officers rewarded me with the occasional piece of chocolate – at the time, a total novelty).

Austria reborn ...

My father had spent the last years of the war in Yugoslavia and, more particularly, Bosnia (to the end of his life, he was deeply distressed by television reports on atrocities committed in places like Banja Luka, Bihac, Bosanski Novy and Kostajnica, where he had once witnessed such horrors himself). Luckily, he had managed to join one of the two 'free' Austrian battalions formed in 1944, and was back in Vienna by the end of July. Our flat was still intact, and so he fetched his family back to the city in conditions unthinkable today – riding on farm carts, walking much of the way with the luggage piled on a hand-cart, and rarely taking trains. Although the Republic had been restored before the war ended, and Renner's three-party government had proclaimed it independent on 26 April, Austria was still not an administrative unit. The regional governments in the western occupation zones, and also the three western powers, were slow to recognise the provisional Government in Vienna (suspecting that the Soviets were behind it [2]), and the only real power lay with the occupation authorities installed by the allies.

The most dangerous part of the journey from Bregenz to Vienna came when we entered the Soviet zone. Exceptionally, the bridge over the Enns was open, although the Soviet sentries on the other side sent men in one direction, and women and children in another. Perhaps my father's discharge papers from the free Austrian battalion did the trick, or perhaps one of the soldiers liked children – at any rate my father was sent to join us on the 'women's side', protesting all the time that he wanted to take us in the opposite direction. Later, despairing families told my parents that the men who had been segregated all landed in Soviet prison camps (some officer was probably trying to meet his 'quota' of prisoners of war, spies and saboteurs). As for us, the end of August found us back in Vienna.

The situation in Austria at that time is certainly best conveyed by the Christmas speech delivered by the Chancellor Leopold Figl, who formed an all-party government after the first free elections, which gave his Christian Democrat *Österreichische Volkspartei* an absolute majority (85 seats, with 75 for the socialists and – disappointingly for the Soviets – only 5 for the communists): 'I can give you nothing for Christmas – no candles for your tree (if you have one), no bread, no coal, not even glass for your broken windows. We have nothing. I can only implore you – believe in this Austria!'

Although we were short of many things – food rationing continued for several years – my parents' sacrifices made sure that I had a happy childhood. I can remember Soviet soldiers sitting in the street and singing sad songs to an accordion. And I remember playing after school – on the bombsites. I was puzzled by the fuss the grown-ups made, talking endlessly about collapsing ruins (we obviously took no notice), and people we had never heard of, who were still buried under them. My own parents hid most of their worries from me: the loss of my father's bicycle, taken from him by a Red Army soldier, who stopped him one morning on his way to the bakery where he worked, or their fear of being caught when they smuggled in food from my aunt's farm.

The politicians also did their best to serve the country under unimaginable conditions. Concentration camps and Gestapo prisons had forged ties between men who had once been bitter political foes, and the plight of their country – occupied and controlled by the four allied powers – encouraged them to seek agreed solutions to its problems. And so, until the State Treaty was concluded in 1955, most differences were subordinated to the one great aim of achieving full sovereignty and ending the occupation. Even before the elections, the provisional government, led by the socialist Chancellor, Karl Renner, had secured the support of the regions in the western occupation zone, mostly controlled by the Christian democrats: a secret emissary had swum across the Enns – the dividing line between Soviets and Americans – for that purpose in September. The one thing which united all the parties (bar the communists) was a total rejection of dictatorship – in any form, old or new. The politicians' consensual, democratic approach carried over into labour relations, where Austria's legendary 'social partnership' was already starting to develop.

... and undivided

The central government was not alone in resisting exactions and interference, chiefly by the Soviet occupiers; regional governments and village mayors stood their ground with equal courage. Partly because of this stout-hearted democratic stance and partly, perhaps, because Stalin wanted to keep a window open to the West, Austria was never partitioned. Of course, there was the 'demarcation line', but this was decided by the occupying powers, and was not an internal frontier. Vienna itself was patrolled by American, British, French and Soviet troops – four to a jeep. The four powers also controlled the first district (the inner city, where the central government offices were located) in monthly rotation. Although Soviet forces were stationed in the east and north of the country, the Iron Curtain lay behind them, on the old frontiers. Unlike Czechoslovakia, for example, Austria was allowed to accept Marshall Aid and could use ERP[3] funds to start rebuilding its economy. It was one of history's tragedies that, apart from Austria itself and the Alto Adige (which had gone to Italy), all the countries which had escaped from the 'dungeon' of the old Dual Monarchy were now under communist rule. In Austria, the watchtowers, minefields and barbed wire, which now kept the peoples of central and eastern Europe truly imprisoned, were so close and clearly visible that the communists stood no chance in free elections. And indeed their share of the vote dwindled steadily from one election to the next, until they finally vanished from Parliament in 1959.

One incident, which I did hear about, took place when the war had already been over for six years. Early in October 1950, there was quite a serious disturbance (I think there may even have been shooting) outside the Communist Party office, about 20 metres down the lane from where we lived. A few evenings later, two men claiming to be police turned up at the door, and started questioning my parents. They, of course, had seen and heard nothing – and wondered afterwards if the visitors had really been policemen. There were reports of a failed communist putsch in the *Courier*, a paper close to the Americans, but obviously – at the age of eight – these meant nothing to me, and I certainly made no connection.

That, I think, was the year when we first went back to the family in the Vorarlberg for our holidays. Apart from visits to my aunt on the farm, I remember that train journey as my first real sight of the country outside Vienna, and its beauty was a revelation. I can still remember marvelling at the glorious monastery at Melk, the tumbling waters of the Salzach, and the stern beauty and spectacular rock formations of the Tyrolean mountains. Austria was still occupied and divided into four zones. The train was stopped at the demarcation line, and identity cards in the allies' three languages were examined – scrutinised by the Soviets and, as a rule, merely glanced at by the Americans. The Soviet guards disappeared into their hut for what seemed an eternity, while the waiting passengers sweated blood. Regularly, someone was taken off the train and not seen again – at least until it was permitted to move off (most, however, were re-routed to the gulag, and did not show up for years, if ever). We, thank God, never had any trouble, but my Vorarlberg relatives – who lived in the French zone – were so frightened of the checks that they never risked coming to see us in Vienna.

Even at the age of nine, the thing that really struck me in this westernmost part of Austria was the difference in living standards and quality of life. It is true that Austria, unlike Germany, had been spared partition and had remained, in spite of its four occupation zones, an economic unit. Nonetheless, there was an invisible dividing line between the 'safe' west, where people invested in the future, and the 'unsafe' east, where the Soviet occupiers had established a privileged economic and industrial complex, the USIA. At any rate, I enjoyed my stay in Bregenz and also the change from the grey poverty of Vienna, with its still uncleared bombsites. Later – I get the same feeling today in some of the poorer new democracies – the contrast was reversed when I visited free Austria's neighbours behind the Iron Curtain, and remembered living in similar conditions myself.

Crossing the border

In today's Europe, I often find myself thinking of another experience during my childhood holidays in the Vorarlberg. Staying there again in summer 1954, we decided to take a boat trip to Lindau, on the Bavarian side of

Lake Constance – the first time I had been 'abroad'! Day-trippers did not need a passport, just an identity card, but (Austria was not yet a free and sovereign country) they also needed a French army permit to cross the border. I still have mine. Today, of course, I can travel from Vienna to Strasbourg without having to show a passport anywhere. But Schengen is not co-extensive with the EU, and I once made the mistake of leaving my passport behind when I went to a conference in Stockholm – before Sweden had accepted the Schengen Agreement. Schengen also forms an invisible wall across Europe, creating a kind of 'inner European' fortress. And so, after four years of travelling as Secretary General of the Council of Europe, my passport is crammed with visas, some of them even from Council member states, and I still have no answer when Haris Silajdzic complains that his grandfather could travel the length and breadth of Europe under the Dual Monarchy, and never need a passport – while he can barely get to Zagreb without a visa.

In the meantime, I had also started to take a first, modest interest in politics. My parents obviously talked about the elections to the National Council, the Austrian Parliament's directly-elected lower house, and the Presidency. As Christians with a social conscience, they were naturally inclined to vote for the ÖVP's presidential candidate, whom they liked in any case. However, my father was a worker (in a bakery) and trade union member, and my parents – who lived in a rented flat – were afraid that traditionally strong safeguards for tenants, which were fiercely defended by the social democrats, might be relaxed. Accordingly, they had to think twice about the parliamentary elections, but I seem to recall that the ÖVP eventually got their vote. The thing I remember most clearly is that, although they differed on certain points with both the democratic parties, the ÖVP and the SPÖ, they were determined to vote – and to vote for one of those parties, and no other. They knew that failing to vote might indirectly favour the communists and so endanger freedom and democracy. I was also aware of the protracted negotiations concerning the State Treaty, mainly with the Soviet Union, and – as the Cold War developed – I could see people openly taking sides on such questions as the Korean war or the German issue. Austrians were, quite simply, on the side of the West.

The Austrian State Treaty

The first Republic (1918–1938) had been a fragile construct, but no one now questioned Austria's viability and independence, and an 'Austrian nation' came into being. In foreign policy, this nation was firmly committed to the 'western' values embodied in the Statute of the Council of Europe, founded in 1949: pluralist democracy, the rule of law and human rights. The young country was also anxious, however, to retain its traditional ties with its eastern, northern and south-eastern neighbours. Ideologically, it was never neutral, either before 1955 or afterwards, but its geographical position made it determined to be nobody's pawn in the Cold War, and – wherever it could – to prise a chink in the Iron Curtain. For obvious, pragmatic reasons, good relations with the Soviet Union were important, but Austria was scrupulously careful not to become dependent on the Soviets or let them dictate its own policy. The Austrian Chancellor, Julius Raab, put it vividly: 'When you've got the Russian bear in your garden, you don't tweak his tail.'

The Austrian State Treaty of 1955 was undoubtedly one of the successes of this policy; acceptance of 'perpetual neutrality' (a formula adopted, on the Swiss model, in the Moscow negotiations) was not the price, but the logical consequence, of Austria's recovered sovereignty. For Moscow, having Switzerland and Austria as a neutral wedge between the Federal Republic of Germany and Italy – both NATO members – was certainly important, strategically and geopolitically. But Austria also stood to gain by not joining either of the massively-armed rival blocs, and not losing its old links with central and eastern Europe. It insisted, however, that its neutrality was military only, and that this essentially committed it to joining no military alliances and accepting no foreign troops on its territory. When the Constitutional Law on Neutrality was discussed in Parliament, the Chancellor explained:

> 'This law in no way restricts the basic rights and freedoms of citizens. Neutrality is binding on the state, but not the individual citizen. The individual's intellectual and political freedom, and particularly freedom of the press and expression, is not affected by a state's permanent neutrality. Nor is there any obligation to observe ideological neutrality. I would also emphasise, ladies and gentlemen, that the military neutrality which you will be voting today will carry no obligations of an economic or cultural nature. The great task of future state policy will be to organise a coalition of free nations to promote and guarantee the rule of law together; this is the idea on which the United Nations is founded. In helping to realise those principles, Austria is remaining true to its innermost nature and is pursuing a policy which has a positive aim of relevance to all citizens and which can, through our neutrality, give preservation of our independence more forceful expression.' [4]

That was why 1955 and 1956 were the years which left a real political mark on me as an adolescent. After endless, abortive negotiations over a State Treaty, which would restore Austria's sovereignty and free it of the burden of having to pay the costs of occupation (the western powers had already waived their claims), a historic window was suddenly opened. A government delegation was invited to Moscow for bilateral talks. Chancellor Julius Raab, Foreign Minister Leopold Figl, Vice-Chancellor Adolf Schärf and State Secretary Bruno Kreisky accepted the challenge, some of them with mixed feelings. As the Chancellor's secretary, Ludwig Steiner – later Secretary of State and Chairman of the Council of Europe Parliamentary Assembly's Political Affairs Committee – was involved in the historic negotiations which brought the breakthrough, and often told me the story.

The whole of Austria was glued to the radio – the only TV programme was experimental, and very few homes could receive it – when Chancellor Raab announced in ringing tones from Moscow: 'Austria is going to be free.'

The returning delegation landed at the Soviet airbase in Bad Vöslau. All the way to Vienna, the road was lined with cheering crowds. My mother took me to the Ballhausplatz, to see the delegates welcomed in front of the government building. People were laughing and weeping at the same time. This was only the first of the many vivid scenes which marked the next few months.

The day on which the State Treaty was signed, 15 May 1955, was unforgettable. The whole of Vienna was in the streets. Whenever the crowds caught a glimpse of the foreign ministers of the four signatory states (soon to be occupying powers no longer), and the heroes of the hour, above all Julius Raab, the 'freedom Chancellor', and Leopold 'Poldi' Figl, probably the most popular Foreign Minister Austria ever had, the cheering broke out afresh. Standing on the balcony at Schloss Belvedere, where the park was black with people, Leopold Figl brandished the treaty and cried: 'Austria is free.' Strictly speaking, this was not entirely true, since it took several months – actually until 25 October – for the last of the occupying troops to withdraw, restoring the country to full sovereignty.

Every stage on the path to freedom was celebrated. I was now 13 years old, but I still had to ask my mother why people became so excited, and why she herself started weeping, when the French, British, Soviet and American flags were lowered on the Allied Control Council building, and Austria's red and white flag was hoisted to replace them. All of this taught me how much freedom and democratic self-determination really mean to ordinary people. I stood proudly with the crowd on the Ringstrasse on 26 October 1955 – the day on which Parliament voted the law declaring Austria neutral forever – as the first units of the newly-founded Austrian federal army marched past. It was those few months which turned me into a conscious Austrian and democrat, and taught me the value of freedom. I little thought that, one day, as an elected MP, I would be helping to shape my country's destiny in the building just over the road from the point where I stood cheering as the troops marched by.

Fighting and dying for freedom – our neighbours pay the price

But all of that lay a long way in the future. The first test of Austria's neutrality came in 1956, when the Red Army crushed the Hungarian rising. Austria's government and people made it unmistakably clear that their sympathies lay with the Hungarian people and the Nagy government. The Austrian embassy in Budapest, under the courageous leadership of Ambassador Peinsipp, first acted as a political go-between and then helped to channel humanitarian aid. But Austria also took its military neutrality seriously and acted accordingly. The newly-formed army was moved up to the Hungarian frontier, and disarmed any soldiers who crossed into Austria. In spite of pressure from Moscow, the border was naturally kept open for the 200,000 or so refugees, who fled to escape the Red Army and the Kádár regime.

When the Hungarian rising broke out on 23 October 1956, I had just turned 14 – possibly the age when one cares most passionately about justice and injustice. The names of Imre Nagy and Pal Maleter imprinted themselves on my memory, like those of Janos Kádár, the Csepel working class district in Budapest or the Petöfi Memorial. Glued to the radio, my homework forgotten, I shared the Hungarians' anguish in their fight for freedom. I was determined to miss nothing. When youth organisations called for volunteers to help organise relief, I joined in at once, sorting and piling the items donated in huge quantities by the Austrian public. I was particularly proud when, one day, I was detailed to help a Hungarian officer from Györ, who was desperately scouring Vienna for vitally needed medical supplies. The exhilaration of the first six days soon turned to despair, which I felt too, when the rebel government was arrested and the freedom fighters broadcast their last desperate cry for help. I could not understand how the British and French could go to war over the Suez Canal – out in the desert, in the middle of nowhere – and simply turn their backs on people locked in a desperate battle for liberty.

Once again, all my afternoons were spent at one of the collection points for items donated – this time for the thousands of refugees who came streaming over the border from Hungary. Some 200,000 managed to slip through the Iron Curtain and make it across the famous bridge at Andau. And the Austrians rushed to help. Needless to say, I pitched in again when schoolchildren started collecting money for the refugees; in just one afternoon, another boy and I managed to collect 2000 schillings – an enormous sum for the time. I had already learned to value democracy and freedom, but I now learned about solidarity with other Europeans and about human rights. In my mind, the European dream was starting to take shape. I now knew that Austria was not an island, and that I had far closer links than I had ever thought with my neighbours and other Europeans everywhere, but I also knew that great wrongs had been done, and were still being done, in Europe. And so, for me, the European dream became inextricably linked with justice, freedom and solidarity, in contrast to their opposites – injustice, tyranny and national egotism.

School for democracy

Just 11 years had passed since the end of the mass slaughter perpetrated during the Second World War and under the Nazi barbarians. A new era had begun, bringing new injustices (above all, behind the Iron Curtain), but the past remained a major problem. People's behaviour and attitudes in that 'past' had simply been too different. Some had cheered when the Nazis marched into Austria and had welcomed annexation by the Third Reich; a few had gone further and had joined at once in ostracising and humiliating the Jews; others again had simply kept their heads down, or had not known how to resist; only a few – too few – dared to stand up and fight back, in the name of freedom and human dignity. Hundreds of thousands were despatched to a war which was not theirs, but which was, they were told, being waged to defend their homeland and families against the invading hordes from the east. Teachers and parents had all been involved, and were afraid to talk about the past with their children and tell them the truth.

I was doubly lucky. Firstly, my parents had no difficulty in talking openly to me about the Nazi era and telling me how they felt about it. Secondly, my history teacher had no inhibitions either: he did not, like so many others, stop dead in 1914, steering clear of all the politically embarassing and controversial developments which followed, but took the story up to the point where my own impressions of contemporary history began, covering the State Treaty, Austria's position in Europe and the world, and the division of Europe by the Iron Curtain. One of the three questions I had to answer orally, in my end-of-school exams in 1960, dealt with Austria's perpetual neutrality, decided by Parliament on 26 October 1955. At that time, Austria had been a genuinely sovereign state for just five years, and for four years a member of the United Nations and also the Council of Europe (which would take another 30 years to become the Council, not just of free, western Europe, but of the whole continent).

My answer was probably not very far from the definition given in Parliament some six weeks later by the future federal Chancellor, Dr Alfons Gorbach, himself a concentration camp survivor:

'Neutrality means keeping out of other people's quarrels, but it never means standing aside from the great international task of working for peace in the economic, social, cultural and humanitarian fields. Austria showed this clearly under the four-power occupation, and showed it again later, when it joined the Organisation for European Economic Co-operation [NB: OEEC, the later OECD] and, after the conclusion of the State Treaty, the United Nations, the Council of Europe and EFTA, and – last but not least – when it recognised the right of asylum at the time of the Hungarian rising.'

Thanks to my parents, and although times were hard, I had a happy childhood and young manhood. Thanks to them, to my teachers (at least some of them) and to responsible politicians, whose closeness to their own people did not stop them from being both cosmopolitan and Europe-minded, I got just the apprenticeship I needed as a young Austrian setting out to become a European.

Rhine, Oder, Adige – mending the bridges

For centuries, the main importance of Europe's frontiers was strategic. By extending them, countries sought to ensure that they could bring their own troops close to the 'enemy' in wartime, while keeping opposing forces well clear of their heartland. They also tried to make them easy to defend. Though they barely affected people living close to them in peacetime – at least until passports and visas were invented – they thus served to divide from a very early stage. Great rivers, like the Rhine (already the border between France and Germany in the 17th century) or the Oder (which became significant in the mid-20th century), or mountains, like those crossed by the Brenner between the North and South Tyrol, were particularly effective both strategically and as dividers. Kings and generals were not alone in thinking 'safe' frontiers worth fighting for. When frictions developed between the new nation-states, security, i.e. safe frontiers, became a matter of vital concern, if not at first to the masses, then to the ruling classes. But did everyone think like this?

'The supranational sense of community among Europeans is a pure invention of the poets – the only ones who preserved it and kept it alive in times of bitter enmity,' wrote Heinrich Mann in 1927. Fortunately, he was wrong, since this sense of community was preserved, not just by poets, but by others too – intellectuals and academics, as well as a few (far too few) politicians and some historians.

Some of the romantics, whose patriotic fervour had initially been ignited by the new concept of the nation-state, were later among the first to warn against the dangers of glorifying the nation, and to voice genuinely European sentiments. Even today, the texts in which they did this make remarkable reading, particularly when the authors came from 'emergent nations', like Italy and Germany. In 1829, Giuseppe Mazzini was already insisting that national independence must not be confused with intellectual isolation, and acknowledging that 'civilisation, carried to its highest point' did not allow peoples to have a clearly individual national character. His central message – in 1829! – was: 'In Europe, there is thus agreement regarding needs and wishes, an all-pervading spirit, a universal soul, which leads all the nations towards a single goal: there is a European movement.'

These words were prophetic, and far ahead of their time, but Mazzini was not the only one. Much the same attitude is apparent in well-known texts by German writers like Novalis, Friedrich Schlegel and Ernst Moritz Arndt – even though some of them later came to think in national, rather than European, terms.

Brotherhood between nations – but not yet

The British poet Shelley's 1812 *Address to the Irish people* is a shining example: 'Fellow men, I am not an Irishman, yet I can feel for you.' He demanded 'universal emancipation – and this emancipation complete and unconditional, that shall comprehend every individual of whatever nation or principles'. He was one of the few to call at that time for equal rights for all Europeans. But he was not alone in wanting Europeans to start thinking of themselves as European. One only has to think of Victor Hugo's *Observations on history* (1827), François Guizot's lectures on *La civilisation en Europe* (1828) and, many years later (1872), Hugo's message to the Lausanne Peace Congress, in which – in spite of his bitterness at seeing Alsace-Lorraine annexed by the German Empire – he called for a 'magnanimous brotherhood of the nations'. One may also think of the famous Sorbonne lecture, *Qu'est-ce qu'une nation?*, in which Ernest Renan proclaimed in 1882, long after the romantics, that: 'The nations are not eternal. They have a beginning and an end. The European confederation will probably replace them.'

Paul Michael Lützeler once wrote: 'In terms of content only, the romantics' essays on Europe have little to teach us today.' But he added that they had 'put thinking about Europe on a level which it would be disastrous to fall short of now'. The truth of this is confirmed by the fact that, for a long time after the romantics, national and indeed nationalist thinking became dominant even among intellectuals. The First World War brought a first change of heart, although this was not – alas – sufficiently widespread. In novels by writers who fought on any side in that war, there is amazingly little hostility towards the 'enemy'. They all shared the *conditio humana* of life in the trenches, the same misery and the same terror – and they all knew that things were no different for soldiers on the other side. This was certainly the experience which gave the European idea a fresh impetus.

Fighting for the Rhine

Tentative moves towards a new start in Europe – reflected in the cautious *rapprochement* between Germany and France, particularly under Aristide Briand and Gustav Stresemann – were broken off when Hitler came to power in Germany. A few weeks before, in December 1932, Julien Benda had completed his *Address to the European Nation*, borrowing his title from Fichte's *Address to the German Nation*. But this arresting plea, from a writer who had denounced the 'treason of the intellectuals' just five years earlier, came too late. The language of the Nazis, the *Lingua Tertii Imperii*, had no term for a 'European nation'. Once again, revenge was to come first. Once again, command of the Rhine and possession of Alsace and Lorraine, the remnants of the kingdom which had come down to Lothar as his share of Charlemagne's empire, and which had been fought over ever since, were to cost millions of young Frenchmen and Germans life, health or – at the very least – years of their lives. Without being asked, Alsatians and Lorrainers were dragged 'home to the Reich', packed into *Wehrmacht* uniforms and sent to their deaths, mainly on the eastern front.

Both during the war and immediately afterwards, Frenchmen – even those in the resistance – were the first to start pondering the need for reconciliation between France and Germany. Jean Monnet had already struck this note, still very soberly, in his Algiers Memorandum. After the war, on 1 October 1945, there came an astounding plea, *L'Allemagne de nos mérites*, from Joseph Rovan, who had been liberated from Dachau just five months previously: 'The greater our enemies' success in masking the face of humanity, the greater our duty to respect, and even glorify, it in them.' And he wrote that the German spirit would have to be loved, even if Germany 'had never produced Bach and Goethe'.

Other French intellectuals – Jean du Rivau, Emmanuel Mounier, Alfred Grosser – were writing in the same vein, but it was still too soon for reconciliation. In his memoirs, Wilhelm Hausenstein, Germany's first post-war Ambassador in Paris, described the atmosphere in 1951, when hardly anyone was left in the city who had not suffered in some way under the Nazis. Similarly, the political *rapprochement* between Robert Schuman and Konrad Adenauer still left the French public unmoved, much as they respected Adenauer's moral integrity and authority.

And so it was left to the 'Chef' of the resistance and liberation, Charles de Gaulle, to acknowledge Germany as a partner and persuade his countrymen to follow him. In his *Mémoires d'espoir*, the man who had once declared that countries had no friends, only interests, spoke of Germany as a friend – he was thinking of Konrad Adenauer – and wrote movingly of the service held in Reims Cathedral (in France, that most secular of countries!) to celebrate the rebirth of friendship between the two nations ('The first citizens of France and of Germany').

There was a strange chemistry between these two old men (Adenauer was 87, de Gaulle 73), which drove them to ignore the opposition of those around them and sign, on 22 January 1963, the Franco-German Friendship Treaty, which remains the basis of relations between the two nations to this day, has weathered all subsequent changes of government, and is still a central element in the architecture of Europe. Everyone knows that François Mitterrand and Helmut Kohl were personally close, but very few people know that Mitterrand accompanied Kohl on a visit to the 90-year old Ernst Jünger in 1985, and asked to see the 'Pour le mérite' medal which Jünger, its last surviving holder, had received from Kaiser Wilhelm for outstanding service in the first World War. When François Mitterrand left office in 1995, a moving farewell tribute by Helmut Kohl appeared in *Le Monde*.

The road to reconciliation: France, Poland, Israel

When his government took office, it was Konrad Adenauer who first set Germany on the path to reconciliation with three countries in particular: France, Poland and Israel. An agreement on reparations opened the way to relations with Israel (although these remained merely formal), and reconciliation was achieved with France, but no headway could be made with communist Poland, which had, on Stalin's orders, annexed huge tracts of German territory. This was a heavy burden on relations, and Adenauer was also careful to stay on good terms with the expellees, whose associations were a powerful force in his party.

After centuries of an ambivalent relationship – war when the land-hungry knights of the Teutonic Order ravaged Polish territories, peace when Saxony and Poland were joined in a personal union – Poland had, since the divisions, suffered repeatedly at the hands of Prussia and later Germany. Hitler's brutal onslaught on Poland had opened the Second World War, and the Hitler-Stalin pact re-enacted the earlier divisions. Later came the Nazis' drive to exterminate the Jews, with Poland as the main arena, and their attempt to wipe the Polish nation off the map – glaringly illustrated by their systematic levelling of old Warsaw after the 1944 rising. Stalin (who had kept the Red Army inactive on the other side of the Vistula, while the rising was brutally crushed) then chose to humble Poland yet again at Germany's expense. In effect, he simply moved the country west: millions of Poles from the east, which became Soviet, were 'resettled' – and millions of Germans from Pomerania, East Prussia and Silesia, all now part of Poland, were driven out. In this way, injustice was piled on injustice, making the rift between Germany and Poland nigh-impossible to heal.

It was Willy Brandt who found the courage to recognise the Oder-Neisse Line in 1970. He did this on behalf of the Federal Republic, not the whole of Germany – a subtle point of treaty law, but important for reasons both of German constitutional and of international law ('the four-power reservation'). Helmut Kohl, who never had any real illusions regarding the permanence of the Oder-Neisse border, started by sticking to the letter of the law as rigorously as any of his predecessors – but he wanted better relations with Poland (and certainly never imagined that German reunification would give him the chance to achieve them). When the time came, he explained to his countrymen that final recognition of the border was a *sine qua non* of reunification, remarking privately to intimates that his signature on the act ratifying the treaty had been: 'The most expensive in my life – 114,000 square kilometres.'

Poland and the reunited Germany actually signed two agreements – one on recognition of the frontier, the other on mutual co-operation. This closed a painful chapter in the history of both nations, and opened the way to good relations. Today it is safe to say that the atmosphere on both sides of the Oder is one of partnership, if not indeed friendship. The commentators and observers who are following the EU's enlargement to the east all agree that Germany is pushing hardest for Polish accession and will insist, for political reasons, on Poland's being included in the first new intake, regardless of possible problems on the economic, and above all agricultural, front.

The Brenner – a 'natural' frontier

And so, step by step, the past's heavy legacy was overcome in western and central Europe. But there were territorial problems in other parts of Europe too: how could Austria, for example, accept a situation which left so many German-speaking inhabitants of Andreas Hofer's Tyrolean homeland – now just a north Italian province – without proper rights of their own?

After the First World War, disregarding the right of peoples to self-determination (one of Wilson's 14 points), Italy had annexed not only the Italian-speaking part of the Tyrol south of the Salorno Gap, but also the German-speaking part south of the Brenner, which Italian nationalists were anxious to secure as a 'natural' frontier. In the three years following

Italy's entry into the war in 1915, the Tyroleans had defended their home-land fiercely and, at a heavy cost in lives, successfully. (My own Alsatian-born grandfather, Johann Baptist Schwimmer, spent three years as a Vorarlberg 'Kaiserjäger' on the Italian front, fortunately surviving to return to his family in Bregenz.) All of this counted for nothing when the armistice was agreed on 3 November 1918. In the 'peace negotiations', Italy backed its claims with maps on which the Tyrolean towns of Bozen, Meran and Brixen appeared as Bolzano, Merano and Bressanone. In fact, a trumped-up Italian name was pinned on every last village, every small-est stream. Annexation was followed, particularly once the Fascists had seized power, by ever-harsher measures to Italianise the region, climaxing in the fatal agreement between Hitler and Mussolini, which gave the South Tyroleans a choice between emigrating to the *Grossdeutsches Reich*, and being absorbed into the Italian population and resettled in southern Italy. The end of the Second World War put a stop to this vicious essay in ethnic cleansing.

All of this obviously made it exceptionally hard for Austria and Italy to reach an understanding on the South Tyrol. Towards the end of the war, there were admittedly some Italian democrats who favoured relinquishing areas inhabited by Austrians – in other words, partitioning the South Tyrol. But the allies wanted to keep the frontier on the Brenner. In September 1946, the Austrian and Italian foreign ministers, Karl Gruber and Alcide di Gasperi (who had represented Trento, then ruled by Austria, as a young man in the Austrian Parliament), concluded an agreement which guaran-teed German-speakers equal rights, schooling in their own language, equal use of German for all official purposes and the 'exercise of regional legislative and executive powers'. But Italy, taking in di Gasperi's home province of Trento, went on to establish a large region, Trentino, with an Italian majority and very limited legislative powers. Moreover, taking a leaf from the Fascists' book, it encouraged immigration, chiefly from the south, with the result that the situation of the German-speaking South Tyroleans worsened steadily. The ensuing disputes dragged on for years – and Austria eventually took the matter to the UN. There were even bomb attacks by extremists (the 'bummser', or blow-up boys). At last, in June 1969, after 23 years of trying, the two countries worked out an agreement which satisfied them both – particularly Austria, since it protected the German-speakers' interests. Even the South Tyrolean People's Party, which had unceasingly proclaimed the South Tyroleans' basic right to self-determination, accepted it. Today, the two states not only enjoy har-monious relations, but regard their solution for the South Tyrol as a model for the settlement of other minority problems in Europe. I saw the fruits for myself when I went to Vienna in spring 2002 to join the Italian Minister for Europe, Rocco Buttiglione, and the Austrian Foreign Minister, Benita Ferrero-Waldner, in celebrating the tenth anniversary of the agreement. The mountain paths laid out by the two opposing armies as they fought for the Tyrol are now used by tourists – and serve to remind both sides of past mistakes.

Like the South Tyrol, the Åaland Islands, which were granted autonomy by Finland, provide a perfect answer to those who argue that autonomy encourages separatism, and see it as the first step towards severance. The islands are mainly inhabited by Swedes and were – like Finland – part of the Russian Empire until 1917. After the First World War, the Åalanders sought union with Sweden, but the international community objected, and the League of Nations calmed their disappointment by making them largely autonomous and demilitarising the islands. When I went there with the Council of Europe Parliamentary Assembly's Legal Affairs Committee, I actually hit the local headlines by asking about the rights of Finnish-speakers. Finland itself has a 6% Swedish minority and, in deference to their rights, Swedish is the country's second language and is taught to all Finns. But Finnish Åaland has just one official language – Swedish! – and ethnic Finns get no basic schooling in their own language. This is a question, not of Swedish nationalism, but of regional rights, and the Åalanders have become loyal Finns – like the South Tyrolean skiers who compete against Austrians from the North Tyrol and win medals for Italy.

It is true that the South Tyrolean People's Party, which represents the German and Ladin-speakers, still insists on the right to self-determination in its programme. In practice, however, it concentrates on exercising the region's existing autonomous rights (far more extensive than those of any Austrian region), co-operates with Italian parties at election-time and has a good relationship with the government in Rome. Obviously, the Ladins, the Rhaeto-Romansch of the Dolomites, have always wanted autonomy and allied themselves with the German-speaking South Tyroleans, but Italian politicians in the Province of Bozen-Südtirol/Alto Adige have discovered the charms of autonomy – and are now their staunch champions. In Brussels, there is joint regional representation, not just of the Austrian North Tyrol and the mainly German-speaking South Tyrol, but also of the 'Italian Tyrol' in the Province of Trento.

Similarly, Poland's German minority is again represented in Parliament today. In Alsace too, the kind of situation Tomi Ungerer evoked, when he spoke to schoolchildren from Strasbourg and Kehl at a Council of Europe meeting against racism and intolerance in 2002, is unthinkable today. Having just celebrated his 70th birthday, he was asked if he had ever been persecuted himself. 'Yes,' he said, 'twice – once when I was beaten at school for speaking French, and again five years later, when I was beaten for speaking German.' Bilingual schools and street names in French and Elsässer-Dütsch show that people now appreciate their double heritage. The removal of frontier controls obviously has greater historical significance on the Pont de l'Europe between Strasbourg (France) and Kehl (Germany) than it does on, say, the Franco-Belgian border – and the same applies to the use of one currency. On the Brenner, the Italians were quicker off the mark than the Austrians in dismantling their border facilities, although removal of the border between North and South Tyrol had been a highly emotive factor in discussion of Austria's accession to the EU. The Oder-Neisse border, too, will soon lose its present significance and acquire a new one.

From enmity to friendship

'Hereditary enmities' have gone, and partnership and co-operation have taken their place. On the Rhine, Oder and Adige, reconciliation – unthinkable for decades, if not centuries – has been achieved. Agreed solutions to territorial and minority problems have been found. Surely Greece and Turkey, for example, should be able to compound their differences too? Surely the Hungarian minorities in Slovakia or Romania need not be a bone of contention? Germany and France have formed a close partnership, Germany and Poland have reached an understanding, Austria and Italy have agreed in the Tyrol – surely the two communities in Cyprus should be able, with benevolent support from Greece and Turkey, to agree and reunite their island? An opinion given by the Council of Europe's Venice Commission has helped Hungary and Romania to reach agreement on the status of Romania's Hungarians. There is no shortage of positive examples – all over Europe, arrangements for autonomous status and protection of minorities are being devised and written into law. Of course, there are still unsolved problems, frozen conflicts, questions of prestige, from Kosovo through Transnistria to Nagorno-Karabakh. But are they insoluble? Permanently intractable? As unthinkable as Franco-German friendship 100 years ago, reconciliation between Poland and Germany 50 years ago, or agreement on the South Tyrol 30 years ago? We must stop merely dreaming of more 'miracles' like these, and remember that many such dreams have already come true.

But they needed help to come true. The courage of an Adenauer or a de Gaulle, the persistence and faith of a Sylvius Magnago in South Tyrol, the humility of a Willy Brandt will be needed again to realise the dream of European unity. I have said there is no shortage of examples – will there be a shortage of people to follow them?

Organising Europe: how it all began

With the Cold War over for more than 10 years, the Maastricht, Amsterdam and Nice Treaties concluded, and EU enlargement firmly on the table, there are many people today who have little idea how the whole European process got started after 1945. The Cold War, which became a reality (at latest) when the four-power conference on Germany collapsed in London at the end of 1947, certainly helped to hasten it. But the European idea was not simply revived by the Cold War – the second World War and events leading up to it had already done that. People always dream of peace in wartime, and Europe's true statesmen were already dreaming of a peace clearly marked by that idea.

In the preamble to the Treaty establishing the European Coal and Steel Community (ECSC), which was signed on 18 April 1951 and came into force in July 1952, the six Contracting Parties (Federal Republic of Germany, France, Italy and the Benelux countries) declared themselves determined to 'to substitute for age-old rivalries the merging of their essential interests; to create, by establishing an economic community, the basis for a broader and deeper community among peoples long divided by bloody conflicts'.

The necessary link between action to preserve peace and prosperity, and action to protect human rights, had already been acknowledged two years before, when the Council of Europe was founded in 1949. In the preamble to its Statute, the 10 founding states had reaffirmed 'their devotion to the spiritual and moral values which are the common heritage of their peoples and the true source of individual freedom, political liberty and the rule of law, principles which form the basis of all genuine democracy'. Thus, from the very beginning, the Council of Europe and the first European Community were not rivals, but twin servants of the European idea, as redefined after the Second World War.

New Europe, vague profile

Many people see Winston Churchill's celebrated Zurich speech of September 1946 as marking the birth of this 'new Europe', but its outlines were still remarkably vague. It is true that, after referring explicitly to Count Coudenhove-Kalergi and Aristide Briand, Churchill called for 'a kind of United States of Europe' – 'or whatever name it may take' – and for the founding of a 'Council of Europe' as a first step. However, the powers and structure of the new body were left completely open.

Nonetheless, his far-sighted vision made an impression: far earlier than most of the European federalists, Churchill had realised that unity on a continental scale was not (yet) a possibility. Some countries might be unwilling or unable to join in taking the first step, but the vital thing was to take it, and involve as many as possible. The first necessity was 'partnership between France and Germany', which must take the lead together. This was Churchill's way of driving home his message that Great Britain and the Commonwealth (like the USA) must be 'the friends and sponsors of the new Europe' – i.e. would not be part of it.

From 1946 on, it was clear that the ideas of the federalists, most of whom still believed in 'pan-Europa', and those of the pragmatic realists were incompatible. In 1948, it became equally clear that they could not afford to waste time fighting each other: in February, the communists (i.e. the Soviets) staged a coup in Czechoslovakia, bringing it permanently under their control. In March, France, Great Britain and the Benelux countries signed the Brussels Treaty as a prelude to the Western European Union (WEU). The Berlin blockade began in June.

In May – at a time when Stalinist rule had already been consolidated in central, eastern and south-eastern Europe, robbing the pan-European federalists of their last illusions – the various European movements had organised a congress in The Hague. Not the least of the reasons for its legendary status and lasting impact was the list of participants from 17 nations. It included: Léon Blum, Jean Monnet and François Mitterrand from France; Winston Churchill, Harold Macmillan and Duncan Sandys from Britain; Alcide de Gasperi, Altiero Spinelli and Ignazio Silone from Italy; and Konrad Adenauer and Walter Hallstein from Germany. The Hague Congress took no binding decisions, but it recommended that an assembly of representatives of national parliaments be established to explore the political and legal implications of a European Union or Federation. This was a prefigurement – admittedly more far-reaching than the eventual reality – of the Council of Europe's Consultative Assembly.

New Europe gets a home – the Council of Europe

On 5 May 1949, 10 states – Belgium, Denmark, France, Ireland, Italy, Luxembourg, the Netherlands, Norway, Sweden and the United Kingdom – founded the Council of Europe. By 1951, Greece, Turkey, Iceland and the Federal Republic of Germany had also joined. This meant that, with the exception of the smaller states, and of the potentially or actually 'neutral' Austria (1956), Switzerland (1963) and Finland (1989), all of Europe's democratic, law-governed states were already, in the early 1950s, members of the Council – an organisation destined to play a permanently leading role in a Europe dedicated to democracy, the rule of law and human rights.

In its Statute, the Council of Europe was given the special task of achieving 'a greater unity between its members for the purpose of safeguarding and realising the ideals and principles which are their common heritage'. Its members were required to respect the rule of law, human rights and basic freedoms. With a dominant Committee of Ministers and a merely 'consultative' Parliamentary Assembly, it reflected the realistic/pragmatic stream in the European movement, although the Assembly itself and a Secretary General elected by the Assembly gave it some of the structural features of a confederation.

The Council was also the first institutional expression of a new trend towards the international protection of human rights. This reflected the vision of humanity which formed part of Europe's heritage, and also an awareness that protecting human rights would help to keep the peace – a function provisionally rounded off when the European Convention for the Protection of Human Rights and Fundamental Freedoms (ECHR) was adopted on 4 November 1950. Like the Council itself, the Convention had also been recommended by the Hague Congress. Few people today realise that this was Europe's first supranational system – even pre-dating the Coal and Steel Community, the germ from which the EU eventually developed.

It is also worth noting that, ever since the ECHR first took effect, the number of states accepting it has always exceeded the number of states within the Communities, which have never achieved an equally stringent level of human rights protection. Indeed, thanks to this and numerous other conventions, and to the long list of requirements it expects new members to satisfy, the Council has ultimately done more to disseminate and consolidate democracy, the rule of law and human rights than many people in Brussels care to admit.

The Council of Europe was barely one year old when Robert Schuman, the French Foreign Minister, sprang a major surprise by announcing, on 9 May 1950, that: 'The French Government proposes that the whole of French and German coal and steel production be controlled by a joint authority, by an organisation open to participation by other European countries.' The German Chancellor had given the plan his blessing in advance. As Konrad Adenauer wrote later in his memoirs: 'Schuman's plan was wholly consonant with the ideas I had long been putting forward concerning the linking of key industries in Europe.'

Coal and steel – the community approach

The international background to the Schuman plan is well known: the Saarland was under French control and its production went to France.

West Germany's heavy industry, centred in the Ruhr, was subject to restrictions and to supervision by the International Ruhr Authority. Once the Cold War had begun, this situation seemed less and less defensible. Great Britain and, above all, the USA realised that they needed an effective, economically viable German partner, firmly tied to the West, on their side of the Iron Curtain. West Germany, however, could not be a partner without having equal rights. France had strong reservations to start with: because of its military potential, it wanted to keep a firm hold on the West German steel industry – and it also feared unwelcome competition.

By spring 1950, it was becoming increasingly clear that the French Government would not be able to maintain this position for long. It accordingly started looking for ways of securing the leading role in western Europe (if nothing else) for France. And so Robert Schuman took over a memorandum drafted by the Planning Commissioner, Jean Monnet, and a few days later went public with the plan to which his name was immediately attached, although Monnet had been its real author.

Reorganising Europe by establishing a federation or *entité européenne*, preventing further war between France and Germany, compromising on absolute state sovereignty in the interests of keeping the peace, Europeanising the metal industry – these were the building blocks from which Monnet and Schuman fashioned their new Europe. In his famous declaration of May 1950, Schuman referred explicitly to armaments, and explained that his plan would make 'war between France and Germany not only unthinkable, but materially impossible'. The establishment of a coal and steel community marked the 'first step towards European federation', which was 'essential to preserving the peace'. Much of this was later incorporated into the Preamble to the Treaty establishing the European Coal and Steel Community.

The ECSC also had a Council of Ministers, an Assembly and a Court. The two organisations served very different functions, but the parallels with the Council of Europe are unmistakable. Today, these similarities still remind us that the European movement, which developed in so many different directions later, had a single origin, and that the various European institutions were founded on much the same ideas.

Getting the ECSC Treaty ratified in France proved difficult, but the efforts finally paid off. However, the French National Assembly blocked efforts to 'communitise' European defence, which would have entailed far more sweeping changes. Interestingly, it was the French Prime Minister, René Pleven, who, in October 1950, first proposed a European Defence Community (EDC) – an initiative which can be seen as an attempt to stop the Federal Republic of Germany from rearming (or being rearmed by the USA).

After strenuous negotiations, the EDC Treaty was finally signed in May 1952. One of its articles, the famous Article 38, stated – quite simply – that development of the EDC into a political union should be envisaged. This part of the text was proposed and put through by the Italian Prime Minister, Alcide de Gasperi. Speaking in the Council of Europe's Consultative Assembly, he explained:

> 'If we expect the armed forces of the various countries to come together in a permanent, constitutional organisation and, in certain circumstances, to defend a greater fatherland, then this fatherland must be visible. The solidarity proposed in the Treaty establishing the European Defence Community, which is a life-and-death solidarity, will never withstand the centrifugal and separatist tendencies which will repeatedly agitate the national parliaments, without a central political authority.'

Since de Gasperi and others like him were unwilling to wait for the EDC Treaty to take effect, the ECSC Assembly was instructed, in September 1952, to start acting on Article 38 in the meantime. Within half a year, the 'ad hoc Assembly', chaired by Paul-Henri Spaak, had produced its draft. The 'Political Union' was to co-ordinate the foreign policy of the member states, gradually establish a common market and finally take over the powers of the ECSC and the EDC. However, as we have said, the project came to nothing. The vote taken in the French National Assembly on 30 August 1954 made it clear that most of the members saw no reason to tamper with the 'holiest' aspect of state sovereignty by communitising foreign and defence policy.

Back to economics

At their conference in Messina in 1955, Europe's foreign ministers set off on a new tack: they decided that a common market was needed, and set up an international committee of experts, chaired by Paul-Henri Spaak, to explore the possibility of integrating certain branches of the economy and setting up an organisation to oversee the peaceful development of nuclear energy.

A year later, the committee proposed that a European Economic Community (EEC) and a European Atomic Energy Community (Euratom) be established. After tough intergovernmental negotiations, the two founding treaties were signed in Rome on 25 March 1957. They came into force on 1 January 1958.

The six (France, Germany, Italy, Belgium, the Netherlands, Luxembourg) founded Euratom to 'create the conditions necessary for the development of a powerful nuclear industry'. The aim they assigned to the

EEC was a general economic one – pooling their economic energies – which was to be achieved by establishing a 'common market' and aligning the member states' economic policies. Joint customs tariffs were seen as a central element in a joint trade policy. Also included in the package were measures covering free movement of commodities, persons and capital, common agricultural and transport policies, harmonisation of legal systems, etc. A 12-year transitional period was allowed for realisation of the 'common market' project.

This programme left plenty of room for manoeuvre, and discussion of the various steps involved in setting up the Community and transferring sovereignty to it was entrusted to the two decision-making bodies: the independent Commission and the Council of Ministers, comprising the specialised ministers concerned. The EEC Treaty introduced a system of ongoing negotiation between the national ministers, and between the Council of Ministers and the Commission. Walter Hallstein (1901–1982) became the Commission's first President, and the mark he left on it outlasted his nearly 10 years in office.

The Parliamentary Assembly was given 'consultative and supervisory powers', but could also dismiss the Commission by passing a vote of no confidence. Its members had to fight hard for the right to participate in decision-making. They emphasised their demands by adopting the title 'European Parliament' – much to de Gaulle's displeasure.

The European Court of Justice started out with far greater powers: from the very beginning, its judgments helped to shape the ever-growing body of Community law, and it remains to this day a body both powerful and feared by many.

In the 12 years of the transitional period (up to 31 December 1969), the EEC laid the foundations of the Common Market – sometimes rapidly (joint customs tariffs in 1960), sometimes as the fruit of a hard-fought, laborious process. Setting up and planning the Common Agricultural Market took the whole of the 1960s (funding was finally settled in April 1970). Of course, there were crises and mistakes as well – they are still, after all, constant features of the EU scene today.

After some hesitation by France, the Foreign Ministers met in April 1962 to decide on the draft Treaty. Belgium and the Netherlands refused to sign, as long as Great Britain remained outside the EEC. The project was therefore shelved indefinitely. Three years later, the three Communities, which already had a common parliamentary assembly and a common court of justice, also got a common council and commission – an institutional symbol of the fact that each was following the same pattern.

Six and six only – but the Council of Europe keeps growing

The United Kingdom, Ireland and Denmark had applied to join the Common Market in 1961, and Norway followed suit in 1962. No purpose would be served here by rehearsing the tale of Britain's tactical errors, and de Gaulle's resentment of Anglo-American links, which he regarded as too close – particularly in defence matters. At all events, early in 1963, he vetoed British membership. A week later, he and Konrad Adenauer met to sign the Elysée Treaty on Franco-German co-operation, under which the two governments were to consult each other 'before all decisions on important matters of foreign policy, with a view to securing, as far as possible, a shared position'. The first questions mentioned were those 'relating to the European Communities and to European co-operation'. It is hardly surprising that many Europeans found themselves wondering whether this was intended as the first move towards a Franco-German duumvirate.

While the Community's membership stayed constant throughout the 1960s – a second application by Britain was again blocked by de Gaulle in 1967 – the Council of Europe admitted three new members: Cyprus (1961), Switzerland (1963) and Malta (1965). Apart from the micro-states, this meant that Finland was the only European democracy still outside. The Council's refusal to admit Portugal and Spain, and the withdrawal of the Colonels' Greece, provoked by the threat of expulsion (1969), came as a reminder that membership constituted a stamp of approval – formal recognition that a state was democratic, was governed by law and respected human rights. Again in the 1960s, the Council extended its range of protective instruments by adopting the European Social Charter (1961) and the fourth Protocol to the ECHR (guaranteeing freedom of movement and prohibiting states from expelling their own nationals).

The EEC's worst moment came in 1965 with the 'empty chair' crisis, when France chose to boycott meetings of the Council. The French leadership objected to a paper in which the Commission put forward slyly linked proposals on funding agricultural policy, giving the Community resources of its own and extending the European Parliament's budgetary powers. France was also alarmed by the imminent introduction (from 1 January 1966) of qualified majority voting for most Council decisions – including those on agricultural policy. It regarded the Commission as power-hungry and felt that it should be called to heel, and it also wanted to ensure that it could not be outvoted on important questions (e.g. agricultural policy).

At the end of January 1966, the six agreed on the 'Luxembourg compromise', ending the French boycott but not (as the resolution expressly declared) the disagreement itself. Concerning majority decisions, the Council members agreed that they would try to find generally acceptable solutions within a reasonable time.

Council majorities in the next 15 years made no further attempts to force the issue – which meant that, in practice, a right of veto was accepted in matters of vital importance.

Planning for economic and monetary union

When President de Gaulle retired, things started moving again within the EEC. 1970 brought progress in six important areas: the problem of funding agricultural policy was finally settled; own-resource funding, particularly from agricultural and customs levies, was introduced for the Community; as a corollary of this, the European Parliament's budgetary powers were extended; the 'Werner Plan' for economic and monetary union was put forward; the first step was taken towards a concerted foreign policy, which later came to be known as 'European Political Co-operation' (EPC); and finally, negotiations began with the four applicant countries.

On 1 January 1973 – exactly three years after completion of the development phase of the Common Market – the United Kingdom, Ireland and Denmark joined the Community. After more than 20 years of adjusting to integration and the supranational approach, this was the first enlargement. The whole question of 'deepening or widening' was to remain one of the EU's permanent concerns.

The plan for economic and monetary union was seriously hit by the first oil crisis, and eventually succumbed to its consequences. Several countries felt unable to meet the requirements of the 'snake' (1972), with its mandatory 2.5% fluctuation margin.

It was not until the late 1970s that the European Monetary System (EMS) and its exchange rate mechanism marked a fresh start on the path to economic convergence of the participating states (all the members, apart from Great Britain). There were also new initiatives in energy, regional development and fisheries. On the structural side, too, some progress was made: the European Council of the Heads of State and Government was institutionalised; the European Parliament's budgetary powers were further extended; a procedure for consultation between the three policy-making bodies on general legal measures with significant financial implications was introduced; and the European Parliament became a directly-elected body.

Human rights – still a Strasbourg monopoly

Nonetheless, the 1970s are rightly regarded as, on the whole, a period of stagnation – in spite of the moves towards 'southern enlargement'. Greece joined on 1 January 1981, Portugal and Spain five years later. When they joined the Communities, all three had already been members of the Council of Europe for several years: Greece had returned in 1974 when the Colonels were toppled, and Portugal and Spain, having put decades of dictatorship behind them, joined in 1976/77. All three had accepted the ECHR. This was clear proof that joining the Council of Europe and accepting the ECHR were – as a sign of sound democratic and rule-of-law credentials – a necessary prelude to joining the Communities.

At that time, the Community treaties made no mention of human rights (this omission was remedied only by the Maastricht Treaty). However, in a joint declaration issued in 1977, the European Parliament, Council and Commission emphasised the priority importance they attached to respect for basic rights. Nonetheless, the codified and institutionalised protection of human rights in Europe remained a Council of Europe monopoly, and the Council extended this protection by adding several new protocols to the ECHR in the 1980s.

Two new instruments were particularly important: Protocol No. 6 to the ECHR on abolition of the death penalty, which was adopted on 28 April 1983, and the European Convention for the Prevention of Torture and Inhuman or Degrading Treatment or Punishment, which was adopted on 26 November 1987, and provided for monitoring by a special committee with authority to visit places of detention. The Council's ambition was – and still is – to extend institutionalised human rights protection to every square mile of European territory. This explains why the micro-states were urged to join as well. Liechtenstein came first in 1978, followed by San Marino in 1988. By the time Andorra joined in 1994, however, the Council had already acquired a wholly new dimension.

Declaring for European union

In the 'Solemn Declaration on European Union', which the European Council adopted in June 1983, the Communities, having overcome the stasis of the 1970s, took a further step towards fuller integration. The Franco-German partnership, now personified in François Mitterrand and Helmut Kohl, provided a fresh impetus. Jacques Delors took over as President of the Commission early in 1985, and proceeded to make the same kind of personal mark on the office as Walter Hallstein in the early days. In Pierre Pflimlin, who served as its President from 1984–1987, the

European Parliament also found a committed and eloquent spokesman to plead, not just its own cause, but the cause of European unity.

Men like these certainly helped to pave the way for the signing of the 'Single European Act' as early as February 1986. This covered amendment and expansion of the EC Treaties and, above all, paved the way for completion of the internal market by the end of 1992, i.e. for removal of all the remaining obstacles to a space without internal frontiers, in which the free movement of commodities, persons, services and capital were to be guaranteed.

A white paper prepared by the Delors Commission in June 1985 had listed these obstacles exhaustively, specified 282 Orders and Directives needed to remove them, and laid down a detailed timetable. Its impact showed what a dynamic Commission could achieve under a strong President.

The range of issues determined by majority decision of the Council was extended, the European Parliament (at last called that in the Treaty) was strengthened, and the EPC was regulated by treaty and incorporated into the EEC. Thus revitalised, and with new or increased powers in the fields of monetary, social and environmental policy, and of research and technological development, the EC was left better armed to face the sweeping changes which lay ahead in Europe.

Union – first step towards unity

When we remember that today's EU started life as the Coal and Steel Community with a brief which, though important, was undoubtedly limited, we may find it less surprising that finalising plans for the common European home is proving such a lengthy process. Moreover, apart from specialised historians and a few surviving contemporaries, there are not many people who know that the original plan was to entrust this brief, not to a separate organisation, but 'only' to a 'high authority' within the Council of Europe.

In addition to promoting sectoral integration and developing institutions, plans were repeatedly laid to 'Europeanise' all relations between EC member states within a single comprehensive organisation. After some vacillation, this project was given the name 'European Union' (EU), which actually provides no indication of its legal character: federal state, association of states, or 'supranational organisation *sui generis*'.

After the European Council's 'Solemn Declaration on European Union' of June 1983, 'European Union' was included as a goal in the Single European Act (i.e. in EC treaty law) in 1986. 'Union' covered three main things: economic and monetary union, political union with a common foreign and security policy, and institutional reforms. Economic and monetary union, a project long cherished by Europeans bent on full integration, received a new – and now decisive – impetus. Discussing the question of national monetary sovereignty in his 1969 memoirs, Jean Monnet noted that it would certainly take a quarter-century 'to dispel the illusions which leave dead realities behind in a people's soul'. We now know just how good a prophet he was.

Once again, a report by Jacques Delors, identifying three necessary stages in the realisation of the project, pointed the way. The Madrid European Council (June 1989) accepted his conclusions and decided that the first phase (unrestricted movement of capital and payments, economic and monetary convergence) would begin on 1 July 1990. A governmental conference would then work out details of what happened next. Sceptics in London and Bonn comforted themselves with the thought that huge quantities of water would have to flow under the Thames and Rhine bridges before the project came to anything.

They were not left waiting for long, however, as the short-order collapse of the communist regimes in central and south-east Europe galvanised the European process unexpectedly. Many people immediately sensed two things: that the Iron Curtain's disappearance had made divided Germany an untenable anachronism, and that the states newly freed from dictatorship and Soviet rule would soon come knocking on the EU's door, and could not be turned away. The Communities' shining example had helped to fuel the drive for freedom in the East, and they now had to accept the idea of opening their doors twice over – to the GDR as part of a reunited Germany, and to the other former Iron Curtain countries as well.

Union or federation?

The 1950s reflex kicked in at once: the aim then had been to bind free Germany firmly to the West, and the aim now was to do the same even more emphatically with reunited Germany. An economically strong West Germany had long been accepted as an integral part of Europe, but a united Germany, stretching to the Oder and with the largest population of any EU state, revived old misgivings and apprehensions. At the end of November 1989, the Federal German Chancellor unveiled his 10-point programme to overcome the division of Germany and Europe, which attracted much attention, but caused some annoyance as well. Already in disarray on other fronts, the French leadership made it tacitly clear that French support for German reunification would depend on German acceptance of monetary union. And so, at the Strasbourg European Council on 8 and 9 December 1989, Helmut Kohl unhesitatingly accepted a resolution providing for a governmental conference on economic and monetary union before the end of 1990. Already outvoted at the Governmental Conference on the Single European Act, Margaret Thatcher, the British Prime Minister – who refused to compromise on monetary sovereignty – was outvoted again.

She found the idea of political union equally repugnant, but her opposition did not stop this decades-old project from resurfacing. Speaking in the European Parliament in January 1990, Jacques Delors called for a 'federation of the 12' (he later spoke of a 'federation of national states'), and for the establishment of an EU institutional structure strong enough to withstand any strain the future might impose. From then on, France and Germany took the lead politically. Two years earlier, they had intensified their bilateral partnership by adopting two protocols to the Elysée Treaty, setting up a Franco-German Defence and Security Council and also a Finance and Economic Council.

In April 1990, François Mitterrand and Helmut Kohl submitted a joint communication to the Irish President of the European Council. At that time, there was no longer any serious doubt that Germany would soon be reunited, since free elections held in the GDR a month earlier had given the parties which wanted this to happen quickly a 75% majority. The French President and the German Chancellor referred to the 'European Union' mentioned as the goal in the Single European Act, and hoped that a governmental conference on political union would be held alongside the conference on economic and monetary union. In fact, such a conference was held on 15 December 1990.

Mitterrand and Kohl were guided by two main considerations. They believed, firstly, that economic and monetary union, with a single currency, needed a firm political framework to be secure and durable, and, secondly, that Europe needed unity – wide-ranging, stable and internally effective – as an anchor-point in a period of turmoil. In their joint communication, they referred to the radical changes then taking place in Europe. In his New Year address for 1989–1990, Mitterrand had warned against a 'tendency towards fragmentation'. Margaret Thatcher and many others in Britain suspected, however, that the Euro-federalists were cooking up a conspiracy which would strip Westminster of its power, reduce Downing Street and Whitehall to subservience, liquidate Britain's 'special relationship' with the USA, and erect a European 'super-state'.

This defensive insularity survived Margaret Thatcher's replacement by John Major, and indeed became increasingly virulent, particularly among conservatives in Parliament and outside. In his autobiography, John Major – a tough, but pragmatic defender of British interests – painted a colourful, and at times near-surrealistic, picture of its wilder forms.

Indeed, his book is an excellent guide to the mind-set of British Euro-sceptics.

In the event, Prime Minister Major made no attempt to block the sign-ing of the truly historic Treaty on European Union in Maastricht on 7 February 1992, although he did secure concessions for Britain on eco-nomic and monetary union and on social policy. Central to the Treaty were the provisions on the Common Foreign and Security Policy (CFSP), and co-operation in the fields of justice and internal affairs. The eleven articles dealing with the CFSP were more impressive on principles than procedure, where many of the proposed arrangements seemed clumsy. On the principle side, the Union was, for example, to act as a 'cohesive force in international relations', while the CFSP was to assert the Union's identity on the international scene, safeguard its common values, funda-mental interests and independence, strengthen its security and that of its member states, preserve peace and strengthen international security.

The 'Common Foreign and Security Policy' – is it coming?

These principles were already impressive, but the CFSP was also intended 'to develop and consolidate democracy and the rule of law, and respect for human rights and fundamental freedoms'. Union and morality were harmoniously fused in this high-minded programme. Procedurally, the way was open to 'joint action', although this required a unanimous Council decision. New ground was broken by the assertion that issues relating to the security of the European Union included 'the eventual framing of a common defence policy, which might in time lead to a common defence'. The Treaty entrusted preparatory work and imple-mentation in this area to the WEU, 'which is an integral part of the develop-ment of the Union'.

In the fields of justice and internal affairs, the Treaty listed matters of common concern, on which the Council might unanimously define joint positions, take joint action and work out agreements. Closer co-operation between two or more member states was expressly permitted. Amend-ments and additions to the Community Treaties also produced some important innovations. For one thing, the European Parliament was given the statutory right to participate in decision-making on certain aspects of Community law and on appointment of the Commission. For another, EU citizenship, chiefly expressed in the right to vote and stand in local elections, and in elections to the European Parliament at the place of residence, was introduced.

The most significant innovation was, of course, the three-stage intro-duction of economic and monetary union, i.e. a single currency. Once stage 3 had been reached, a European Central Bank was to be established, with exclusive power to approve the issuing of banknotes within the Community. This was not to 'seek or take instructions from Community institutions or bodies, from any government of a member state or from any other body' – was, in other words, to be independent.

The EU Treaty embodies a monetary constitution for the Union and is, to that extent, already a form of constitution itself. Since the single currency was introduced on 1 January 1999, some EU institutions have had authority in monetary matters, i.e. partial sovereignty, while some member states have had their sovereignty curtailed, insofar as monetary matters are excluded from their purview (the EC's exclusive responsibility for external trade is one important aspect of this). The resultant complex of powers is not easily described or indeed classified in legal terms. Obviously, the member states retain control of the Treaty, since they alone (and not some Community body) have power to amend it. The fact that amendment requires a unanimous decision is often seen as an obstacle to progress. This may be true – but it is also true that giving every member state a veto helps to ensure that the Community does not retreat from ground already won.

Whatever one thinks of this strange combination of partial sovereignty for the EU and limited sovereignty for its member states, the single currency still represents a step towards political union, since monetary policy is 'policy in the full sense' (Walter Hallstein). Only 11 of the 15 member states joined in the final economic and monetary union. Greece came on board on 1 January 2001, but Britain, Denmark and Sweden stayed outside (the first two demanding special exemption clauses). Britain also chose not to sign the agreement on social policy. All of this highlighted the trend towards integration in smaller groups, i.e. fragmentation – and the Amsterdam Treaty pushed it still further.

Unity – and its opponents

There were several countries where substantial opposition needed overcoming before the Maastricht Treaty could take effect on 1 November 1993. In Denmark, two referendums proved necessary. In France, one was enough, but the 'pro' majority was small and the prior discussion fierce. In Britain, Prime Minister Major needed all his political guile to outwit Eurosceptics in his own and other parties and steer the Treaty through Parliament. Germany was the last to ratify, having to wait until the Constitutional Court had decided whether the text was compatible with its Basic Law. Many EU citizens found monetary union hardest to stomach, less because the Treaty provisions were complicated (hardly anyone actually understood them – not entirely reassuring, one might think), than because they were loath to part with banknotes and coins which they regarded as permanent fixtures on the home scene. For post-war Germans and Austrians, for example, the Deutschmark and Schilling were part of their country's and their own success story – and so had sentimental value too.

None of this augured well for the 'Revision Conference', provided for in the Treaty. By the time that Conference's final negotiations got under way in mid-June 1997, many faces had changed since the Maastricht European Council: Jacques Chirac (forced into double harness with a Prime Minister from a rival party just a few weeks before) had replaced François Mitterrand; Tony Blair had recently taken over from John Major; José-Maria Aznar had replaced Felipe Gonzalez; and Jacques Santer had succeeded Jacques Delors. It may have been partly because of the changes that the new Treaty, agreed in Amsterdam, was in certain respects a disappointing one.

Some progress was made with the plan to turn the Union into an 'area of freedom, security and law'. Certain aspects of the Common Justice and Internal Policy – particularly controls on external frontiers, and asylum and immigration policy – were henceforth to be determined by the Community, and not worked out among themselves by governments. The European Parliament was given a bigger role in these areas, and its status was generally upgraded by extension and strengthening of its right to participate in decision-making. Also, the new British Government's acceptance of the Agreement on Social Policy meant that its provisions could be incorporated into the EC Treaty.

The points secured at Schengen, i.e. the agreements now concluded between 13 member states on removing controls on shared internal frontiers, were also incorporated into the Treaty. Admittedly, in the fields of justice and internal policy, there were special arrangements for Britain, Ireland and Denmark – a further example of increasing differentiation inside the Union or Community.

The Common Foreign and Security Policy was another area where the new Treaty diluted the Community's 'united front' principle: it was agreed that a member state which abstained from voting on a resolution requiring a unanimous decision would not stop it from going through – but would not be required to implement it. 'Common strategies' were added to the CFSP instruments. Defence, however, was the area where the EU's reach was extended most strikingly: closer links with the WEU were to give it 'access to an operational capability' for military action, including crisis management and peace-making tasks. Preserving the 'integrity of the Union' was accordingly included among the aims of the CFSP.

From 15 to 27?

When the European Council met in June 1997, the Union already had 15 member states, and a further 12 had applied to join: Malta, Cyprus, the three Baltic states and seven countries in central and south-eastern Europe – all of them now members of the Council of Europe. Admittedly, Latvia's membership was only a few months old: with its very large Russian minority, it had not been given the green light until it had – after difficult discussions and with Council experts' help – drafted and passed a nationality law acceptable to Strasbourg. It was also required to give a whole series of commitments, one of them being to adopt a law on the rights and status of non-nationals, again with the help of Council experts. Without these rule-of-law reforms, it would have been unable to join, not only the Council of Europe, but also the EU. It is no coincidence that the 'Copenhagen criteria', i.e. the political conditions for EU membership, are identical to the Council of Europe's basic principles. This explains why Latvia was nearly two years behind Estonia and Lithuania in applying to join.

Clearly, with so many countries already in the EU (since 1995), and nearly as many on the waiting list, the Amsterdam Conference should have agreed on comprehensive institutional reforms. Its failure to do this was the plainest sign of all that the momentum of the late 1980s and early 1990s had been lost. Strangely enough, the decision to postpone reform – taken in a mood of glum helplessness – was itself embodied in an agreement or, specifically, special protocol. Belgium, France and Italy entered a joint declaration in the Final Act, stating that reform should not simply cover the Commission's composition and the weighting of votes on the Council, but should also involve 'a significant extension of recourse to qualified majority voting'.

Unresolved in Amsterdam, these three questions were certain to figure prominently on the agenda for the next Intergovernmental Conference. A fourth was 'closer' or 'enhanced' co-operation. This was an Amsterdam Treaty innovation, and allowed a majority group of member states (i.e. eight or more) to co-operate more closely than provided for in the Treaties, and use the EU/EC's institutional framework for that purpose. Strict conditions were attached. Any such project would require qualified majority authorisation by the Council, and any member might veto it 'for important and stated reasons of national policy'. The CFSP was a no-go area, and the existing exemptions (particularly those accepted for economic and monetary union) meant that closer co-operation within a smaller circle was not really new territory. Here again, after some initial movement, things ground to a halt.

A remark by President Chirac sums up the Intergovernmental Conference on Institutional Reform of the European Union, which took place in Nice in the second half of 2000: 'Building Europe takes determination and a vision – and today the visionaries are tired'. The conference nonetheless reached agreement on abolishing the *de facto* right of veto on enhanced co-operation, and extending the latter to the CFSP, applying the following yardstick: 'Enhanced co-operation [...] shall relate to implementation of a joint action or a common position. It shall not relate to matters having military or defence implications.' Co-operative CFSP initiatives could also – unlike others – be vetoed.

The Political and Security Policy Committee was made responsible, under the Council's authority, for political supervision and strategic conduct of crisis management operations. Otherwise, the Nice Conference did not concern itself with the Common Security and Defence Policy, although the European Council did – briefly.

In fact, the year 2000 brought a breakthrough towards making a European Security Union an integral part of the EU. The WEU's tasks were increasingly transferred to the EU, and its members gave undertakings on supplying troops for a rapid reaction force under EU leadership. It was decided that a Military Committee and a Military Staff would be established alongside the Political and Security Policy Committee, the idea being to ensure that the EU could always – and particularly at times of crisis – draw on the combined expertise of all its members. The existing EU Treaty already provided a legal basis for the various steps involved in setting up a Common Security and Defence Policy, so there was little need for the conference to discuss them.

Welcome to the bazaar

Indeed, institutional reform was more than enough to keep it busy. Enough angry ink has already been spilt on the results it achieved and the tug of war needed to get them – 'Welcome to the bazaar' was one newspaper's headline – so we shall simply note them here (in any case, they speak for themselves). Some member states were wary of extending qualified majority voting to certain areas: Britain did not want it for tax harmonisation and social policy, Germany for asylum and immigration policy, Spain, Portugal and Greece for regional development, and France (mainly) for cultural policy. They dug in their heels, and concessions on specifics were the outcome. To take just one example, Spain finally accepted qualified majority decisions for the Regional Structural Fund from 1 January 2007, but only on condition that a six-year programme, running to the end of 2012, was agreed in advance.

Concerning the composition of the Commission, the Intergovernmental Conference decided to play for time and take the path of least resistance. From 1 January 2005, every member is to have one representative on the Commission, up to a maximum of 26 states. Once membership tops that figure, rotation will be necessary, and the Council wil have to take a unanimous decision on the details. If Commissioners continue to serve for five years in a 27-member EU, each state will have to miss a turn once in 130 years. This may sound workable, but the unanimity rule means that some unselfish state will have to set the ball rolling – unless the Treaty is amended, or 'associate commissioners' (like France's associate ministers) are introduced. In short, there is little reason to suppose that Nice found any permanent answer to the problem of making the Commission effective.

The question of national representation in the post-enlargement European Parliament clearly did not exercise the conference unduly (although Hungary and the Czech Republic, for example, are unlikely to accept an arrangement which leaves them with fewer members than countries with the same, or even smaller, populations, like Belgium, Greece and Portugal). Interest focused instead on the weighting of votes in the Council. The large countries' voting power was slightly increased – Spain's rather more than that of the 'big four' – with 71.3% remaining the quorum for qualified majorities. Above all, the countries which account for more than 38% of the EU population were effectively given a veto. In a declaration – which is not, of course, legally binding – the conference provided for raising of the quorum to over 73% in a 27-member EU. This would allow three of the four large countries, solely on the strength of their population, to form an obstructive minority – in other words, stop the other 24 from taking qualified majority decisions.

Nonetheless, the applicant countries declared themselves satisfied, feeling that the presumptive allocation of votes in the Council gave them a fair deal. Just before the European Council and the Governmental Conference which ended it, their leaders had met their colleagues from EU countries. This was not the first 'European Conference' – an EU term since March 1998 – but the European Council broke new ground when it proposed that countries involved in the stabilisation and association process, as well as EFTA countries, be invited to future conferences as prospective members. This leaves the door wide open to meetings of nearly 40 state representatives in future.

A policy for Greater Europe

It is hard to see what useful purpose this is meant to serve. Inviting applicant countries is understandable, but the point of involving countries which will not be able to join for years is less obvious. Perhaps a clue can be found in a speech delivered by Javier Solana, the High Representative for the Common Foreign and Security Policy, early in March 2001. In it, he made the point that enlargement would alter the Union's geopolitical environment, giving it not only lengthy frontiers with Russia, but also frontiers with Belarus, Ukraine, Moldova, Georgia, Armenia, Iran, Iraq and Syria. He added that regions adjoining the enlarged Union in the east and south were undoubtedly major priorities, and that the European Union would have to devise a 'policy for Greater Europe'.

In fact, the best platform for the kind of general, multilateral dialogue on political, economic and social issues the EU seems to want is the Council of Europe, which has, for the last 54 years, been predestined to play just that role. At the Vienna European Council in December 1998, there was talk of a 'European Conference', to serve as 'a forum for political consultation on questions of general concern to the participants'. Consultation on questions of common interest is, however, exactly the task which those same member states entrusted to the Council of Europe in its Statute. It is – to put it mildly – a pity that the EU does not make better use of the Council's profound knowledge of the countries of central, eastern and south-eastern Europe. That knowledge extends to the three trans-Caucasian countries, which have all concluded partnership and co-operation agreements with the EU (and are thus potential guests at the 'European Conference', which is still little more than a glorified lunch party). Instead of 'the appropriate forms of co-operation with the Council of Europe' referred to in Article 303 of the Treaty on the European Community (not the European Union!), is more institution-building going to complicate the picture even further? It is doubtful that this will really help the EU towards a clear foreign policy.

In the field of basic rights too, the EU's ignoring of the Council of Europe – at least until the Convention met – is hard to fathom. With the Charter of Fundamental Rights, proclaimed by the Council, Commission and European Parliament at the end of 2000, it again went its own way. The text, which various experts (including two of the Council of Europe's leading human rights specialists, whom I appointed as observers) helped to prepare, has undoubted qualities. But the obvious solution – the solution which would prevent fragmentation and divergent case-law – was, and is, Community accession to the European Convention for the Protection of Human Rights and Fundamental Freedoms, and Community acceptance of the Strasbourg Court's jurisdiction. The legalities of this step have long since been worked out. It is simply a question of deciding to take it.

Since the EU has had 25 members, Europe's political landscape has radically altered, both inside and outside the expanded Union. The result of the change must not be new dividing lines. There is only one Europe: the whole continent with over 800 million people. Since 1989 – 40 years after it was founded and given the task of overcoming conflicts – the Council of Europe has been making shared values a viable basis for emergence of that 'one Europe'.

Human rights and freedom in a basket

When the Final Act of the Conference for Security and Co-operation in Europe (CSCE) was signed in Helsinki on 1 August 1975, many people hoped that the threat of nuclear conflict, created by the Cold War, had been exorcised forever. Some even hoped that the lives of people behind the Iron Curtain might improve. Hardly anyone imagined, however, that the Final Act could actually heal the great divide in Europe. And yet the events of 1989 were the final stage in a process which had started 14 years before in the Finnish capital.

People still look back on the fall of the Berlin Wall as a watershed event, and the cry, 'We are the people!' has not been forgotten. At the same time, we may wonder whether the wall would have come down without the Hungarians' brave decision, a few months before, to facilitate a mass exodus to the West of 'tourists' from their brother-state, the GDR – a decision fully in line with the Final Act and with the promise which Hungary and the other signatories had given in Helsinki to promote human contacts.

From Molotov's proposal for a treaty on collective security in Europe (at the Berlin Conference in 1954) through the 1958 Rapacki plan for a nuclear-free zone in central Europe, to the CSCE's opening session in Helsinki on 3 July 1973, the way had been a long one. The CSCE itself was both part and provisional culmination of an overall policy, which found its most striking expression in the German-Soviet and German-Polish treaties, in the talks held between the two Germanys in 1970, and in the Berlin four-power agreement of September 1971.

From balance of terror to balance of interests

The aim of this policy was to achieve *détente*, end the Cold War and chart a course from a balance of terror to a balance of interests. The Helsinki Final Act was designed to pave the way for permanent normalisation of relations between states with different political, economic and social systems. It was part of an attempt to devise a common crisis management strategy, covering both disarmament negotiations and closer contacts, based on ongoing, generalised co-operation.

The 35 signatories declared themselves 'convinced of the need to exert efforts to make *détente* both a continuing and an increasingly viable and comprehensive process'. Co-operation was seen as holding the key to peace and security, and suitable areas for co-operation were divided into three 'baskets': the first contained a list of 10 principles and a document on confidence-building measures; the second was concerned with co-operation in the fields of economics, science and technology, and environment; and the third covered co-operation in humanitarian and other fields, including human contacts, information, culture and education. A declaration of intention concerning security and co-operation in the Mediterranean was also part of the package.

In its scope and content, the Final Act marked a new departure in East-West relations. Inevitably, it created expectations, but it also raised questions. For one thing, it was a political agreement containing very real commitments, but not legally binding – and so every party tried to impose its own interpretation on the text.

In spite of all the difficulties, the Final Act soon developed a momentum of its own. The following year, Professor Arbatov, a respected member of the Soviet Academy, noted complacently that 'to their chagrin, cold warriors in the West have been unable to misuse the principles laid down in the Final Act to influence internal processes in the socialist countries and undermine their societies' social foundations'. What he was saying was that *détente* had not given the West things that armed force or other forms of pressure from the Cold War arsenal had failed to deliver.[5]

Same text – different readings

The Soviet Union took Helsinki as a sign that, politically speaking, the Second World War was over at last, and assumed that recognition of existing frontiers would help to consolidate the *status quo* in eastern Europe. At the same time, it stuck to its policy of 'peaceful coexistence' (the Brezhnev doctrine, which actually meant that the international class struggle would continue, using all means, short of war). The West saw the CSCE as offering a chance to revive the post-war vision of a free and peaceful Europe by implementing the various baskets across the East-West divide. This certainly meant trade and economic co-operation, but it also, and above all, meant developing human contacts and human rights, which had already proved an effective source of unity in western Europe.

The reactions of the non-aligned countries, particularly Yugoslavia, made it clear that the Final Act was not just an East-West affair, but included the idea of transcending blocs and democratising international relations. Whether this was accepted or not, the many different interpretations of the text promised critical dialogue, not stasis. And the number of participants in that dialogue soon started to grow, and kept on growing. States which had signed the Final Act were required to publish the text, and their citizens were able – to their own surprise, and for the first time – to see exactly what those at the top had agreed to.

This soon made it plain that one of the principles laid down in the Final Act, namely the right of every state to 'choose and develop its political, social, economic and cultural systems, as well as its right to determine its laws and regulations', was self-contradictory.

The people demand their liberties

Obviously, freedom of choice is also a basic principle of pluralist democracy – and the basic political right of anyone living in a democratic state. It was thus not surprising that, having seen the Final Act, people living under 'democratic socialism' should begin to question that system, and demand the basic freedoms promised in the text.

The positive response and support which their demands received in the West were a logical consequence of the latter's value system. In fact, public debate on human rights in the signatory states and action to promote human contacts across frontiers were one approach to buildimg confidence, strengthening co-operation and creating security. They were based on Principle No. 7 ('Respect for human rights and fundamental freedoms, including the freedom of thought, conscience, religion or belief'), and on co-operation in humanitarian and other areas, covered by the third basket. Here, the Final Act had introduced a shared responsibility which was in no way incompatible with Principle No. 6 ('Non-intervention in internal affairs').

The Final Act had expressly linked respect for human rights and basic freedoms with peace, friendly relations and co-operation. Obviously, therefore, the firing of shots at people trying to cross the border from East to West Germany, and the prosecution of dissidents who invoked the Final Act in signatory states, were seen as incompatible with the text.

Détente – *a waiting game*

Admittedly, the Final Act, and particularly the debate over the third basket, did not put a stop to the ideological dispute, which continued and actually became more acrimonious – but nor did it consolidate the *status quo*, as the eastern signatories had hoped, or lead to socialism's being universally confirmed and acknowledged as a new (and in some states triumphant) social system. On the contrary, people in the East increasingly took the Final Act as a basis for questioning it.

In 1977, the Soviet Union launched a new arms drive, setting out –
among other things – to modernise its medium-range missiles and make
them more accurate. Suddenly, western Europe found itself facing a new
threat, which NATO countered by introducing Pershing II medium-range
missiles and cruise missiles in 1979. Both sides were blamed for restarting
the arms race, but the only open protests took place in the West (the East
suppressed them in the usual way). An agreement on medium-range missile reduction, the INF Treaty, was not secured until 1987.

The CSCE also triggered processes which regrettably led, in the short
term, to increased repression within the communist systems – the reaction of leaderships which felt their authority slipping. In the long term,
however, the points of agreement so vital for peace and security in Europe
won through.

It was not diplomacy, nor implementation of an unusually effective
text, but – quite simply – the human factor, which brought this about.
Vaclav Havel put this vividly when he addressed the Council of Europe's
Parliamentary Assembly in May 1990, and argued convincingly for the
power of dreams. He spoke of the dream he had shared with his Charter
77 associate and friend, Jiri Dienstbier, in prison – the dream of a 'Europe
free of blocs', in which no constraints, ideological or other, would interfere with respect for human dignity and human rights. Derided by the
'realists' who accepted the *status quo* and the East/West divide, they still
clung to their dream of another, better Europe – knowing full well that
renewed imprisonment might be the price of doing so.

The things they dreamed of should have existed as a matter of course,
and their dream eventually came true. The conclusion Havel drew from
this holds a lesson for all of us: 'Everything seems to indicate that we must
not be afraid to dream of the seemingly impossible if we want the seemingly impossible to become a reality. Without dreaming of a better Europe
we shall never build a better Europe.' A year later, it was his fellow
campaigner, Jiri Dienstbier, who, as Foreign Minister and Deputy Prime
Minister, sealed democratic Czechoslovakia's accession to the Council of
Europe and signed the European Convention on Human Rights on its
behalf.

The same basic freedoms for all Europe

The CSCE had recognised that peace depended on co-operation, had
turned co-operation into a political principle and had set that principle
down in a text available to everyone. From that point on, attempts to
impose ideological uniformity, and stop people from going their own way
and speaking out freely, were doomed. The citizens of Prague, Warsaw,

Moscow and Sofia were as much a part of Europe's history and culture as the citizens of Rome, London, Stockholm or Vienna. What justification could there be for denying them the same basic freedoms – of thought, conscience, religion or belief? These were human rights which everyone, everywhere, must be guaranteed – a point hammered home by the massive demonstrations in Berlin, Leipzig and Dresden in 1989, when the cry, 'We are the people!', constituted a direct challenge to the Central Committee and People's Chamber of the GDR.

In the years immediately after Helsinki, there were widespread, bitter complaints that the Final Act and its ratification of post-war frontiers spelt victory for the Soviet Union. Vague hopes of humanitarian and human rights concessions were dismissed as illusory. Fortunately, the sceptics were wrong on both counts. In fact, the Final Act became the central reference text for all bilateral and multilateral diplomatic, political and summit meetings between East and West, fuelled countless parliamentary debates, and provided a rallying point for all those dissidents who accused their own countries of failing to honour the promises they had given. At NGO level, 'Helsinki committees' were even established to keep defaulting governments up to the mark.

Human rights – which belong to everyone, and which neither national sovereignty nor ideology can affect – had acted as a unifying factor once before, when the Council of Europe was founded in 1949, and now they did so again. The third CSCE basket can thus be rightly seen as a vital, very real building block in construction of the common European home.

Clausewitz was wrong

During the Second World War, as during the First World War, people were already trying to devise an effective international system to ensure peace afterwards – a system to replace the old League of Nations and remedy its defects. The result was the United Nations Charter, which was signed by 50 states in San Francisco on 25 June 1945 and came into force on 24 October 1945. This had been preceded by a declaration naming the future organisation, issued on 1 January 1942 by the 26 states of the 'anti-Hitler coalition', and by lengthy negotiations, eventually leading to hard-won compromises, between Roosevelt, Churchill and Stalin. The USA did most of the planning work. The League of Nations officially ceased to exist in spring 1946.

Collective security – the UN approach

The UN Charter established a system of collective security – pithily described by Karl Doehring, an expert on the law of nations, as 'an inward-looking system, in which the members undertake to act together against anyone who attempts to achieve his goals by using force against partners in the system'. Article 51 recognised the right to self-defence, but the use of force was banned in all other cases by Article 2, paragraph 4: 'All members shall refrain, in their international relations, from the threat or use of force against the territorial integrity or political independence of any state, or in any other manner inconsistent with the purposes of the United Nations.'

The Charter entrusted 'primary responsibility for the maintenance of international peace and security' to the Security Council. Its functions in this area were determined by Chapter 7: in the event of a threat to the peace, a breach of the peace or an act of aggression, it could impose economic sanctions (Article 41) and, if necessary, take military action (Article 42). However, any of the five permanent members (China, France, United Kingdom, Soviet Union, USA) could veto such resolutions.

From the very start, therefore, it was clear that the UN 'collective security' system would work only if these five privileged states basically acted together to preserve peace between the nations. However, the anti-Hitler coalition collapsed soon after the war. Admittedly, the Security Council did threaten action under Chapter 7 when the first Israeli-Arab war broke out in mid-1948 (the Soviet Union had recognised the state of Israel as soon as it had been proclaimed). The Soviet Union also did nothing to block the three resolutions of June/July 1950, in which the Security Council authorised the deployment of UN-led forces in Korea, but only because it was boycotting Council sessions at the time – in protest at China being represented by the Taiwan Government. But apart from these two special cases (and, much later, the even more special cases of Rhodesia and South Africa), Chapter 7 stayed a blunt sword for decades.

The five permanent members of the Security Council used their veto to protect not just themselves, but their allies and *protégés* worldwide. And so nothing was done to prevent a whole series of wars – including many 'proxy wars' between the USA and Soviet clients – or at least to end them quickly. It was all too clear that Chapter 7 would be even less able to prevent a war between the two principal powers. It was not until Mikhail Gorbachev took over as Soviet leader that the Security Council recovered some of its freedom of action. The breakthrough came when it adopted Resolution 678, authorising military action to expel Iraq from Kuwait, on 29 November 1990.

The Cold War

It is no coincidence that the UN collective security system recovered its relevance at a time when the East–West conflict was winding down, and one of the two great military alliances was poised on the brink of dissolution. This East–West conflict, or Cold War, had begun soon after 1945, when – Roosevelt's 'one world' vision having proved an illusion – the USA and the Soviet Union parted company. As early as February 1946, the American ambassadorial adviser, George F. Kennan, had been warning from Moscow of Soviet expansionist aims. As month followed month, events in various countries showed how right he had been. In March 1947, Roosevelt's successor proclaimed his 'Truman doctrine', declaring that 'We must assist free peoples to work out their own destinies in their own way'. This was followed a few months later by Kennan's public, but anonymous, plea for a policy of containment.

This prepared the ground for the 'Vandenberg Resolution', in which the US Senate invoked the right of collective self-defence and demanded that the US join appropriate military alliances for that purpose – the first time the country had envisaged this (June 1948). The way was now clear for the founding of NATO by 12 states on 4 April 1949.

In the meantime, Stalin had consolidated his hold on five central and south-eastern European countries, and on the Soviet-occupied part of Germany. By 1949, Poland, Czechoslovakia, Hungary, Bulgaria and Romania had concluded 15 bilateral security agreements with the Soviet Union and one another. Soviet troops were still stationed, in near-wartime strength, on the border between the two Germanys, and were clearly ready to march. The UN founders' noble ideals had been eclipsed by the grim reality of a dividing line – ever more fixed and ever more permanent – running through the heart of Europe. My own home city of Vienna was the only place where 'four to a jeep' patrols still operated (amicably enough, I daresay, on that level). In the Allied Control Council for Austria, the four still sat at the same table, but the atmosphere was heavy with mutual suspicion.

All but suspended, the UN collective security system was replaced by a North Atlantic collective self-defence alliance in the West, and a Communist/ imperialist military bloc in the East. Disarmament gave way to massive re-armament, and finally a nuclear arms race. Instead of a universal security community, carefully monitored by the five main powers on the UN Security Council, the world got a situation in which two diametrically opposed social and value systems confronted each other in mutual hostility.

Alliances were not a thing of the past after all – but shifting alliances were. America's partners were fully aware that, in the long term, only the US nuclear shield stood between them and a Soviet takeover – and this helped to curb centrifugal tendencies. In Soviet-ruled areas, non-compliance was mercilessly crushed. This rigid division into rival fronts set its mark on Europe. West Germany joining NATO and the WEU (not an ersatz EDC, but a body mainly responsible for internal arms control) early in May 1955, and the signing of the Warsaw Pact (by the GDR, among others) a few days later, merely confirmed this bi-polar confrontation, which was literally cemented by the building of the Berlin Wall in 1961. Then, as now, there was no middle way between freedom and dictatorship.

After Stalin's death in 1953, the new Soviet leadership announced a policy of 'peaceful coexistence', but the arms race continued, with the emphasis on nuclear warheads and delivery systems. The public was bombarded with a whole new military and strategic vocabulary, backed by mystifying acronyms: destructive capacity, first strike, counter-strike, second strike capacity, all-out nuclear response, flexible response, deterrence, intermediate range ballistic missile (IRBM), intercontinental ballistic missile (ICBM), nuclear stalemate, balance of terror, total nuclear war and – like a last, savage joke in the darkness which had fallen on peace-keeping – mutual assured destruction (MAD).

Unheard-of sums were spent on producing weapons of mass destruction, and then up-dating them repeatedly, simply to ensure that they would never have to be used. Humanity – and not just humanity, but reason itself – was left teetering on the edge of a vertiginous abyss. For the first time in history, humanity's survival depended on preventing war between the major powers. With or without veto rights within the Security Council, this was clearly too much for the UN system to handle. Indeed, the UN would have had neither the time nor the means to react to breach of the peace by nuclear attack. Mutual fear of MAD was the only thing that kept the peace – looking back, it seems little short of a miracle that NATO was right in assuming that the Soviet Union would always retreat before the worst happened.

Coexistence and world peace

The Cuban crisis of 1962, provoked by the Soviet plan to station missiles on the island, proved the point. Humanity had never been closer to the ultimate nuclear disaster. The Soviet leadership finally backed down, but then poured even more money into arms, for the purpose of achieving parity with the USA. At the same time, the crisis made people on both sides realise that there was no alternative to coexistence and dialogue, particularly on arms control and 'confidence-building measures'.

Speaking on 'world peace' in June 1963, John F. Kennedy declared: 'If we cannot end now our differences, at least we can help make the world safe for diversity [...] We can seek a relaxation of tension without relaxing our guard.' The first tangible signs of *détente* between the superpowers were the treaty banning nuclear weapons testing in the atmosphere, under water or in space (1963) and the non-proliferation treaty (1968). These visible attempts to reduce the tensions, this promise (at least) to cut back on these fearful weapons, are probably one of the reasons for the aura which, for a whole generation, still surrounds Kennedy today.

Kennedy was also responsible for shifts in America's policy *vis-à-vis* its allies, emphasising shared political goals and calling for economic co-operation throughout the free world, as well as fairer burden-sharing within the Atlantic Alliance. He argued that America and Europe, as the 'twin pillars' of the Alliance, must assume equal responsibilities within it. Nonetheless, decades were to pass before EC/EU Europeans made a serious effort, around the turn of the century, to devise a common security and defence policy, and set up the instruments it needed.

In the field of economic co-operation, and in spite of 'chicken wars', 'banana splits' and other trade skirmishes, agreement was achieved more rapidly. A first major round of negotiations (the 'Kennedy Round') on a general reduction of customs tariffs within GATT (today the World Trade Organisation/WTO) led to a series of joint, if not always consensual, efforts by America and Europe to liberalise world trade – efforts which continue today. The effects of this on relations between the allied trading nations in Europe and North America were particularly beneficial.

The strongest tie, however – the one which held the Alliance together and gave it a moral dimension – remained shared values. The preamble to the NATO Treaty proclaims the parties' determination 'to safeguard the freedom, common heritage and civilisation of their peoples, founded on the principles of democracy, individual liberty and the rule of law'. These ideals were restated in the NATO Council's pioneering 'Harmel report' of 1967, which spelt out a double strategy, based on military strength and security, and on a policy of *détente*.

The fact that the Alliance owed its solidity, not just to shared vital interests, but also to shared values and ideals, explains why the Soviets failed in all their efforts to divide it, especially in the crisis-years of the early 1980s, when they tried to stop NATO from neutralising their new medium-range missiles by deploying equivalent systems, and cruise missiles as well. This, together with the 1983 clash over President Ronald Reagan's Strategic Defence Initiative (SDI) – a plan to intercept and destroy enemy missiles in outer space – was the last major clash between East and West.

Arms race – round two

In the 1970s, a sense of their special responsibility for keeping the peace had led the two 'superpowers' (as they were now called) to strive for a direct understanding. They actually scored a number of successes: the first strategic arms limitation treaty (SALT I), plus extensive renunciation of anti-missile systems (the ABM Treaty) in 1972; the agreement on preventing nuclear war in 1973; and the SALT II agreement, after lengthy negotiations, in 1979. But the wind had already changed when SALT II was signed. In 1972, the USA had all but acknowledged the Soviet Union's equal strike capacity, but this did not stop the Soviets from pressing ahead with arms production and constantly up-dating their arsenal. They also began to deploy missiles with a range of up to 5500 kilometres. By the time the Red Army marched into Afghanistan late in 1979, the NATO countries' patience was exhausted. With President Carter still in office, the US decided to increase its defence spending significantly.

However, this return to Cold War confrontation was to prove a mere interlude.

In fact, the Soviet Union could no longer afford to spend lavishly on arms. On the contrary, cuts were now essential. Even before Mikhail Gorbachev took office in March 1985, agreement had been reached on resuming arms control talks with the US. But it was the Soviet Union's new leader who committed it to effective disarmament, which meant accepting on-the-spot monitoring, i.e. admitting outside inspectors. This might have proved a serious obstacle, but the CSCE's final document on confidence and security-building measures, and disarmament – which allowed participating states to observe one another's military manoeuvres – opened the way to a breakthrough in September 1986.

Fifteen months later, Mikhail Gorbachev and Ronald Reagan signed the INF Treaty, which covered the dismantling of all Soviet and US missiles with a range of 500 to 5,500 kilometres. This was the first ever disarmament treaty, and its benefits extended beyond the signatories to the five NATO and three Warsaw Pact countries where these missiles were deployed in Europe – taking a particularly deadly class of weapon off the scene on both sides of the Iron Curtain.

Planning the common European home

The psychological effects of this on people living in a region with more weapons per square kilometre than any other in the world can easily be imagined. Suddenly, after decades of a peace guaranteed only by the hideous certainty of mutual destruction if anyone actually pressed the button, they could at least breathe a little more freely. Again, there was a general sense that people on both sides of the European divide had a shared destiny – and shared responsibilities too. Gorbachev's oft-repeated metaphor of the 'common European home' took the process further.

Speaking before the Council of Europe's Parliamentary Assembly on 6 July 1989, he declared: 'The time has come to put the assumptions of the Cold War, when Europe was seen as an arena for confrontation, as a subject of military dispute, as a battleground, divided into zones of influence, behind us. The idea behind the concept of the "pan-European home" excludes the probability of armed conflict, and indeed the possibility of using or threatening to use force.' The Austrian Chancellor, Josef Klaus, had actually used the same metaphor in the Assembly 20 years before, but he had been speaking for a neutral country, wedged between the blocs – and it made a big difference that the speaker now using it had power to make the vision come true.

In principle, this meant that the way was already clear for redefinition of the relationship between the alliances, and of the peacekeeping strategy, even before the Communist regimes in the Soviet Union's partner countries collapsed. In 1990, a line was drawn and a new start was made. In July the NATO countries' leaders adopted a declaration, in which they spoke of the Cold War as a thing of the past, and extended the 'hand of friendship' to the countries of central and eastern Europe. The Alliance was to strengthen its political components, could help to lay the structural foundations of a more united continent, and must become a forum for co-operation on the building of a new partnership with all the countries of Europe.

A full four months later, on 19 November, those same leaders joined their counterparts in Bulgaria, Poland, Romania, Czechoslovakia, Hungary and the USSR in confirming 'that the age of division and confrontation, which has lasted more than four decades, is at an end'. They also approved the text of a treaty on reducing conventional forces in Europe. All of this was done on the fringes of the CSCE's Paris Summit, which solemnly proclaimed the 'Paris Charter for a New Europe'. A few days later, the UN system of collective security was revived to deal wih the Iraq-Kuwait conflict. Some months after that, the Warsaw Pact and COMECON were dissolved.

Coming home to Europe

It was now up to the organisations which had always worked for democracy, the rule of law and human rights to help the new democracies to 'come home to Europe'. An imaginative grasp of the problems and anxieties of neighbours who had suffered the effects of autocratic rule, rigid economic planning and Soviet domination for so many years was a vital part of this. Speaking at the Council of Europe in January 1990, Tadeusz Mazowiecki, Poland's first democratically elected Prime Minister in over

60 years, had already put his finger on the issues: 'The wall between free and subjugated Europe has already been removed. The gap between poor and rich Europe remains to be bridged. If Europe is to become a "common home", in which some may not close the door on others, then discrepancies like these must not be allowed to last for long.' Are we living up to our responsibilities? Have those discrepancies already lasted too long? Has the Iron Curtain been replaced by a series of locked doors, stylishly padded on one side, and hung with old sacks on the other? If it has, this is certainly not the Europe of which I, and millions of others, used to dream.

Mazowiecki's own country will be joining the European Union on 1 May 2004, but the problem he raised remains unsolved for large parts of eastern and south-eastern Europe. The key to a solution lies, I am convinced, in a pan-European approach, and not in the use or threat of force. This indeed is the greatest change we have witnessed. No one today would dream of suggesting a military solution. Perhaps it is true, as cynics suggested (and as the very name implied), that the Cold War was simply a continuation of war by slightly less bellicose means – but in Europe at least, war is no longer a continuation of politics by other means.

I wrote this chapter before the Iraq war, which left Europe divided over the action taken unilaterally – with no explicit Security Council resolutions to back it – by the US/British coalition. That war, and the problems it caused in Europe, have merely strengthened my conviction that strengthening, not weakening, the UN system is vital for Europe. Imperfect that system may be – but it is the best we have.

Tanks and barbed wire – farewell to freedom

The origins of the East/West split in Europe are usually traced to the Yalta Conference of February 1945. The accepted version is that Roosevelt and Churchill on one side, and Stalin on the other, used the meeting to divide the world, and particularly Europe, between them. This is certainly true to the extent that the USA was prepared to allow the Soviets to exercise a powerful influence in the countries east and south-east of Germany (the argument that close links with the Soviets were their best defence against future German aggression seemed convincing). There is no indication, however, that the establishment of communist dictatorships in those countries was part of the bargain for Churchill and Roosevelt. They joined Stalin in signing a 'Declaration of Liberated Europe', in which the three governments promised to help 'establish conditions of internal peace', and to 'form interim governmental authorities broadly representative of all democratic elements in the population and committed to the earliest possible establishment, through free elections, of governments responsive to the will of the people'.

The rift opens

Roosevelt, at least, never suspected that the Soviet 'protectors', with their ideological conceptions of peace, democracy and the will of the people, meant to use these clauses to ensure that the provisional governments included communists, who would then eliminate 'enemies of peace and the people'. But that was the pattern of events between 1945 and 1948. There was, it turned out, no question of getting Soviet influence without Soviet-style societies and Soviet-style government. On the contrary, the Soviet Union tightened its hold through a series of bilateral 'friendship, co-operation and mutual aid' agreements, concluding the first with the Czech Government in exile as early as December 1943. In the event of a future attack by Germany, the two parties promised to 'use all the means at their disposal to provide each other with military and other assistance'. There was also an ominous mutual undertaking 'to conclude no alliances and participate in no coalition directed against the other High Contracting Party'. By the time the Warsaw Pact was signed in 1955, the Soviet Union's partners had long been enmeshed in this web of treaties.

Like Czechoslovakia, the Polish Government (which was dominated by the communists' 'Ljublin Committee') signed a bilateral agreement of this kind with the Soviet Union before the war ended. A glance at the map is enough to show why Stalin was so anxious to move quickly with these two countries. Obviously, too, he was determined to keep a firm grip on the occupation zone in Germany which the Soviets had been promised at the Teheran Conference in 1943 – although the proclamation of the Truman doctrine in March 1947, and the help the USA gave the Greek Government in its fight against the Communist guerrillas, made him realise that there was no immediate prospect of bringing the whole of Germany under Soviet control. Increasing difficulties in their negotiations with the Soviet Union forced the three western powers to admit that the chances of securing a consensual peace plan for the whole of Germany, on acceptable conditions, were receding rapidly. They drew three conclusions from this.

Picking up the pieces: the Marshall Plan

The first was that a vacuum must not be allowed to develop west of the Soviet zone, which was rigidly controlled and dominated by the massive presence of the Red Army. They accordingly set out to devise a state system for the three western zones. This involved a whole series of steps, of which we shall mention only the following: economic and administrative merging of the three zones to form a British-US 'bi-zone', and eventually a 'tri-zone'; the convening of a Parliamentary Council to draft a constitution, under allied supervision; and proclamation of the Basic Law for the Federal Republic of Germany on 23 May 1949. A key date along the way was 20 June 1948, when currency reform gave West Germany the *Deutschmark*, setting it on the path to a spectacular economic recovery.

The second conclusion, indeed, was that Europe must be put back on its feet, and the USA played a major part in this. Its response to the tightening Soviet hold on eastern Europe was the Marshall Plan for European reconstruction of June 1947, the brainchild of the US Secretary of State, George Marshall. In his celebrated Harvard address, Marshall promised that the US would do everything in its power to help restore sound economic conditions, without which there could be neither political stability nor lasting peace. The Soviet Union rejected the plan, and forbade Poland and Czechoslovakia to accept the massive economic aid the US was offering. This was not just a blow for European unity – it was also a tragedy for the peoples deprived of desperately needed assistance.

Marshall had called on the Europeans to agree among themselves on priorities and on how to use American aid most effectively. This led to the founding of the Organisation for European Economic Co-operation (OEEC) by 17 countries in April 1948. The three Western occupation zones in Germany, represented by their military governors, were members of the new organisation and thus entitled to development aid as well. The OEEC's main aim at the outset was to ensure that American aid was effectively used. This it succeeded in doing, but it provided no significant impetus for the unification of (western) Europe.

This was even truer of the Economic Commission for Europe (ECE), a United Nations subsidiary founded in March 1947. Its primary task was to plan and participate in joint action for the economic reconstruction of Europe – and particularly of devastated European countries within the UN. Another was to promote Europe's economic development, and to help preserve and strengthen national economic relations – always with the proviso that no action affecting any country must be taken without its government's consent. Germany and Austria did not belong to the United Nations at that time, and neither did Finland, Italy, Albania, Bulgaria, Romania or Hungary. The USSR, Ukraine and Belarus were founder members of the ECE, and so were Poland and Czechoslovakia. It accordingly spanned the European divide, although the East-West conflict largely paralysed it for quite some time. Nonetheless, it did valuable standard-setting work, particularly in the field of transfrontier traffic and transport.

Berlin blockaded, Germany divided

The third conclusion was that the West must organise its own defence, and this led to the founding of NATO in 1949. At that time, Berlin was still under blockade, i.e. there was no land access through the Soviet zone to the city's three western sectors. Three months before the blockade started, in April 1948, the Soviet representative had withdrawn from the Allied Control Commission for Germany – a clear sign that the Soviets were now focused on rounding off their empire in territorial terms.

The Berlin blockade failed, since the three western powers kept their heads, and airlifted supplies to Berliners and their own troops in the city for close on a year. At the end of that time, the Soviets were forced to accept the continued existence of a 'western island' in the heart of their occupation zone. This at least made it clear that the four wartime allies still had shared rights in the city, if only in such matters as supervision of the Spandau prison for war criminals, brief inspection trips to one another's sectors and similar symbolic acts. In fact, they retained four-power responsibility for Berlin and Germany as a whole until 1990, although this – on the Soviet side and in relation to East Berlin and the GDR – was reflected in subtleties only.

The German Democratic Republic was founded on 7 October 1949 as the final element in the 'eastern bloc', which now confronted western Europe and its trans-Atlantic ally. Geography and old mind-sets seemed to have been neutralised – Erfurt and Prague were again in the East. In effect, the only surviving part of central Europe was Austria, formally under four-power administration. Its system of government and social organisation made it part of the West, like Finland, Sweden and Switzerland, and – like them – it became neutral in 1955. Of course, these four countries owed their neutrality to very different causes, and so their international relations after 1945 are not reducible to a single pattern.

Finland concluded a friendship and assistance treaty with the USSR in 1948. It was obliged to stay on good terms with its powerful neighbour, and did not join the Council of Europe until 1989. Switzerland stayed outside the United Nations and its peacekeeping system, while Finland, Austria and Sweden took leading parts in many of its peacekeeping operations. A 1992 referendum also stopped Switzerland from joining the European Economic Area, causing its application for EU membership to lapse. In contrast, referendums held in Austria, Finland and Sweden produced pro-EU results. Once the East-West conflict had ended, and these three countries were no longer in an exposed (and sometimes precarious) position, they saw no reason to remain outside the EU – regardless of their special positions on the Common Security and Defence Policy. All the four neutrals have one thing in common, however: during the Cold War, they repeatedly helped, through discreet diplomacy, to forge contacts between the rival camps.

Compromise and isolation: Tito's Yugoslavia and Hoxha's Albania

Other countries which helped to nuance the picture of a bi-polar Europe in the East-West conflict included: Ireland, whose determination to stay out of NATO as a neutral was compounded by disagreement with Britain over Northern Ireland; Portugal and Spain with their autocratic regimes (although Portugal, which had furnished the allies with bases during the Second World War, was a founder member of NATO); Yugoslavia and Albania. Albania and its communist leader, Enver Hoxha, were less dependent on Stalin then on Tito's Yugoslavia. The country steered a zigzag course: joining the Council for Mutual Economic Assistance (COMECON) in 1949, boycotting it from 1961; becoming a founder member of the Warsaw Pact in 1955, leaving it again in 1968; breaking with the Soviet Union in the early 1960s and forging ties with China, then parting company with China in the mid-1970s. The last stage in this process was total isolation, eased gradually only after Hoxha's death in 1985. This paranoid fear of the outside world left (literal) concrete traces as well. The whole country is dotted with mini-bunkers, of which there are said to be 800,000. Passengers landing at Tirana Airport get a good view of them; at one time indeed, guests at the city's Europa Hotel were given tiny replicas as a memento of their stay.

Unlike Stalin's satraps in Warsaw, Prague, Budapest, Bucharest, Sofia and East Berlin, Yugoslavia's Marshall Tito did not owe his power to the Soviet dictator. It is true that Yugoslavia concluded a bilateral pact with the Soviet Union in 1945. It is also true that, in 1947, the Yugoslav Communist Party became a founder member of the Communist Information Bureau (COMINFORM), which had the task of co-ordinating the activities of the various Communist parties by mutual agreement; in other words, it was used by Stalin to supervise and discipline. However, Tito was unwilling to be kept in rein, and his party was excluded one year later for betraying Marxism-Leninism. In 1949, the bilateral pact was revoked. Tito adopted a policy of consistent non-alignment, and Yugoslavia remained a leading member of the non-aligned movement, even when relations with the Soviet Union improved after 1955.

The revolution devours its children

The USSR reached a grudging understanding with Yugoslavia, and let Albania go its own way – but expected all other partners to toe the party line unswervingly. In most of the so-called peoples' democracies, leading communist functionaries were purged, some after show trials, like those staged in Moscow in 1936–1938, some after secret hearings. Stalin was personally responsible for the purges, using them to rule the Party by terror. Trumped-up accusations of Titoism, economic sabotage, anti-state activity, collusion with the West, etc, served as pretexts for public humiliation and punishment, which drove home the message that slavish obedience to Moscow was the first and only commandment. Wladyslaw Gomulka survived in Poland, but Albania's Kotschi Dodse, Hungary's Laszlo Rajk, Czechoslovakia's Rudolf Slansky and Bulgaria's Traicho Kostov were sentenced to death and executed.

People in the public eye were the prime targets, and anti-Semitism was clearly a significant contributory factor. This is reflected in the last murderous project planned by Stalin for the Soviet Union itself. The intended victims were doctors, most of them Jewish, who were accused of causing or plotting the deaths of leading Soviet politicians and senior army officers. We should not forget, however, that some of the leading Party functionaries killed on Moscow's orders had themselves played a major part in liquidating non-communist politicians and colleagues in the post-1945 'People's Front' governments. Matyas Rakosi, dyed-in-the-wool Stalinist leader of the Hungarian communists, coined the now familiar term 'salami tactics' for this gradual process of eliminating 'enemies' or – putting it euphemistically – bringing them into line. At a later stage, Hungary also gave a name – 'goulash communism' – to a brand of national communism which gradually detached itself from Moscow.

Many now (regrettably) forgotten names deserve a mention here. They include György Donath of the Hungarian Small Farmers' Party, which took 57% of the vote in 1945, and Nicolas Petkov of the Bulgarian Peasants' Party. They were liquidated by Rajk and Kostov, who were themselves executed later. Stalin's persecution mania focused first on people who had fought in Spain and distinguished themselves as resistance fighters in their own or other countries, i.e. people who had not come through the war as 'Muscovites'. Today, while making the necessary distinctions, we can think with pity of all the murdered victims of this inexorable yet arbitrary tyranny.

Puppet judges and the gallows were enough to deal with alleged deviants and enemies of the state, but tanks were needed when whole peoples rebelled. This happened first in the GDR, when protest demonstrations staged by angry workers on 17 June 1953 led to general uproar. Later, when the people of Hungary rose against communist dictatorship and Soviet rule in October 1956, the Moscow leadership was – we now know – at first uncertain what to do. In fact, it issued a statement, indicating its willingness to discuss withdrawal of its troops from the countries where they were stationed. But before Hungary could seize its chance to leave the Warsaw Pact and declare itself neutral, the hard-liners, who refused to accept a 'brother' state's seceding, had carried the day in Moscow. After several days of fighting, Soviet armoured divisions succeeded in crushing the rising, and some 200,000 Hungarians fled the country. Prime Minister Imre Nagy was deposed, tried in secret and sentenced to death. The Soviet Union had shown that escape from its rule was impossible.

Nonetheless, the stage was already set – just one year on from conclusion of the Warsaw Pact – for a development which would lose the Soviet Union its original monolithic character. Tito's insistence on going his own way had caused, not just anger, but uncertainty too – and Yugoslavia's being given the right, in 1955, to follow its 'own road to socialism' inevitably added to the latter. But it was Khrushchev's settling of scores with Stalinism at the 20th Congress of the Communist Party of the Soviet Union which made it abundantly clear to all the faithful that – even at the centre of world communism – infallibility did not exist. Soviet troops were not needed to quell the serious disturbances in Poland in 1956, but the re-emergence of Gomulka (condemned for nationalistic right-wing aberrations in 1948) confirmed that even communists could err. The rehabilitation and ceremonial interment of Laszlo Rajk early that October, shortly after the dismissal of the Stalinist Rajk, probably helped to make Hungarian communists feel even less sure of their ground.

From de-Stalinisation to the Prague spring

De-Stalinisation helped to make the machinery of repression less brutal after 1956 – but without, in any sense, giving dictatorship a more human face. Churches and churchmen were still persecuted, and everything was done to stop the old democratic parties or independent trade unions from re-forming. Any move towards a civil society, in which people could say what they thought and make up their own minds on political issues, was instantly crushed. Indeed, the oppressors came up with new and ingenious stratagems – for example, incarcerating dissidents in lunatic asylums or forcing them to leave the country.

How would the Soviet leadership react when, at a time of relative *détente* at home and outside, its Marxist-Leninist line was publicly questioned? Those who wondered got their answer on 21 August 1968, when the Soviet Union again – and for the last time – used tanks to enforce its rule in eastern Europe. Faced with the 'Prague spring', it had warned five weeks before: 'We cannot allow hostile forces to divert your country from the socialist path, and create a danger of Czechoslovakia's leaving the socialist community. These are no longer your concerns alone. They are the common concerns of all communist and workers' parties, and of all states united by alliance, co-operation and friendship.' This warning encapsulated what became known as the Brezhnev doctrine. In fact, the principle of Socialist internationalism had already been stated in November 1957, when the communist parties promised one another 'fraternal assistance' when needed.

The reform movement in Czechoslovakia was crushed, but Alexander Dubcek, its symbolic figurehead, escaped the fate of Imre Nagy: instead of being liquidated, he was merely sidelined. Brezhnev had already employed this relatively civilised approach to removal in 1964 – with Khrushchev, whom he simply nudged into retirement. In Prague, the Soviet Union found willing helpers, but chose not to install a puppet government immediately. Dubcek's successor, Gustav Husak, had actually served a nine-year prison sentence for allegedly pursuing a nationalist line in Slovakia. He could take the measure of the satellite states' independence exactly, and that was enough for the Soviets.

The real master, when it came to gauging national room for manoeuvre and making the most of it, was Hungary's Janos Kadar. He too, like Gustav Husak, had once been sentenced to imprisonment – for life – under his own party's rule. In 1956, he betrayed Imre Nagy and his country by agreeing to serve as Soviet governor, but he later managed to convert his loyalty to Moscow into numerous 'mini-liberties' for his countrymen. Even if he had not died on 6 July 1989 – the very day on which the Hungarian Supreme Court officially rehabilitated Imre Nagy – his fate would certainly not have been that of Nicolae Ceaucescu in Romania.

Even under Ceaucescu's predecessor, Georghiu-Dej, Romania had achieved a certain latitude in its dealings with the Soviet Union. It was Moscow's attempt to impose central planning on its satellites which the country's communists found hardest to accept. In 1964, they proclaimed that every Socialist state had a 'sovereign right to choose its own path' (the parallel with the concessions extorted by Yugoslavia was unmistakable). An ambivalently sympathetic attitude to the Chinese 'heretics' earned some external backing for their own chosen path. Unlike Bulgaria, Poland, Hungary and the GDR, Romania did not join in invading Czechoslovakia in 1968, although Ceaucescu certainly had no time for the reformers around Dubcek. Blithely styling himself *Conducatore* – a title with sinister echoes of *Führer, Duce* or *Caudillo* – he ended his days as one of history's most hated leaders.

Solidarnosc paves the way for change

The death-knell of communist rule in Europe was finally sounded in Poland, where the Soviet Union had never risked military intervention, but had always relied on the managerial talents of its loyal partners to keep things in order. In 1970, Gomulka was sacrificed to the strikers in the Baltic ports, and particularly Danzig, and Gierek succeeded him. However, when strikes erupted once again in 1980, and the free trade union, *Solidarnosc*, and its charismatic leader, Lech Walesa, came on the scene, the communists were lost for an answer. General Wojciech Jaruzelski's appointment as Prime Minister was a clear indication of what lay ahead: in December 1981, martial law was declared. At least, armed intervention by the Soviets had again been averted.

But *Solidarnosc* kept going, and its power and impact were such that – when Mikhail Gorbachev took over, with *glasnost* and *perestroika* as his watchwords, and civil society started to develop – it could no longer be ignored. In August 1988, the Polish leadership decided to start negotiating with it. The elections held on 4 June 1989 were still not genuinely free, but this did not stop the Poles from using them to eject the communists. In August 1989, Tadeusz Mazowiecki, a democrat and member of *Solidarnosc*, became Prime Minister.

Communism had played its last card. One after another, the communist regimes in central and south-eastern Europe crumbled and collapsed. On 29 December 1989, Vaclav Havel was elected President of Czechoslovakia. This was indeed a powerful symbol: the world-famous dissident dramatist, once forced to work in a brewery for a living, was now the leader of this country at the heart of Europe. The East-West conflict was over, and Prague was no longer in 'the East' – but back where it belonged.

'Never again!' – new Europe's necessary motto

The Austrian dramatist Franz Grillparzer, who died in 1872, wrote prophetically of a process which led 'from humanity through nationality to bestiality'. The path, not just to the First World War, but also to the Second – the most bestial in history – was marked out in advance, since rabid nationalism was near-universal in early 20th-century Europe. Anything akin to European consciousness was conspicuously absent in 1914 – unless Germany's desire to dominate the continent counts as a perverted version. There were no friendships between nations, merely affinities and, above all, alliances (and the Triple Alliance between Austria, Hungary and Italy was sufficient proof of their fragility).

The road to destruction

'Each nation had its own special impulse behind that general mid-summer madness of joy which greeted the outbreak of war', as British historian Gordon Brook-Shepherd puts it at the start of the section, 'The Road to Destruction', which he devotes to the origins of the First World War in his book on Austria.[6] He goes on: 'The Germans saw in it their call to arms as the predestined masters of Europe; the French, revenge for the humiliations of 1870; the Russians, the fulfilment of their duty as the protectors of all the Slavs; even the British […] could draw on jingoistic memories of their great naval rivalry with Germany'. For the people of the Dual Monarchy, 'next to the Italians (still *the* enemy in the popular mind, despite the fact that Italy had been an ally since 1882), the Serbs, with their dream of "Greater Serbia", were perceived as the greatest menace on their borders'.

The German Emperor, Wilhelm II, dreamed of a 'final battle' between Germans and Slavs. 'Serbien muss sterbien' (Serbia must die), as the Vienna *Kronenzeitung* put it in a vicious bit of xenophobic wordplay. And the tone of most headlines in the rest of Europe was little better. Nationalism was in the air people breathed, every nation despised every other, and every nation was convinced that its cause – being the only just one – was certain to triumph. For *Gott, Kaiser und Vaterland* and for *la patrie*, the troops marched away to the 20th century's first Armageddon. On all sides, social democrats forgot the internationalism they had preached so fervently, Christian democrats the injunction to love their neighbours and enemies, and liberals the freedoms so painfully won. Almost without exception, people espoused their own nation's imperialist goals, summoned God to their standard, and submitted slavishly to military discipline. The Kaiser declared that he now knew nothing of political parties and recognised only Germans, while in faraway Baku (then a Russian province, now capital of independent Azerbaijan), a general strike was called off for patriotic reasons.

Nationalism gets its chance

The urban elites of peoples with no states of their own prepared to seize their longed-for independence. The Poles were first off the mark, but the Czechs and irredentists like Cesare Battisti, who had represented the Trentino in the Austrian Parliament, also felt that their hour had come. When everything was over and the dust had cleared, many of these peoples had simply traded one foreign ruler for another, sparking new liberation movements – with results which were still affecting Europe in the

1990s. In 1914, it looked as if nationalism's chance had come, and in 1918, when the greatest conflict since the Thirty Years War had ended, it looked as if nationalism – or at least the nationalism of the victorious or liberated peoples – had triumphed. This is why Otto Molden prefers to call the first war (and the second) a 'great nationalistic war for leadership in Europe', rather than a world war.[7] Very few people saw the dangers: either the dangers disastrously realised in 1914, or the dangers not only unremoved after 1918, but carefully stoked and – not deliberately, perhaps, but with the best intentions – exacerbated. At all events, the protagonists had played totally into the hands of virtuoso performers on the nationalist and racist registers, who – as Otto Molden puts it again – succeeded in plunging the continent into an even greater war to secure one nation's hegemony.

And so, when the First World War ended, no one reflected on its causes, and nothing was done to curb nationalism. The losers were humiliated, and only the losers were called to account for the wrongs they had done. Moreover, as a well-known German historian[8] pointed out, the war 'was also an unparalleled intellectual disaster, destroying the moral energies that had made Europe great and giving evil fearful scope for action'.

Evil included not just flagrant violations of international law, like the flouting of Belgian neutrality at the outset, the use of poison gas or Germany's declaration of 'unrestricted submarine warfare' (bringing America into the war) in 1917, but also the cynical support given to the Bolsheviks by the Germany army leadership, who certainly had no sympathy for communism.

Over 10 million Europeans were killed in the actual fighting, and countless others died of malnutrition, for want of medical treatment, etc. And no one could have guessed that a Second World War would bring greater – immeasurably greater – horrors.

Deadly mixture

Before they could finally learn the right lessons, Europeans had to be shown a second time what a deadly mixture words could produce – words like 'our cause is God's cause' or 'my country right or wrong'. Dangerous and perverted ideas had helped to prepare the ground. 'To rule is to have power to suspend the law,' declared Carl Schmitt, one of the 20th century's most celebrated and controversial constitutional lawyers and – intentionally or otherwise – the spiritual father of 'enabling law' in Germany. This paved the way for Nazi totalitarianism, which made up the law as it went – all the way to genocide. Not all of Hitler's subjects were 'willing helpers', but, fatally, too many Germans had lost sight of the values which might have helped them to use their voting rights properly. Germany was not the only country where 'us v. them' thinking and total obedience were seen as the basic political rules; even after the changes of 1989–1990, these same attitudes and values resurfaced in the former Yugoslavia – again with appalling consequences.

But let us return to the 'inter-war period' (significant term!). Happily, there were also political thinkers who took a different line – men like Max Weber and his French disciples, Raymond Aron and Julien Freund. In dark and difficult times, ethics are no longer a matter of attitude, but of responsibility. Indeed, individual responsibility becomes vital at such times, when ethics must not be suspended, the real priorities must be grasped, and principles which shine like a beacon in the dark are needed. But Nazi Germany's rulers had a very different programme. The far-sighted thinkers and politicians who were already looking to reconciliation between supposedly hostile nations for an answer were preaching in the wilderness. True, Briand and Stresemann were awarded the Nobel Peace Prize for their efforts, but the effects of those efforts soon faded.

The world might have been spared so much if Aristide Briand's words, when he spoke after Gustav Stresemann and welcomed Germany to the League of Nations in Geneva in 1926, had proved accurate:

> 'And now, you gentlemen who mock, surely even you must admit that the things we have seen today, just a few years after the most terrible war which ever brought confusion on the world, while the blood on the battlefields is not yet dry, have been deeply and genuinely moving? Here we see the very same peoples, who have just clashed so fiercely, sitting down quietly to work together for world peace. I know that there are still differences of opinion between our countries, but in future they will settle their differences in court, like private individuals. That is why I say, away with the rifles, the machine-guns, the cannons! Make way for reconciliation, arbitration and peace!'

The mockers were right

To start with, alas, the mockers were proved right. Way was made, not for reconciliation and peace, but precisely for the rifles and the cannons. The war itself, and the failure to secure a real peace afterwards, had strengthened the extremists, right and left – not the moderates who wanted reconciliation. A brand of communism which rode roughshod over individuals and their rights had taken over in Russia, and Fascist dictatorships were shortly to emerge in Italy and Germany. When that happened, the road to the ultimate horror was a straight one.

Totalitarian regimes cheat and ignore the rules from the start – which is why watching for the first symptoms is so vital. Vigilance and commitment are the hallmark of a free political system, and must never be relaxed. It was because they were neither vigilant nor committed that people in Germany, and other countries too, were so easily led astray between the wars. Many - and particularly those who had fought at the front – had been robbed of inner balance by their wartime experiences, and shattered by the glaring contradiction between nationalist fervour (by no means limited to governments) and the grim reality of the trenches, where the greatest of all assets – life itself – was cynically squandered in massive battles. People are always susceptible to promises, even the promise of a thousand-year Reich, one of those constantly recurring myths which feed insatiably on hereditary and national enmities – until death takes everyone. After 1918, however, they were particularly susceptible. Wounds had been left, not just by the war, but also by the peace treaties, which were inspired less by Wilson's 14 points than by 19th-century nationalist principles.

The European democrat's first duty has always been to spot trouble coming and point to it in time. Perhaps family tradition, and particularly my later intellectual and political activity, have helped to make me watchful. Like many others, I was inoculated against the devil's language by the recent past – my own country's and Europe's. But democrats must not rely on a sense of their own immunity; they, and political office-holders, must always remember how fragile the political process is. Democracy stands and falls with the clear-sightedness, vigilance and strength of character of each and every individual.

Patriotism v. nationalism

An important part of this is knowing the difference between patriotism and nationalism. In Europe as in other parts of the world, a sense of affinity with one's own country and people (which has nothing to do with looking down on others) is – and will always be – a virtue. Nationalism, on the other hand, is associated with a lust for power, an urge to dominate others (seen as inferior), intolerance and an 'us v. them' outlook. Hitler, Mussolini – and possibly Stalin too, to some extent – were able to accumulate power so easily because nationalist politicians in Europe's surviving democracies secretly sympathised with some of the things they were doing, feeling that they would have done 'the same in their shoes'. This may be one reason why the Reich's annexation of Austria was tacitly accepted – Mexico was the only country to protest. The same applies to the famous (or notorious) Munich Agreement, and the European powers' failure to react when Czechoslovakia was occupied – an event which opened many people's eyes, but too late.

Probably, too, people believed these excesses were temporary. This (overlooking the covert anti-Semitism of many of Hitler's western opponents, let alone Stalin) may also be the only, inadequate, explanation for their persistent blindness to the Nazis' systematic persecution and extermination of the Jews – an atrocity unparalleled in history. Neither Hitler's *Mein Kampf* (contrary to popular belief, widely read), nor the Nuremberg Laws, which stripped German Jews of their rights and nationality in 1935, should have left room for any doubt. Far outside Germany, the burning of the synagogues on 9 November 1938 (*Kristallnacht*) is now seen as the emblematic last warning signal to democracies everywhere. And Hitler proclaimed that he intended to 'destroy the Jewish race in Europe' seven months before the Second World War began.

The vital lesson: never again!

For Jews in my country, terror followed hard on the heels of the *Anschluss* (13 March 1938). Adolf Eichmann installed himself in the Palais Rothschild and began by 'merely' putting pressure on Jews to leave the country. I remember hearing at home how difficult the decision to leave (while they could) had been for Jewish friends and neighbours. They already knew about Buchenwald, Dachau and the other 'final destinations', but the thought of going was still unbearable. Doctors, artists, architects, lawyers, bank managers and war veterans (in short, the so-called assimilated Jews) were unable to grasp the stark choice before them: New York, London, Paris – or hell, and a one–way ticket from the cafés to the camps! And this was the land of Mozart and Haydn, Hofmannsthal and Musil, Klimt and Kokoschka, not to mention the indispensable Sigmund Freud. All of this weighs on me even today. I still find it hard to realise that I actually grew up in the second district of Vienna without meeting a single Jewish boy at my school in Leopoldstadt. At that time, of course, I had not read Freud's pre-war letters to Stefan Zweig, written shortly before he left for London.

Today, we all know that racism, anti-Semitism and xenophobia are the regular concomitants of rabid nationalism – nationalism which is endemically anti-European, since it denies or rides roughshod over basic values. That is why, even in today's Europe, I always warn against thinking 'it couldn't happen to us'. Alas, 'never again!' and 'it couldn't happen now' are very different things. We have certainly learned from the past, but still not enough, as the excesses of the last few years – far from just verbal – show all too plainly.

After Auschwitz and Theresienstadt, nothing could ever be the same again. Auschwitz is not a mere scar – it remains an open wound in the very heart of Europe. This and the other wounds hurt, but they are the spiritual source of all the political efforts being made today – by the Council of Europe, among others – to achieve reconciliation. They are part of the European soul we all share, which is itself a metaphor for European identity. Auschwitz was, and remains, unthinkable, but it did not make postwar Europe a moral desert. On the contrary, our scale of references had been sea-changed, and an imperishable inner memorial – beyond the reach of revisionists and all the others who falsify the past – had been raised. Collective guilt does not exist, but collective responsibility does, and is part of our shared European heritage.

Joint heritage

European co-operation, in all its steadily intensifying forms, acts as a positive counterweight to the burdens of the past, and is the heartening side of our grief and our efforts to come to terms with our destiny. The EU citizenship introduced by the Maastricht Treaty is – after the European Convention on Human Rights – another important step towards European legislation on nationality. We have, thank God, come a long way from the 'blood and soil' politics, aggressive expansionism, perversion of healthy patriotism, ugly colonial wars and militarization of whole societies which we saw between 1914 and 1945 – and earlier.

We often talk today (and the Council of Europe's Statute does too) about our common European heritage. When we do, we normally think first of culture and civilisation, but we must never forget that shared trauma – two world wars, the ravages of nationalism, and genocide of the Jews (as well as the Sinti and Roma, then known as Gypsies) – is part of our heritage too. Our collective memory is not filled simply with gothic cathedrals, museums, composers, poets, Santiago de Compostela and the Magna Carta. The European pattern remains a complex one, and many different strands are woven into it. We cannot reduce it to a series of rose-tinted images. Even a healthy body retains the memory of illness, and the fear of its recurrence. Indeed, everything humanly possible must be done to prevent it recurring. Countless efforts have been made for that purpose, none more important than the various initiatives for European unity launched since 1945 – and particularly the instruments devised to protect human rights, especially the right to life and respect for human dignity, at international level.

But we must not forget the ageing generals, the politicians, dictators and warped utopians of the first half of the last century, the military parades in Berlin, the militias, the SS volunteers, the collaborators, the Nazis' Aryanising of the German economy, the Vienna Jews forced to clean the streets on hands and knees, the Jewish musicians playing classical music even in the camps, the tireless Simon Wiesenthal, still uncovering Nazi crimes and tracking down the criminals worldwide – and also the ageing veterans still dreaming of the good old days in the SA. What is this bundle of contradictions, this Europe we have inherited? Making sense of it all and shaping the future with an eye on the past, with a clear vision and an emphasis on values, is certainly a job for people who can bring enthusiasm to the task. But the story of Europe since 1945 – first of the West and later (since 1989) of the East as well – gives reason to hope that today's Europeans, disagree though they may on certain points, have the qualities needed to do it.

NOTES:

1. Figures supplied by the Vienna Military Studies Institute.
2. The 'western' Länder did not contact the provisional government until 24 September, and it was recognised by the four occupying powers on 20 October 1945.
3. ERP = European Recovery Programme.
4. Mayrzedt, Hans, and Hummer, Waldemar, *20 Jahre österreichische Neutralitäts- und Europapolitik (1955–1975)* (Wilhelm Braumüller, Vienna), 1976, p. 90.
5. *Entspannungspolitik nach Helsinki – eine Zwischenbilanz. Bergdorfer Gesprächskreis*, Protokoll No. 55, 1976.
6. Gordon Brook-Shepherd, *The Austrians* (London, Harper Collins Publishers Ltd), 1995.
7. Otto Molden, *Die Europäische Nation* (Munich, Herbig), 1990, p. 89.
8. Michael Salewski, *Geschichte Europas* (Munich, C.H. Beck), 2000.

CHAPTER FOUR

1989 – a year when a million dreams came true

The Berlin Wall comes down

The anniversary which the Council of Europe celebrated on 5 May 1989 was no ordinary one. Forty years old, with Finland just admitted as its twenty-third member, it now comprised all the European states which respected its values – pluralist democracy, human rights and the rule of law. To top things off, the Council's member governments decided to mark its 40th birthday by issuing a political declaration on its future role in the ongoing process of building Europe. In that declaration, they reacted to reform initiatives in some of the central and east European countries by raising the question of future relations. A clear political signal was given, and prospects for co-operation were outlined – with political and legal reform (including improved human rights protection) as obvious first targets. This co-operation was intended to promote closer transfrontier ties between Europeans, both individuals and groups. The fact is, social problems call for joint solutions – and a European identity rooted in a shared history and culture, with democracy and freedom as underlying values, can help us to find them.

The declaration of May 1989 confirmed a policy of gradually increasing openness, which dated back to an initiative taken by Hans-Dietrich Genscher, Federal German Foreign Minister, when he was chairing the Committee of Ministers in 1985.

This had been a fresh attempt to initiate dialogue, contact and practical co-operation with the other half of Europe. After all, the Council of Europe was not set up to serve just part of the continent. Its spiritual fathers (I am thinking primarily of Winston Churchill and his Zurich speech of 1946) shared the vision of a European family of peoples, living in concord and freedom, with no frontiers to divide them. The fact that

the Council's foundation in 1949 coincided with the opening of the ideological rift in Europe reflected contemporary power politics, and not
some permanent historical necessity. This was clear from the existence
within the Parliamentary Assembly, from the 1950s on, of a 'Committee
on Non-Member Countries', which listened to the victims and opponents
of Europe's anti-democratic regimes, and prepared reports and Assembly
debates on the situation in their countries.

In the mid-1960s, the then Secretary General, Sir Peter Smithers, had
explored possibilities for dialogue and co-operation with a number of
central European countries, and particularly Poland. When the 'Prague
Spring' movement was brutally suppressed, this initiative was dropped,
and a chill set in. In 1975, the Helsinki Final Act gave East-West relations
a new reference text – and the Parliamentary Assembly began to hold
regular debates on the CSCE and the Council's connections with it. It
invited parliamentarians from Canada and the US to take part – and also
parliamentarians from Yugoslavia, a non-aligned country firmly committed to the CSCE process.

Yugoslavia – first contacts

From then on, Yugoslav parliamentarians were invited to attend whenever the Assembly or its committees were discussing questions of interest
to both sides (chiefly Mediterranean and CSCE issues), and Council of
Europe parliamentarians and Secretaries General were in frequent touch
with Belgrade. On an inter-state co-operative basis, Yugoslavia came to
participate in various aspects of the Council's work, and this led to its
signing the European Cultural Convention in 1987, and so becoming a
full member of the Council for Cultural Co-operation.

In May 1990, the President of the Socialist Federative Republic of
Yugoslavia, Janez Drnovsek (later Prime Minister and currently President
of independent Slovenia), addressed the Parliamentary Assembly and was
welcomed by President Björck as the representative of a country on the
point of becoming a full member of 'our European family'. He spoke of
economic and political changes in his country, which would allow it to
apply, in two or three years' time, for membership of the European
Community. He also spoke of the transition to political pluralism, with
free elections in the Republics and to the Federal Parliament. He insisted
on Yugoslavia's determination to protect human rights, and said that this
would allow it to sign the European Convention on Human Rights and
so join the Council of Europe very shortly. He also spoke, however, of
problems in Kosovo, where rabid nationalism had been undermining
economic and political stability for the past 10 years. Political and demo-

cratic solutions must be found, since ethnic conflicts could not be settled by using force and imposing solutions from the top. This was an area where faster integration within the structures of European co-operation could help Yugoslavia. He hoped that it would become a full member of the Council of Europe as soon as possible, and join the other members in helping to shape tomorrow's Europe.

Unfortunately, internal developments in the next few months put an end to change and improvement. Drnovsek had said that the existing economic and political balance was fragile. It collapsed. He had made no secret of the danger that old enmities might resurface. They erupted with savage force. As early as September 1990, Milosevic took away Kosovo's independent status. Instead of joining in the European process, Yugoslavia plunged into internecine conflict – and 10 years were to pass before large sections of the former federal community again had prospects of joining the democratic family of European peoples.

The Helsinki Final Act marked the start of a new phase in East-West relations. At the end of the 1970s, this prompted my fellow countryman and Secretary General, Franz Karasek, to put out new feelers in the East and suggest areas for co-operation. Political, diplomatic and parliamentary contacts over a long period had encouraged him to do this, and a number of indicative policy speeches had prepared the ground. Then, in late December 1979, Soviet forces marched into Afghanistan. Yet again, political developments on the broader East-West scene had frustrated a pragmatic Council of Europe initiative to improve relations across the European divide.

It is true that François Mitterrand, speaking in the Parliamentary Assembly in 1981, insisted on the Council's potential for pragmatic co-operation with the countries of eastern Europe in non-ideological areas; but, as we have seen, four years were to pass before Hans-Dietrich Genscher made a fresh political start in that direction.

A new eastern policy – for the Council too

In January 1985, Genscher called a special meeting of the Committee of Ministers to discuss policy on eastern Europe, and all his fellow ministers attended. The meeting itself was something of a novelty for the Council of Europe. It led to a resolution on European cultural identity, which was then adopted at the Ministers' regular meeting in May 1985. This emphasised the importance of culture and a shared historical and cultural heritage as a connecting link and basis for co-operation, regardless of ideological divisions. It insisted that the relevant Council of Europe instrument – the European Cultural Convention – must be put to good use, and invited non-member states to seek contact with Strasbourg. In the wake of this resolution, the Ministers also adopted basic rules, allowing the Secretary General to initiate dialogue with the central and eastern European reform countries. Under its various Presidents, the Parliamentary Assembly had already done much to develop such contacts and make them regular. In 1987 and 1988, Secretary General Oreja visited Budapest and Warsaw.

In October 1988, these contacts were alluded to in the Assembly by a very special Polish visitor – Pope Jean Paul II, who invoked Europe's shared destiny and deep-rooted solidarity, and called on it to be true to itself by bringing all its peoples together.

At this point, the Presidency of the Assembly had already floated the idea of inviting President Mikhail Gorbachev to Strasbourg. The suggestion was initially greeted with some scepticism, but later won acceptance, and a special sitting was scheduled for 6 July 1989.

In the run-up to the visit, the Assembly – at the prompting of Peter Sager, its Swiss Rapporteur and expert on eastern Europe – proposed special guest status for parliamentarians from central and eastern European countries which had embarked on political reform. It was suggested that sitting in on Assembly sessions and committee meetings would give them a chance to see pluralist, parliamentary democracy in action. Special guest status was accordingly granted to the parliaments of Hungary, Poland, Yugoslavia and the Soviet Union, whose representatives attended for the first time on the occasion of President Gorbachev's visit.

Gorbachev at the Council

On 6 July 1989, just a few months before the Berlin Wall came down, the President of the Soviet Union, the official representative of an ideology still unwaveringly focused on world domination, addressed the Assembly of another 'community of belief', seen in Moscow until very recently as a bastion of the Cold War in western Europe. Not content with addressing its Assembly, he openly espoused that community's political credo – pluralist democracy, individual human rights and the rule of law – and hailed the Council of Europe as one of the pillars of his vision of a common European home. While affirming that *glasnost* and *perestroika* had put his own country on the road to reform, he admitted that it still fell far short of the Council's requirements – but added that increased co-operation, and particularly active help with the reform process, should enable it to join this European community of states in the foreseeable future.

No one could have dreamed that, in the same place just eight years later, Boris Yeltsin, President of a Russia now fully part of the Council, would be speaking, at the Second Council Summit, of a Europe without dividing lines – a Europe in which no state would seek to impose its will on any other.

There can be no doubt that 6 July 1989 marked a major turning point in the ideological revolution – particularly since the full text of President Gorbachev's speech was printed, as usual, in the party press. This meant that his ringing statement of his beliefs could be read by anyone, bringing unexpected encouragement and probably (to start with) unintended support to reformers and dissidents in the Soviet Union – and particularly satellite countries where totalitarian power structures were still firmly intact.

Gorbachev's visit to Strasbourg was not just a matter of making a speech which was epoch-making in its implications for the future, but not necessarily registered by the public at large. After addressing the Assembly, he withdrew to an adjoining room with the previous, current and next Chairmen of the Committee of Ministers (Hans van den Broek, Netherlands; Thorvald Stoltenberg, Norway; and João de Deus Pinheiro, Portugal), to discuss details of his appeal for co-operation and support. The room, specially refurbished for the occasion, is still known at the Council as the 'Gorbachev Room', and in it he found himself facing, not just the three ministers, but also a mediaeval print of Strasbourg, one of the great centres of European humanism – an ideal setting for discussion of reform. Gorbachev told his hosts that the Soviet Union was aiming at a new form of European partnership, and intended to reform its own legal system and establish democratic institutions. It was agreed that a joint steering committee would oversee co-operation and specialised aid in those areas. To that extent, 6 July 1989 also sowed the seeds of the assistance and co-operation programmes ('Demosthenes' and 'ADACS'), which the Council later set up to help all the countries of central and eastern Europe to introduce democratic reforms as an essential step towards full membership.

Healing the rift

Strasbourg was a calculated stage on the path which the partisans of reform in the Soviet Union were following. One of the movement's leaders, Foreign Minister Edward Shevardnadze, who had accompanied Mikhail Gorbachev on his visit to the Council of Europe, confirmed this some months later – when the radical changes in the Soviet imperium were fully underway – in a *Moscow News* article. He insisted that Europe's political, military and economic divisions must be overcome and saw the Council itself as the embodiment of 'European cohesion', giving the concept of 'Europe from the Atlantic to the Urals' its full meaning. The then Secretary General, Catherine Lalumière (France), had said that the Council of Europe must become the Council *of Greater Europe*, and he agreed, adding that this Council of Greater Europe should include the Soviet Union. At the Second Council Summit eight years later, in the Assembly Chamber at the Palais de l'Europe (which had now itself become the 'common European home'), he again spoke eloquently – this time as President of Georgia – of the shared cultural and historical heritage which bound his Caucasian homeland to the rest of Europe.

These changes in the Council's political life – special guest status for four eastern European countries, and acceptance of its basic values and principles by the leader of the communist world – were discreet, but their impact was far from being marginal or limited. In fact, they affected the whole of Europe, and this became even clearer on 10 September 1989, when Hungary's Government, and above all its Foreign Minister, Gyula Horn, took their historic decision to open the borders and let thousands of GDR citizens pour through to freedom in the West. The avalanche had started to roll, and the communist empire crumbled. The Red Army stayed in their barracks, and the satellite countries' rulers – deprived of the military backing which had saved their predecessors at the time of the Prague Spring in 1968 – were swept from office.

At its regular meeting early in November 1989, the Council of Europe's Committee of Ministers gave a clear political sign of its readiness for dialogue and co-operation with the democratic movements and reformers. It invited the foreign ministers of three reform states, Poland (Krzysztof Skubiszewski), Hungary (Gyula Horn) and Yugoslavia (Budimir Loncar) to attend, and instructed the Secretary General to devise a co-operation and support programme to promote the process of democratic reform. Their intention was to make the experience gained by the Council in over 40 years of European co-operation, and the rules and working methods it had worked out for democratic institutions, available to the young democracies.

In Berlin, when the Wall came down, Honnecker fell with it. In Prague, Dubček and Havel reappeared, bringing hopes, not just of a new spring, but of a return to Europe. In Bucharest, Ceaucescu was toppled.

The Council of Europe brought the right kind of political pragmatism to its new tasks. It exerted itself in support of democratic reform and sought to bring these countries rapidly into its Europe-wide co-operation system. Early in March 1990, the Chairman of the Committee of Ministers, João de Deus Pinheiro, and the Secretary General, Catherine Lalumière, visited Warsaw, Moscow, Bucharest, Sofia, Belgrade, Budapest,

Prague and East Berlin in lightning succession. Next came a special Committee of Ministers session in Lisbon, where the Council's special role as the reform states' door to the European democratic family was emphasised. Guidance and support were provided as a prelude to joining, and admission was made conditional on strict respect for democracy, human rights and the rule of law. The Parliamentary Assembly (by granting special guest status and monitoring the accession procedure) and the Committee of Ministers were acting in full political accord.

New members – and warning signs

With Spain chairing the Committee of Ministers, contacts in the applicant states' capitals were renewed early in 1991, and the Committee itself held a special session in Madrid in February. There were grounds for satisfaction, but also for concern. The use of troops in the Baltic states and the worsening of the situation in Yugoslavia were both sobering. On the other hand, the admission of the first reform states to the Council – Hungary on 6 November 1990, and now Czechoslovakia on 21 February 1991, in Madrid – was powerfully symbolic. Indeed, Jiri Dienstbier, who signed for Czechoslovakia, had – with Vaclav Havel – been one of the figurehead leaders of the democratic resistance. Again on 21 February, the Soviet Foreign Minister signed the European Cultural Convention. At least in the areas covered by that text (education, culture and heritage), this meant that the 'greater Europe' embodied in the Council now stretched to the Pacific – and that Churchill's vision of 1946 was edging towards fulfilment.

Symbolically significant this opening of the doors to the Soviet Union might be, but the background was still one of tension and uncertainty. Only a few weeks before, the President of the Assembly, Anders Björck (Sweden), had gone to Vilnius, Riga and Tallinn with a number of other parliamentarians, to assure the Baltic republics of their solidarity and support. The conditions in which President Landsbergis received them in the Lithuanian Parliament, which the Russians had sealed off with tanks, suggested that the threat of force was stifling all hope of democracy and freedom. The delegation travelled on to Moscow, where they voiced their concern and insisted on the need for dialogue and democratic decision-making. It was thus an emotional moment when, a few months later, guest delegations from Estonia, Latvia and Lithuania made their first appearance in Strasbourg, at the Assembly's September session. Half-way through his speech, Mr Ivans, leader of the Latvian delegation, produced, with a mixture of pride and emotion, the passport issued to him just the day before by his country's new authorities – number one in the series.

Moreover, the delegation had travelled to Strasbourg via Moscow, where their new travel papers had been accepted without question.

The months between February and September also witnessed Boris Yeltsin's election to the Russian Presidency, and the failure of the old communists' attempted coup in August. It may be worth noting that – in those days and hours, when the Soviet Union's political future was hanging in the balance – Boris Yeltsin despatched Andrei Kozyrev, his right-hand man on foreign policy, to assure western governments of his determination to stick to the democratic path and, if the worst happened, establish a democratic government in exile. A few weeks before, one of the European Parliament's political groups had invited Yeltsin to Strasbourg, giving him an opportunity to contact the Council of Europe as well, and discuss prospects for help with democratic reform in Russia (still a constituent republic of the Soviet Union) with its Secretary General, Catherine Lalumière. This meeting was clearly regarded as important, since Andrei Kozyrev later made a special trip from Paris to spend an evening in Strasbourg and brief her on developments in Moscow and on Boris Yeltsin's intentions.

All change in Europe

True to its post-war political role and statutory mission, the Council of Europe led the way in welcoming the reform states to Europe.

Apart from Yugoslavia (where war had followed war, since the Serb-controlled federal army had invaded Slovenia in June 1991, and Vukovar had been destroyed), the countries of central and eastern Europe all wanted – after decades of nationalism, totalitarianism and ideological division – to rejoin democratic Europe.

Basically, this meant that Europe itself needed to be rethought and redefined. Now that the ideological rift, which had marked its post-war history, had happily been healed, a new and comprehensive political vision was essential. Once again, as in the early 1950s, the Parliamentary Assembly became a platform and forum for the planners and prophets of the new Europe.

Vaclav Havel, the Czech humanist, thought back to the 'European dreams' he had shared in prison with his Charter 77 friend, Jiri Dienstbier. The time had now come to organise the states of Europe on the basis of the spiritual and moral values embodied in the Council of Europe, which had for a time – and only for sad historical reasons – been limited to western Europe. The only way of helping the seemingly impossible dream of a better Europe to come true was to keep on dreaming it, with passionate conviction.

Lech Walesa, the charismatic but pragmatic trade union leader, warned that a new divide – economic, not ideological – now threatened Europe. He hoped that the appeal he was making at the Council of Europe, at the heart of democratic Europe, would be heard. He was speaking to the Europe which had always shared destinies, but now shared interests too, the Europe in which East and West would henceforth have to share both successes and failures.

Delight at being free and united was obviously part of the transition to a Europe without dividing lines, but so was the fear of fresh divisions. The idea of a genuinely undivided Europe immediately became the main challenge – a challenge which has still to be met. Unprecedented wealth and unimaginable poverty are both part of the picture. Some people have literally boundless freedom to travel, others face endless queuing for visas they may never get. Is the dream of a better Europe acceptable only as long as it stays abstract and demands nothing of us, or are we prepared to sacrifice something for it? The fact that a majority of (EU) Europeans are currently prepared to do just that to permit enlargement is encouraging. But beyond the EU's new external ('Schengen') frontier lies Europe again – and the great challenge of the next decade!

Advise, help, hope and pray – Russia joins the Council

'Like a river returning to its bed, Europe has reconnected with its past and its true geographical dimensions.' When he uttered these words a few weeks after the fall of the Berlin Wall, François Mitterrand could have had no idea that the process would prove so tumultuous that Europe's geo-political map would emerge from it totally redrawn.

The differences are instantly apparent if one compares the map of Europe on 1 January 1991 and 31 December of the same year. In those 12 months, the accounts left open by the First and Second World Wars were finally closed off, and the order shaped by the Versailles Treaty of 1919, the German-Soviet Pact of 1939 and the Yalta Agreements of 1945 lost its *raison d'être*. Two multi-ethnic, pluri-national federations – one covering 40% of the Euro-Asian continent and one-sixth of the world's land mass, and often described as the last colonial empire, the other an increasingly shaky jigsaw in the most volatile part of Europe – were simply swept off the map.

Redrawing the map of Europe

'We have hard times before us. The proud European tower is still only a dream. It must be built on the most solid foundation of all, democracy embracing all of Europe. If one country, one region, fails to meet demo-

cratic standards, it will be enough to make the whole building unstable.'
These were the words with which the Parliamentary Assembly's Swedish
President, Anders Björck, described the challenge facing Europe and the
Council of Europe.

This instantly raised the question of where 'Europe' ended. The geographical scope of both the Council of Europe and the European
Communities is limited by definition, since only 'European' countries can
join them: being part of Europe is thus a necessary condition, though not,
of course, the only one. This question had never seemed urgent before, but
the pioneering role the Council was set to play in reconnecting the two
halves of Europe would soon make it vital for the Strasbourg Organisation.

Maastricht and the birth of the EU

In the meantime, meeting in Maastricht on 9 and 10 December 1991, the
EC countries' leaders concluded a historic agreement and created a new
entity: the European Union. Officially signed in Maastricht on 7 February
1992, the 'Treaty on the European Union' marked a major step forward on
the path to European integration: it strengthened the European
Community, extended its powers, and completed the single market by
setting up a Central Bank and introducing a single currency, which was
to come into use at the end of the decade. It then added two further
elements, to provide a basis for a common foreign and security policy,
and for co-operation in the fields of justice and internal policy. And so, by
a quirk of history, the establishment in Western Europe of a kind of federation, within which 12 (soon 15) states were preparing to divide their
sovereignty, coincided, in Eastern Europe and the Balkans, with the
collapse of authoritarian federalism and the final implosion of two state
entities, undermined by nationalism. Almost overnight, 20 new states
emerged from the wreckage to take their places on the European and
world scene.

Political leaders in western Europe thus had to decide, as a matter of
urgency, what attitude to take to these new states – and particularly the
Russian Federation. They obviously realised that the potentially disastrous
effects of the USSR's imploding (and above all the danger of nuclear pro-
liferation) must be controlled, and this was one of their reasons for giving
Yeltsin's Russia access to know-how and capital which they had withheld
from Gorbachev's Soviet Union. In fact, the new situation created by the
fall of the Berlin Wall was reflected only peripherally in the fundamental
changes which the two most important 'European' organisations were forced
to accept in the winter of 1991–1992.[1] NATO had founded the 'North
Atlantic Co-operation Council' as a political platform for co-operation

with the former Warsaw Pact countries, and the European Community had, by signing the first 'European Agreements' with Poland, Hungary and Czechoslovakia, established its own structures for co-operation with the countries of central and eastern Europe. Outside the Council of Europe, however, genuinely equal rights for the 'new' states were still a long way off.

The dream of a better Europe

At this point, it is worth quoting two distinguished visitors from the new democracies who, addressing the Council of Europe's Parliamentary Assembly, voiced their hopes – and fears. Vaclav Havel, President of (the still extant) Czechoslovakia, spoke of hopes and dreams: 'To me, the twelve stars in your emblem do not express the proud conviction that the Council of Europe will build heaven on this earth. There will never be heaven on earth. I see these 12 stars as a reminder that the world could become a better place if, from time to time, we had the courage to look up at the stars.'

But there were (and are) fears as well, and the Polish President Lech Walesa expressed them:

> 'We, citizens of the poorer part of Europe, are getting the impression that the richer and more prosperous part of Europe is closing itself shut against us, that it is becoming a posh club for those who are better off and live in stable conditions. Poland, finding itself in the middle between the West, looking intently into and after itself, and the changing Soviet state, is now bound to look forward to a time with no friends. But that does not apply only to Poland, it applies equally to our neighbours, those from the South and those from the East.'

This was the background when François Mitterrand addressed the Assembly on 4 May 1992. In a Europe 'in search of a new equilibrium', as the Assembly's new President, Miguel Ángel Martínez (Spain), put it, he laid the foundation stone of the Council of Europe's new Human Rights Building and told an enthusiastic Assembly how the Organisation might take on the role he had earlier intended for a 'European confederation' (a short-lived project): 'the Council of Europe could be one of the crucibles – and if it is ambitious and succeeds, the crucible – of this confederation which seems to me so necessary'. And he added: 'I urge you to make that great hope a reality. Incarnate a little more each day the great idea of the Greater Europe.'

However, the Council of Europe started 1993 by taking one step back and two forward. The loss of one member state (Czechoslovakia) on 31 December was followed by the promise of two new ones, when the newborn Czech and Slovak Republics applied formally to join on 1 January. On a more basic level, 1993 saw the Council forced to make a difficult choice between strict (if not over-strict) adherence to its principles and affirmation of its pan-European vocation, between staying at home to guard the temple and going out to meet the challenge from the East, while endeavouring to hold a steady course. And indeed, the storm raging in Bosnia and Herzegovina was enough to shake the very foundations of an organisation whose whole *raison d'être* was grounded in the vow of 'Never again!' fervently uttered, immediately after the Second World War, by political leaders and ordinary people traumatised by atrocities which (they believed) they could stop from recurring, if not throughout the world, at least in Europe.

In spite of the savage fighting and disastrous developments in the former Yugoslavia, which had indeed seemed unthinkable, Europe's leaders continued to believe in the Council of Europe's peacekeeping role. One of them was Franz Vranitzky who, as Austrian Chancellor, hosted the first Summit of the member states' heads of state government in October 1993:

> 'We have become aware that the Council of Europe also plays an important role in maintaining peace on our continent. Security is not confined to military or socio-economic considerations, but has also become a question of the mentality, the outlook and the democratic attitude of European citizens and European society. This is the Council of Europe's great task: to form a factor for integration in Europe which, through respect for human rights, humanist values and democratic principles, helps to ensure that, together, instead of creating new frontiers in Europe, we continue to forge our European identity or, in the words of Edgar Morin, our "common destiny".'

The vision of 'one Europe'

Paradoxically, the concept of 'Europe', as used by politicians and the public, has actually been narrowed at the start of this 21st century by the prospect of the EU's enlargement (in itself a good thing) to take in five former Warsaw Pact countries, the three Baltic states, Malta and Cyprus. Many people now equate Europe with the (enlarged) EU, but participants at the first Council Summit had a clear vision of one great Europe – a Europe of shared values and standards.

As Helmut Kohl, the German Chancellor, pointed out, a dynamic balance between openness and firmness was particularly important in the case of Russia:

> 'When Russia knocks on the door here and says: "We want to join", then the answer should be "yes", but on one condition, namely that the high standards set by the Council of Europe are adhered to, so that a show of special good-

will does not lead to a lower standard. That would be quite the wrong policy. If the demands made here correspond to the standards required, that offers a man like Boris Yeltsin the best chance of moving things forward at home.'

At a safe distance from the slaughter in Bosnia, the Council was heading for a historic spring – one that would see its membership rise, in the space of a few weeks, from 26 to 31.

Spectacular this second wave of new accessions may have been, but others were set to follow shortly, as no fewer than nine other countries were officially waiting to join.

Thus, on the eve of its first Summit, the 'one Europe' embodied in the Council was not simply growing faster than ever before, but was also preparing – while insisting more than ever on the statutory values which gave it its identity – to change character: originally a 'club' for accredited democracies, it gradually evolved into a 'college' for 'students' of democracy, both advanced and beginners. But this was a college with no teachers and pupils, no masters and apprentices: all its members were equal in law and in dignity, all were equally engaged in pursuing an ideal of democracy which could be sought, but never totally realised, and learning and teaching were reciprocal.

The first Council Summit

The Committee of Ministers having confirmed the Assembly's 'yes' to Romania on 7 October, 32 full member states were present when the Heads of State and Government met in Vienna on 8 and 9 October 1993 for the Council's first-ever summit. Unique in the Organisation's history, the meeting passed its first test with flying colours, since no fewer than 29 of those countries sent their top political leaders. The 'family photo' taken at the Summit, featuring seasoned European statesmen like François Mitterrand, Helmut Kohl, Jacques Santer, Felipe Gonzales and Franz Vranitzky, alongside 'newcomers' like Vaclav Havel, Vladimir Meciar, Hanna Suchocka, Zhelyu Zhelyev and Ion Iliescu, offered a striking image of a new Europe 'full of both promise and turmoil', as Catherine Lalumière put it in her welcoming address. There could, she pointed out, be no forgetting that they were meeting 'to talk about Europe, peace and democracy at a tragic moment in our history: thousands of dead in former Yugoslavia and, in Moscow, scores of dead in a struggle for or against reform, for or against democracy'.

In fact, this new Europe was omnipresent in the Austrian capital, where the Congress of Vienna had – for better or worse – established a 'concert of the nations' in the early 19th century. Now, 178 years later, the Council of Europe's Heads of State and Government were sketching in the outlines of a new 21st-century 'concert of Europe', in which every instrument (state, nation, people or international organisation) would have its own appointed part to play in guaranteeing stability of the continent and security of its inhabitants.

The twin keynotes of the Vienna Summit were hope (first of all, the hope of uniting the continent on the basis of values acknowledged and shared by all its countries) and urgency. In fact, there was a powerful sense of urgency, of the need to find an institutional framework for this new, extended unity, and also political solutions to the terrible dangers which continued to weigh on Europe's future – in Bosnia, the Caucasus and Russia.

The aim defined by the Assembly and by François Mitterrand clearly proved too ambitious: the Vienna Summit marked neither the birth nor even the conception of a European confederation, which remained a mere dream without substance. Nonetheless, this first top-level meeting of the member states' leaders did mark a decisive phase in the building of a new Europe:

- by confirming the Council's status as 'the pre-eminent European political institution capable of welcoming, on an equal footing and in permanent structures, the democracies of Europe freed from communist oppression' and by making their accession 'a central factor in the process of European construction based on our Organisation's values';

- by confirming 'a policy of openness and co-operation *vis-à-vis* all the countries of central and eastern Europe that opt for democracy' and defining an enlargement policy based on two requirements: fidelity to the Council's values and respect for the obligations of membership;

- by sending, in this context, an important positive signal to Russia,[2] which had, as Boris Yeltsin stressed in a message to the Summit, opted irrevocably for democratic reforms – reforms designed to bring this 'integral part of European civilisation' into the Council in due course; and

- by taking, finally, a whole series of decisions on such questions as the establishment of a single Court of Human Rights, the protection of national minorities (with the help of confidence-building measures, legal aid and new legal instruments), the launching of a pan-European policy against racism, xenophobia, anti-Semitism and intolerance, and the setting-up of an advisory body to give local and regional authorities a part in building greater Europe.

First of all, however, one basic question – a question which had been exercising both the Assembly and the Committee of Ministers since 1991 –

needed definite answering: where could, and should, the Council's growth stop? In a word, the time had come at last to determine the contours of a concept which politicians, intellectuals and the media had been using for close on 50 years, without ever quite defining it: Europe.

In its Recommendation 1247 on the enlargement of the Council of Europe, the Assembly confirmed the Council's specifically 'European' character and set geographical limits to its expansion. Dropping the idea of imposing artificial boundaries on areas where no natural ones existed, it took a pragmatic line and listed states which qualified for membership. Specifically, it:

- confirmed the 'European' status, not just of the Council's 32 member states, but also the nine 'special guest' countries;

- formally recognised the 'potential member' status of Andorra (on which it had recently adopted a positive opinion, and which the Committee of Ministers admitted as the 33rd member state a month later), and of the Federal Republic of Yugoslavia (Serbia and Montenegro), once it had rejoined the international community; and

- 'in view of their cultural links with Europe', acknowledged that applying for membership was a 'possibility' for Armenia, Azerbaijan and Georgia, provided they clearly indicated 'their will to be considered as part of Europe'.[3]

This made it clear, once and for all, that the sense of belonging to Europe was the main criterion in deciding how far Europe extended. And so, following in the footsteps of Altiero Spinelli, who saw the peoples' acceptance of the European idea as an essential element in European identity, the Assembly opted for a fluid, adjustable definition of Europe and its boundaries. Implicitly approved by the Committee of Ministers, this decision launched the Council (and the whole European process) on an enlargement trajectory which none of the 'founding fathers' – not even the most visionary – would have dared to predict.

Better include than exclude

Relatively quickly, in the space of a few weeks, the Council of Europe successively opened its doors to Moldova, Albania, Ukraine and 'the former Yugoslav Republic of Macedonia', taking Daniel Tarschys's dictum, 'Better include than exclude', as its motto and assuming that membership would encourage these countries – all of them having enormous difficulty in making the transition to democracy and market economics – to persevere on the right path.

The first element in this 'therapeutic accession' was a series of core requirements applying to all new members. Specifically, they were expected to:

- sign the European Convention on Human Rights and its main protocols on joining, and ratify them within a year;
- impose an immediate moratorium on enforcement of the death
  penalty, as a prelude to abolishing it (by ratifying Protocol No. 6 to
  the European Convention on Human Rights) within three years;
- sign the European Convention for the Prevention of Torture on
  joining, and ratify it within a year;
- sign the Framework Convention for the Protection of National
  Minorities and the European Charter of Local Self-Government on
  joining, and ratify them within a year;
- examine other Council of Europe conventions – particularly those
  on extradition, mutual legal assistance, the transfer of sentenced
  persons and the laundering, tracing and confiscation of the proceeds
  of crime – with a view to ratifying them, and apply the basic principles enshrined in them;
- examine the European Social Charter and the European Charter of
  Regional or Minority Languages, with a view to ratifying them;
- undertake to resolve international and internal disputes peacefully –
  an obligation which applies to all member states;
- co-operate in implementing the monitoring procedures set up by the
  Assembly and the Committee of Ministers.

In addition to this impressive list of 'universal' requirements, there was
another, equally substantial list of 'specific' requirements, often very
detailed and reflecting the situation in the state concerned.

In the general requirements, applying equally to all new members, the
Council of Europe or, more accurately, its Parliamentary Assembly had set
European standards of pluralist democracy, governance by law and
human rights, which were essential to 'one' Europe's political identity.

None of the new member states has ever seriously questioned these
'greater European' principles, although some have fallen down on the
timetable for implementing them. Some dissatisfaction is admittedly
caused – and not just in 'new' member countries – by the obvious fact that
these principles do not automatically apply in the same way to 'old' ones.
It is true that the European Convention on Human Rights, including its
6th Protocol on abolition of the death penalty in peacetime, and the Anti-
Torture Convention are now universally applied (even though Great

Britain, for example, only incorporated the Human Rights Convention into domestic law two years ago, thus making it directly enforceable by British courts), but other agreements, which new members are expected to accept as a matter of course, such as the Framework Convention for the Protection of National Minorities and the Charter of Local Self-Government, still encounter problems in some 'old' member states – which does not necessarily help the Organisation's credibility. Hence occasional complaints (not wholly unjustified) that double standards are being applied. Nonetheless, I am convinced that the Assembly's requirements for new members will eventually be satisfied by everyone.

Russia joins the Council

Ukraine's accession in November 1995 brought the Council's membership to 38 states, including five former Soviet republics, of which two – Ukraine and Moldova – were also members of the CIS. An application to join from the Russian Federation had also been on the table since 7 May 1992. Russia, of course, was not instantly comparable to any other European state – larger than all the other members together, it had a population running to a quarter of their collective total, and had decisively shaped the recent history of Europe and the world. Its transition from a Bolshevik single-party state to a parliamentary democracy, from central rule by the Communist Party to a federation of 89 'subjects', had by no means been an easy one – as the attempted coup against Gorbachev in August 1991 and the battle for the 'White House' at the time of the 'second October Revolution' in 1993 remind us.

Russia's own admission had run into problems, and the procedure had actually been 'frozen' for nine months. Russian military action against the 'rebel' Chechen Republic had prompted the Parliamentary Assembly, at its first part-session in 1995, to postpone giving an opinion on Russia's membership request (a mandatory prelude to admission) until it saw fit to restart the procedure (which improvements in Chechnya, and particularly the agreement concluded between the Russian commander in Chechnya, General Anatoly Romanov, and the Chechen leader, Aslan Maskhadov, allowed it to do that summer). The decisive (and provisionally peace-bringing) agreement of Kasavyurt was signed only one year later by Alexander Lebed and Maskhadov, in the presence of the Swiss OSCE representative, Tim Guldimann.

The debate on Russia's application for membership took place on 25 January 1996. There was still great uncertainty. For one thing, the situation in Chechnya remained extremely tense. For another, the elections held on 17 December 1995, in which the democrats had again lost ground to the ultra-nationalists and communists (who had increased their score from 44% to 55% of the total vote since December 1993), had thrown fresh shadows on Russia's political future. Admittedly, the large electoral turnout and the satisfactory conduct of the elections (judged 'free and fair' by all the international observers, including the Council's parliamentary delegation) were positive factors, but the future of the problem-fraught democratic reform process was clearly in the balance. The 'disaster' scenario (disastrous both for Russia and the whole of Europe) – a relapse into communism, or even Czarist-type autocracy – never seemed likelier than it did in those first six months of 1996, when an ailing and politically weakened Boris Yeltsin was preparing once again to face the electorate.

In these circumstances, the decision facing the Assembly was anything but easy: on the one hand, it seemed sensible to wait a few more months, since the outcome of the presidential election would certainly clarify the situation; on the other hand, it seemed wise to send Russia a positive signal and respond, while there was time, to Sergei Kovalev's urgent plea ('democrats in the West must help democrats in the East'). The Council's member governments already knew which way they meant to go, and Danish Foreign Minister Niels Helveg Petersen made this utterly clear on 24 January when he delivered the Committee of Ministers' traditional communication in the Parliamentary Assembly: 'The democratic security, which was highlighted at the Vienna Summit in 1993 as the most important vocation of the Council of Europe in these years, will be fully obtained and secured only with Russia as a member of our Organisation.'

Tilting the balance

At the beginning of that very session week, Leni Fischer (Germany, CDU) replaced Miguel Angel Martinez (Spain, Socialist) as President of the Assembly. I was unanimously elected to succeed her as Chair of the Group of the European People's Party (EPP) – the Assembly's second-largest political group, which incorporates the Christian Democrat and centre parties. At the very first meeting I chaired, I was faced with the task of determining the EPP's line on admitting Russia. The discussion, involving Group members from Russia's special guest delegation (independents and members of the 'Our Home Russia' party), was highly emotional, and the ensuing vote was exactly split between advocates and opponents of immediate Russian accession – the result every chairman dreads. Pitched in at the deep end, I had to give a lead. It was clear that this was a question which would also divide other groups, but it was equally clear that the position we adopted would influence waverers among the Conservatives (whose chair was against) and Liberals (whose chair was in favour). One thing was sure: sitting on the fence or failing to agree on our own group's position before going on to vote in the Assembly would not help the latter to reach a definite decision.

I called a meeting of the Bureau and invited representatives of the 'pro' and 'con' factions in the group to attend. We weighed the arguments, and the Bureau finally authorised me to recommend, on the whole group's behalf, that the Assembly vote to admit Russia. Most of those who opposed immediate accession (the only question!) were prepared to accept this recommendation or, quite simply, abstain. The preliminary decision had therefore been taken: it remained to be seen how much support it would get in the Assembly. The ensuing debate was one of the most important in its history – and I was deeply conscious of our duty to help bring the European dream a little closer to fulfilment.

While Vladimir Zhirinovsky's blustering rhetoric ('If the Council shuts its doors on Russia, it will be doing me a great favour: millions of Russians will vote for me, for I shall be standing in the next presidential election') produced the reverse effect of that probably intended, his compatriot Vladimir Lukin found words to fit the occasion:

> 'If Russia is admitted, it will join the Council of Europe in the state that it is in at that moment. The rule of law has not been completed and there are people, even those in high places, who are trying to slow the process. [...] However, if the Assembly admits Russia, it will not simply be admitting politicians who say one thing and do another: it will be showing solidarity with a great country which, for the first time in its history, has embarked on the path to the rule of law and has guaranteed freedoms the Russians have never had before. [...] If the Assembly refuses to admit Russia, there is a danger that the Iron Curtain may come down again. If it admits Russia, Russia will become a state ruled by law.'

Speaking for the EPP in the debate, I declared:

> 'A majority of the members of my group feel that we should help Russia to advance towards democracy, strengthen the rule of law and respect human rights, and that we should, above all, give the people of Russia the chance to turn to the Council of Europe's human rights institutions. For these reasons, Russia should be admitted. We should not allow it to join just because it is a great power. It is up to countries to become great powers at the Council by developing democracy, protecting human rights and respecting the rule of law. Geopolitical power, at any rate, counts for nothing at the Council now, and must not count for anything in future.'

At the close of an impassioned and unusually earnest debate, the Assembly finally adopted a positive opinion on inviting Russia to join by

164 votes in favour, 35 against and 15 abstentions (i.e. considerably more than the requisite two-thirds majority). This decision marked a new stage in the theory of 'therapeutic accession', since the Assembly's 'yes' to Russia was coupled with three series of commitments.

On the way to European standards

The first series comprised the traditional 'core' requirements imposed on all new members, covering signature and ratification of the main Council of Europe conventions, particularly those relating to human rights; the second series supplemented the first by detailing, as had been done in the case of countries like Albania, Moldova, Ukraine and 'the former Yugoslav Republic of Macedonia', a wide range of specific measures which Russia was expected to take – in the medium or longer term – to bring itself into line with Council of Europe standards; the third series differed from the two others (and from all the requirements previously made in the case of new member states), in reflecting Russia's special responsibilities as heir to one of the 20th century's two superpowers, and a major Eurasian power in its own right. The Assembly started by asking it to take just measures to erase the last effects of the Second World War; it noted that it was henceforth determined to settle its international disputes, not only 'by resolutely rejecting all threat of using force against its neighbours', but also 'respecting the existing international treaties' in questions relating to frontiers; it finally asked the Russian authorities 'to denounce as mistaken the concept of two different categories of foreign country, which involves treating some of them, which are known as "the near abroad", as a zone of special influence' (a criticism aimed at the vision, then widely current in Russia, of a police role for the zone corresponding to the former Soviet Union, a role which Russia had tried unsuccessfully to get the UN to recognise).

In Russia itself, after months of uncertainty, the drive for reform and the attempt to resolve the Chechnyan conflict peacefully were given fresh impetus by the outcome of the presidential elections on 16 June and 3 July. The political success achieved in Chechnya by the short-lived Yeltsin-Lebed alliance was greeted with immense relief by the international community, whose decision to trust to Russia's good intentions now seemed fully justified.

Russia's accession was followed the same year by that of Croatia – again after lengthy debates, in which the main issues were the part played by the country (and above all its President, Franjo Tudjman) in the Bosnian conflict, its retaking of territory mainly inhabited by Serbs, and freedom of the press and opinion. The states still outside in eastern and south-eastern Europe were now Bosnia and Herzegovina, still torn in spite of the

Dayton Accords, Milosevic's Federal Republic of Yugoslavia (obviously), Belarus, which was plainly having more trouble than Russia itself with democratic reform, and the south Caucasian countries, still rocked by conflicts dating back to the dissolution of the Soviet Union.

The second Summit: Europe reconciled with itself

But the 'grey' zones on the map of the European democracies were shrinking, and the continent was becoming steadily more aware of its shared features and identity. This was increasingly plain to us in the Assembly and its political groups, where the young democracies' new political parties quickly allied themselves with Conservatives, Liberals or Christian Democrats. Most of the former Communists and post-Communists in countries like Poland, Slovakia, Hungary, Romania and Bulgaria (who had seized the chance to democratise their parties as well as their countries) made common cause with the social democrats. Even those communists who wanted to stay communists accepted the principles of pluralist, parliamentary democracy and found, in the Assembly, a suitable and recognised home with the 'Unified European Left'.

What better place, in these circumstances, for the continent to make peace with itself than the Council of Europe? This, in a fundamental sense, was what the second Summit, held in Strasbourg on 10 and 11 October 1997, was all about. From the impressive turnout, it was clear that Europe's leaders were aware of this. No fewer than 46 heads of state and government, representing nearly all the countries of Europe, accepted French President Jacques Chirac's invitation. Symbolically, the extraordinary 'family photo' was taken almost 50 years to the day after the Marshall Plan's rejection, under Soviet pressure, by the countries of central and eastern Europe (a move which sealed the division of Europe into rival blocs, making the Iron Curtain, which Winston Churchill had seen descending over Europe in 1946, a fixture). What the Summit really expressed – coming back yet again to Jacques Santer's phrase – was Europe's reconciliation with itself. Never in all its long history had the continent seen such a massive gathering of all its leaders. Did those leaders know that they were making history? Perhaps not – but that, nonetheless, is what Jacques Chirac, Lionel Jospin, Helmut Kohl, Romano Prodi, José-Maria Aznar, Tony Blair, Boris Yeltsin, Vaclav Havel, Mesut Yilmaz, Leonid Kuchma, Edward Shevardnadze and all the others were doing in that month of October 1997.

All of this was striking and symbolic, but symbolic significance was simply not enough to make the Summit a success. To outlive the 'family photo', Europe's reconciliation with itself needed firm foundations to make it permanent.

The first of those foundations was provided by the Council's 'fundamental principles'. This was why the Final Declaration adopted at the Summit expressly declared:

> 'We, Heads of State and Government of the member states of the Council of Europe, meeting in Strasbourg on 10 and 11 October 1997 for our Organisation's second Summit, [...] solemnly reaffirm our attachment to the fundamental principles of the Council of Europe – pluralist democracy, respect for human rights, the rule of law – and the commitment of our governments to comply fully with the requirements and meet the responsibilities arising from membership of our Organisation'.

This solemn, shared commitment to the fundamental values written into the Council's Statute did not simply hark back to the sources of the European project. It was also, and above all, a message for the future – a collective task entrusted to the Council and its members.

The second foundation was equality of all the states of Europe. For the purpose of stifling, once and for all, that spirit of confrontation and conquest which had caused so much tragedy throughout the continent's history, a partnership pact, based on mutual respect and enrichment, was concluded: 'All different, all equal'! The statements made at the Summit by the leaders of Europe's largest country and one of its smallest are worth recalling here. The conviction voiced by Russia's Boris Yeltsin ('We are now poised to begin building together a new, greater Europe, free from dividing lines: a Europe where no state will impose its will on others, a Europe where big and small countries are equal partners united by common democratic principles') was echoed by Liechtenstein's Mario Frick: 'When the fundamental values of a community are seriously challenged, a clear commitment is necessary. In this context, it is precisely the smaller countries which can never be accused of pursuing hidden interests and which are called upon to combat lawlessness, unscrupulousness and violence.'

The third foundation of Europe's nascent unity was the dual emphasis placed on internal diversity and external openness. Europe is necessarily a plural entity, and its diversity is a matter, not just of differences between states, but of differences within states and between transfrontier communities – in short, that extraordinary mosaic of peoples, nations, and cultural and linguistic communities which together make up the continent. But Europe also has responsibilities to the rest of the world and needs to remember them (this was the force of the paragraph in the Final Declaration which called for 'understanding between the citizens of the North and the South, in particular through information and civic education for young people, as well as initiatives aimed at promoting mutual respect and solidarity among peoples').

Realisation of the European dream invoked at the Summit – the dream of 'one Europe', united yet diverse, stretching from the Azores to Vladivostok, from Akureyi in Iceland to Limassol in Cyprus – seemed so close in 1997. True, there were still conflicts. But surely Chechnya and Bosnia had shown that the shooting at least could stop, that human rights and freedoms could be given a chance, and protection for minorities ensure that the past's basic errors could never be repeated?

Europe's past is a chronicle of conflicts. Its present is not, of course, conflict-free, but it does seem set to become a chronicle of conflicts resolved – of reconciliation. Will its future be a chronicle of co-operation, of unity in the midst of diversity? At all events, we can be sure that its present and future will be shaped, not by any institution or organisation and its members, but by a bewildering array of different factors. The 'common European home' has been built to no uniform plan. Many different architects, builders and foremen, both professional and amateur, have gone at the job in their various ways – planning, replanning, building, rebuilding and extending. This chapter has chiefly focused on the Council of Europe as a building site, from the Vienna to the Strasbourg Summit, but we need to look at the other blueprints (or should I say dreams?) as well.

My dream comes true – destination Strasbourg

When election-time came round in Austria in 1990, two 'pillars' of the ÖVP and the Austrian delegation to the Strasbourg Assembly – Marga Hubinek, second President of the Austrian Parliament, and Ludwig Steiner, the party's long-term spokesman on foreign affairs and a former State Secretary – decided not to stand. The two vacant places in the Strasbourg delegation went to my friend and former party chairman, Fritz König – and to me. Fritz saw this as a stepping-stone to the European Parliament (a logical move for a man who had been an early proponent of Austria's joining the EU). But I saw enlarging the Council of Europe and spreading democracy in central and eastern Europe as the great challenge which had to be met if the whole reform process, which had just begun, was to be made irreversible. Moreover, not all the reformers were firmly in the saddle, and some countries, e.g. the Baltic states, were still struggling to achieve independence.

New boy at the Palais

And so, in April 1991, I arrived, as a member of the Council of Europe's Parliamentary Assembly, at the 'Palais de l'Europe', or Palace of Europe – the kind of high-flown title that sounds natural only in French. With the exception of the Assembly Chamber or 'hemicycle' (so-called because of its semi-circular shape), the 'Palais' is actually a plain and functional office building. Without striving for architectural effect, it still looks impressive when approached from the city centre – on its artificial mound, with a fine park across the road, a sweeping lawn in front, and the member states' flags (then 26, now 45) flying proudly on the forecourt. Until a special new building was opened nearby in 1999, the European Parliament also used it for its sessions.

Impressed by the building, I was equally impressed by the Assembly, of which I was to remain a member for over eight years. One distinctive (and still controversial feature) is its seating plan: members are seated alphabetically, and not divided into national or political groups. The resultant mosaic may not be ideal for day-to-day parliamentary purposes, but I still feel that this is the arrangement which best embodies the spirit of European unity. People from different countries and parties make contact quickly and become friends, regardless of political differences. Thanks to these personal contacts, and the open discussion they generate, the Assembly's decisions are not just a reflection of national and party-political interests and influences, but the product of a genuinely European opinion-forming process, based on partnership.

Logically, in view of my longstanding interest in home affairs, my Assembly career began in the Social, Health and Family Affairs Committee, and the Committee on Economic Affairs and Development. In the Political and Legal Affairs Committees, I started by merely deputising for my colleagues, Fritz König and Martin Strimitzer. The issues we dealt with were fascinating. Moreover, I had arrived just in time for what was, very probably, the most interesting period in the Council's and the Assembly's history. The first 'new' members, Hungary and Czechoslovakia (still undivided), had already joined – the latter very recently, on 21 February 1991. Others were in mid-procedure, and already had 'special guest' delegations. But tragedy was in the offing too: under Slobodan Milosevic's authoritarian rule, Serbia had embarked on an aggressively nationalistic, 'greater Serbian' course, indirectly dealing the old – non-democratic, but at least multi-ethnic – Yugoslavia the death blow. Kosovo, which had lost its autonomous status and seen the rights of its Albanian majority drastically curtailed, was a time bomb, and the inevitable explosion was to shake, not just the Council of Europe, but the whole international community.

I soon found my feet in the Assembly and became actively involved in its work, both in committee and at plenary sessions. In the Social, Health and Family Affairs Committee, I worked on a European policy to give people with disabilities greater independence, and, for the Committee on Economic Affairs and Development, I prepared the Assembly's first report on the recently founded European Bank for Reconstruction and Development.

Yugoslavia at war

The Assembly soon had to deal with developments triggered by the former Yugoslavia's dissolution, which had not, alas, gone peacefully. The Yugoslav federal army, under Milosevic's *de facto* command, attempted to crush Slovenian and Croatian independence by force. At the end of June, Yugoslav and newly-formed Slovenian units clashed on the frontier with Austria – which the Austrian army moved up to defend. Shortly before, on 25 June, the Assembly had held its 'mini-session' in Helsinki. Inevitably, the Yugoslav crisis was the number-one topic both inside and outside the meeting room. I supported the efforts of Slovenia and Croatia to achieve independence, but not everyone agreed. Here I found, as I was to do later on other occasions, that foreign policy is an area where governments and parliaments tend to stick doggedly to the old line, seeing yesterday's 'friends' and 'foes' as today's. I am still convinced that Milosevic got away with so much for so long because some foreign ministries still saw 'his' Serbia in 1914 terms and regarded it as an ally, dismissing Austrian and German attitudes to the new states as an anti-Serb reflex. There were also a few states (some in western Europe) with 'separatist' problems of their own, which tended to take a jaundiced view of 'secessionism' anywhere. A leading Spanish member of the Assembly, who has since become a good friend, defended Milosevic with the words: 'If Catalonia declared itself independent, we'd send in the Spanish army too.' Europe took some time to form even a partial idea of what was really happening in the former Yugoslavia.

At that time, not all the signs were yet threatening. Bosnia had been multi-ethnic and multiconfessional for centuries, and its various communities seemed likely to agree and find a peaceful way to independence. Nonetheless, we were getting some disturbing reports, and my optimism vanished after a meeting with Haris Silajdzic, Bosnia's Foreign Minister, arranged for me in January 1992 by the President of the Austro-Bosnian Association, Mr Urban, an Austrian of Bosnian descent, who acted as Bosnia's unofficial ambassador in Vienna. We met in the Café Sacher – entirely the wrong setting for the things he had to tell me. He painted an utterly bleak picture of a greater Serbia and a greater Croatia, both equally bent on dismembering Bosnia, and made it clear that the worst was bound to happen. Whether or not Bosnia declared itself independent, aggression, atrocity and expulsions would follow, and Bosnia's Muslims would be the helpless losers. The basic problem was a clear one. Here was a state with three indigenous communities. Two regarded themselves as forming part of adjacent states and rejected the present one, while the third had no state but the one it shared with them. I little suspected how much the fate of Bosnia and its three peoples (linked, in the fullest sense, for better or for worse) would concern me, after one of Europe's most savage conflicts, in which genocide and rape were used as weapons, when the Dayton Accords had produced a flawed peace.

Yugoslavia had emerged from the old Dual Monarchy, and was now a prey to the very same problems of nationality which had proved fatal to the latter. While it was being torn apart in a welter of violence and terror, another state, which had also inherited a mix of different peoples and communities from the Habsburg system, was redivided – if not quite amicably, at least peacefully – after 75 years' existence. Czechoslovakia (or, as it finally styled itself, the Czech and Slovak Federative Republic, CSFR) split on the strength of a decision, not necessarily by the people, but by the Prague and Bratislava leaders, that this was in their best interests. The CSFR had had little trouble gaining admission to the Council of Europe, as the second reform state to join – but the applications immediately lodged by the two new republics were looked at more closely.

From the Halonen Order to monitoring

The Committee for Legal Affairs and Human Rights, which would increasingly absorb my interest, appointed me rapporteur for its opinion on Slovakia's application. The Political Affairs Committee's rapporteur was the Finnish Social Democrat, Tarja Halonen (whom I later welcomed, as Secretary General, when she visited the Council as President of her country), and the Committee on Non-Member Countries (which no longer exists) had opted for the Danish Liberal, Hanna Severinsen.

Our task looked easy to start with – and this was reflected in the fact that our reports were due for the Assembly's session at the end of June 1993 – but proved politically explosive.

In fact, the fall of communism had given the former Soviet satellite states and republics the freedom they had lacked for so long, but had also brought previously hidden problems to the surface. Internal conflicts, particularly concerning national minorities and the Roma, were among the most serious. The communists had seen everything in terms of the class struggle, and had concentrated on stripping the 'capitalists' (the source of all social evils) of their property and socialising the means of production. This fixation had blinded them to other conflicts, which they thus had no desire to settle. National minorities had extensive rights on paper – above all in education, whose actual content was dictated by the Party, and culture, which was state-controlled in any case – but majorities and minorities were not reconciled, as they had been in nearly all parts of western Europe.

As a result, most of the new democracies were again left exactly where they had been before the communists seized power. The wounds inflicted by territorial disputes and imposed settlements had never healed properly, but had simply been perfunctorily concealed beneath the scab of communist dictatorship. As for the Roma, they had been 'treated like everyone else' and had – supposedly for their own good – been rehoused in faceless, jerry-built flats, and forced to adopt a totally alien lifestyle.

These problems were particularly acute in Slovakia (and also in Romania). In the 10-year period preceding the communist takeover in Czechoslovakia, Slovaks and Magyars in the south of the country had both been winners and losers, and also, to some extent, expellees and expellers. At an earlier stage, when the state itself had been founded, Slovaks had soon come to see themselves as a minority, or at least as less favoured by Prague. Hitler had exploited this in crushing Czechoslovakia, and had granted Slovakia a kind of pseudo-independence under a nationalist president. In return, extensive territories in southern Slovakia, which had a mixed Slovak and Hungarian population, were surrendered to Hungary. Some of the Slav population were forcibly resettled, while others – still smarting at the memory of compulsory Magyarisation in the Hungarian half of the old Dual Monarchy – preferred to leave their homeland semi-voluntarily. When Hitler's Germany was defeated and the Czechoslovak Republic was restored at the end of the Second World War – events in which a Slovak rising played an honourable part – the lost territories were restored. It was now the Hungarians' turn to be expelled. Like Germans in Czech territory under the Benes decrees, they were collectively stripped of their rights and declared enemies of the state, which confiscated their property (some of it owned by churches and Hungarian associations). As the parallel expulsion of the several hundred thousand Slovaks, who had traditionally lived in scattered settlements in Hungary, made clear, all of this had little to do with individual guilt (even cumulative individual guilt). For nearly a thousand years, from the time of St Stephen to the end of the First World War, Hungarians and Slovaks had lived together in one kingdom; for several hundred years, Pressburg (German), Poszony (Hungarian) or Bratislava (Slovak) had even been the Hungarians' capital, where their kings were crowned.

Unlike the Germans, who were expelled wholesale from Czech territory, not all the Hungarians settled in Slovakia had been expelled by the time the communists took over (conversely, nearly all the Slovaks in Hungary had been forcibly resettled in Slovakia). Under the Communists, the Hungarians again had extensive cultural rights on paper, although they were subject to various bureaucratic restrictions (e.g. Hungarian first names for children had to be chosen from an official list of about 200).

When freedom returned, there were thus many scores waiting to be settled. The minorities wanted new rights granted and old ones restored, while the majority, for historical reasons, dreaded a resurgence of separatism. On both sides, expellees and their descendants had been nursing resentments, and the Slovaks were convinced that Prague had, in all those years, been privileging the Hungarians at their expense.

Truly self-governing for the first time in its history, Slovakia had as its Prime Minister Vladimir Meciar, who liked to pose as the father of his country's independence. In fact, he had merely raised the stakes with Prague in an effort to extract more rights for his regional government – only to find himself facing, in Vaclav Klaus, an opponent who thought chiefly in economic terms, and was only too happy to sever the link with a less developed entity, which he regarded as a ball and chain.

Meciar responded by calling even more stridently for independence and playing the nationalist card. This at once made him suspect at European level, although the peaceful parting of the ways in Czechoslovakia was contrasted with the tragedy which had befallen the former Yugoslavia. Relations between majorities and minorities always suffer first when the nationalists move in. When those relations are also burdened by unsolved problems left over from the past, the resulting mixture can be potentially explosive – as it was in the situation we found ourselves facing as rapporteurs.

The tensions, of course, were genuine, but they were certainly exaggerated by the politicians – both by Meciar's governing party, the HDSZ ('Movement for a Democratic Slovakia') and the Hungarian coalition's representatives. In most of the villages and towns which we visited in southern Slovakia, the two communities lived harmoniously together, and we even found Hungarian mayors in places where Hungarians accounted for only 30% of the population. The political alarm was caused more by intentions (sometimes merely alleged intentions) than by actual measures. On the other hand, we did find that most of the bilingual place names and signposts had been removed on the flimsy pretext that they had no basis in law.

We also found, of course, that reforms were needed. After all, the Velvet Revolution was little more than three years in the past, and a sizeable part of the communist legacy remained to be dealt with. On minority policy, we obviously urged the government to apply the Strasbourg Assembly's celebrated Recommendation 1201(92) – and specifically to abolish the list of officially approved Hungarian names and make bilingual signs a legal requirement in areas with a minority population (obviously not just Hungarian) of at least 20%.

Meciar's nationalist posturing had gone down badly in the West; for the first time, a membership application from a new central European democracy got a less than totally favourable reception. During the Assembly's mini-session in Malta in spring 1993, the Ministers' Deputies invited me to a private meeting, so that they could question me about the situation in Slovakia, and find out what I basically thought myself.

However, after several visits and intensive talks with, among others, Prime Minister Meciar, who was always charming face-to-face, Tarja Halonen, Hanna Severinsen and I had already decided that Slovakia deserved – like the newly founded Czech Republic (and the new democracies which had already joined) – to be admitted to the Council of Europe on certain, clearly defined conditions. We all felt indeed that joining the Council, and accepting its standards and the principles written into Recommendation 1201 by the Assembly, would help it to solve its minority problems more easily. More particularly, we had also agreed that the obligations it accepted, and the commitments it gave, would require special watching.

This was how the Council of Europe's 'monitoring procedure' originated. Introduced by the Parliamentary Assembly in the 'Halonen Order' (named after Tarja), it was initially operated by the Political and Legal Affairs Committees, working in tandem, and began automatically six months after accession. A year later, the Committee of Ministers followed suit with a separate – and different – procedure of its own.

The Council gets my vote

Like Tarja Halonen, I had made a name for myself in the Assembly with the report on Slovakia, and also as a 'founding' rapporteur when the monitoring procedure was launched. I became a full member of the committee, already unusual enough, and was also chosen to follow Martin Strimitzer as its Vice-Chairman. From then on, things moved quickly.

When Austria joined the EU on 1 January 1995, my friend and colleague, Fritz König, 'migrated' to the European Parliament. For two months, from the signing of the agreement to Austria's actual accession, I was myself an 'advisory member' of the European Parliament, and was entitled to attend committee meetings without voting. However, the things I saw did not impress me unduly. There was simply too much discussion for my taste, and the Parliament and its committees tended –

whenever areas of EU concern in which they had no real powers were the issue – to talk about everything and nothing. By comparison, the Council of Europe's Parliamentary Assembly seemed far more purposeful, far more bent on getting results, far quicker in coming to the point and – as the driving force behind a possibly less powerful, but still essential institution – markedly more effective. And so, to many people's surprise, I rejected the chance to become one of Austria's first 'real' MEPs, although these were still appointed by parliaments, and not directly elected. (I prefer 'MEP' to the more common 'Euro-MP' – a term which should really apply, I believe, to members of the Council of Europe's Parliamentary Assembly.)

As Fritz König's successor, I became a full member of the Political Affairs Committee, certainly the Council's most important and prestigious, and also succeeded him as rapporteur on the monitoring procedure for Romania. Like Slovakia, Romania was beset with minority problems, again chiefly concerning the sizeable Hungarian minority, which was represented by an active party of its own. There were also many Roma, as well as residual Transylvanian and Banat Germans, Bulgarians, Ukrainians and even Italians. Other huge problems concerned the restitution of property arbitrarily confiscated under the communists, former political prisoners demanding rehabilitation, the supposedly still powerful influence of the Securitate (Ceaucescu's notorious security service), general poverty, and one terrible legacy of the Ceaucescu era – the 'abandoned' children, who were left to vegetate in appalling, prison-like institutions (they certainly did not deserve the name 'homes') or survive as best they could on the streets. Politically polarised between the former communists and an opposition which harked back to pre-Ceaucescu times, and did not score its first election victory until 1997, the country still made extraordinary efforts to overcome all the obstacles and find a path to democracy, market economics and membership of the European family. Monitoring the undertakings it had given the Council of Europe constituted a real challenge.

As with Slovakia, I found myself playing a double role. In Romania itself, and in dealing with representatives of its government or parliament, I saw myself as a Council of Europe spokesman, as an ambassador for its values, with the task of persuading, guiding and helping. This was also the spirit which informed any criticisms I made in my reports. I was not trying to blame, let alone punish, but to show where changes needed to be made and action taken. In Council of Europe committees, on the other hand, and in talking to fellow Assembly-members and to member states' ambassadors, who followed my work with great interest, my main concern was to explain Romania's anxieties and problems. Given its history and the situation it had inherited, I was fully aware that it could not solve its problems from one day to the next, and could not satisfy all of the Council's requirements to the letter and at once.

A difficult mission: Turkey

All of this had earned me a name as a non-judgmental, fair-minded politician, who thought carefully before acting – which is probably why I got the new jobs that my passionate interest in the challenges presented by an ever-changing European scene repeatedly made me look for.

In 1994–1995, human rights violations and action outside its own frontiers (e.g. in the Kurdish areas of northern Iraq) increasingly made Turkey the target of European criticism. The Legal Affairs Committee asked me to prepare its opinion on the reports prepared for the Political Affairs Committee by the Hungarian Socialist, Andras Bársony (now State Secretary in the Hungarian Foreign Ministry). It would have been easy just to condemn Turkey and demand immediate total compliance with European standards, and the whole Assembly would certainly have backed us. In spite of the differences in our political backgrounds (the Hungarian Socialists had emerged from the old Communist Party, and Andras Bársony had, as a young man, been a state trade union official), we essentially agreed that doing this and nothing else would leave Turkey resentful and defiant, without improving the admittedly lamentable situation. Turkey had been in the Council since 1949, but had experienced some serious crises, including two takeovers by the army, which was still a force to be reckoned with – and it needed help and guidance as well. We accordingly took care never to criticise without immediately pointing to the remedy and saying exactly what needed to be changed. Turkey was the first 'old member' to be subjected to the Assembly's monitoring procedure – and it accepted this. Andras Bársony and I were also appointed rapporteurs for this procedure by the Political and (in my case) Legal Affairs Committees.

When a special Monitoring Committee was established early in 1998, we were again appointed to serve it as equal-ranking rapporteurs on Turkey. The procedure for Romania, which had essentially honoured its obligations, had now been successfully concluded. I had to resign as rapporteur on Slovakia, which was still a little short of that point, since the new Committee's rules allowed rapporteurs to deal with one country only, and I had chosen Turkey. But most of the things that needed doing for Slovakia had been done, and this was confirmed when it was included on the EU's 'enlargement list' and, having satisfied the Copenhagen criteria, among the countries due to join on 1 May 2004.

In Turkey, too, things were moving. Our first report, and the influence of the Turkish delegation to the Parliamentary Assembly, prompted Europe-minded members of the Grand National Assembly in Ankara to start pushing for the constitutional amendments we had recommended, which were secured – in diluted form, admittedly – in 1995. The Turkish Government also appointed a separate Human Rights Minister. From one visit to the next, we could see slight improvements in the conduct of criminal proceedings and, above all, the attitude of the security forces. But there were problems and reverses too. Not only were the DEP (Democracy Party) and HADEP (Freedom of the People and Democracy Party) parties, which were close to the Kurds, prohibited or harassed, but the Refah (Welfare) Party, led by Necmettin Erbakan, and its successor party, Faselet, were also banned, although Erbakan himself even served as Prime Minister in a coalition government. In defiance of strong protests by the Parliamentary Assembly, four DEP parliamentarians were stripped of their immunity, charged with supporting terrorist activity, convicted and sent to jail. The same fate befell Recep Tayyip Erdogan, now Prime Minister, who was Istanbul's progressive and successful mayor when we met him. For making a speech and reading out a poem (i.e. for voicing his opinions), he too was sentenced by the courts.

We were actually allowed to visit Laila Sana and the three other DEP parliamentarians in the high security prison at Ankara, but could not obtain their release. Early in 1999, when the leader of the PKK terrorist organisation, Abdullah Öcalan, was apprehended by Turkey, after an odyssey which said little for legal co-operation in Europe, and was tried on the prison island of Imrali, the Parliamentary Assembly secured the presence of international observers at the trial. I attended the opening myself, and so heard Öcalan's surprising confession of his guilt. Like other leading Council of Europe politicians, I had spoken out against sentencing him to death. After many contacts, and although public and media opinion in Turkey was inflamed against him, I felt confident on this score. After all, Turkey had observed a self-imposed moratorium on executions strictly since 1984 (although the courts continued to pass the death sentence).

Campaigning – and fact-finding

The very next morning, after roughly three hours' sleep at the Austrian Consul General's residence, I flew straight from Istanbul to Rome, to canvass parliamentary and government support for my candidature for the Secretary Generalship of the Council of Europe. Having spent a day in Rome, I flew on to Athens, and from there to Nicosia. A week later, I was in Helsinki and Tallinn and then, a week before the Parliamentary

Assembly's session, I flew to Tirana in an Austrian military aircraft, and on by helicopter to Skopje, where some 5000 refugees from Kosovo were housed in a camp run by the Austrian army. I was quite as anxious to get a first-hand picture of the situation as I was to push my campaign. From Tirana I went on by car to Macedonia, where I visited a UN camp for some 30,000 refugees, and saw the border with Kosovo, 20 kilometres north of Skopje. After Skopje, it was back to Turkey – this time Ankara, where I met the Turkish parliamentary delegation. This was the last stop on the 'election trail' which had, in the space of seven months, taken me to nearly all the Council of Europe countries.

In Moscow too, there had been considerable interest. Nearly all the members of the Russian delegation to the Assembly had attended a reception at the Austrian embassy; at the Duma, I had spoken to the speakers of both houses, Gennady Seleznov and Yegor Stroyev; at the Foreign Ministry, I had met the Deputy Minister, Yevgeni Gusarov, and the President's Office had also invited me for talks. All these contacts proved useful after my election, having shown me that the Russian authorities are perfectly prepared to accept criticism – provided it is well informed.

Twelve Stars for Europe

During my campaign, my ordinary work went ahead, both in the Austrian Parliament – I was Chairman of the Buildings Committee and my Party's spokesman on building projects and housing – and in the Assembly, where I had been chairman of the second largest political group, the European People's Party, since early 1996. My prominent function in that group had not prevented me from working on numerous issues with parliamentarians from the other four: the Socialist Group, the European Democratic Group (Conservatives, National Conservatives), the Liberal, Democratic and Reformers Group, and the Group of the Unified European Left. I had attended hearings organised by the Ministers' Deputies and by the Assembly's Standing Committee, and had been invited to present my programme to all the political groups. I had made 'Twelve stars for Europe' my campaign motto, and my programme covered the following 12 points:

1. Strengthening the Council of Europe as a pan-European political forum for democracy, the rule of law and human rights.
2. Giving the European Convention on Human Rights (ECHR) currency throughout Europe by securing formal EU accession to the text, and its recognition by the OSCE as the decisive human rights standard.
3. Promoting co-operation and exploiting synergies with the EU and the OSCE.

4. Establishing a permanent EU presence at the Council of Europe and attendance by the CFSP representative at meetings of the Committee of Ministers.
5. Establishing a timetable and list of measures for implementation of the Second Summit's Action Plan.
6. Using well-known people to act as goodwill ambassadors for the Council and publicise the aims of the Action Plan.
7. East-West youth exchanges (training, jobs, social service) to help Europe grow together.
8. Definite decision-making and financial powers for the Assembly as a parliamentary body with a decision-making, and not just consultative role.
9. Linking the monitoring procedures of the Parliamentary Assembly and the Committee of Ministers.
10. Consolidating the Organisation's financial resources.
11. Sufficient and guaranteed provision for future pensions.
12. Funding certain activities via 'Council of Europe foundations'.

Belonging to Europe

And so I approached the election in good spirits. There were two other candidates: Britain's Terry Davis, standing for the Socialists, and Poland's Hanna Suchocka, backed by her government. I was standing for the EPP, and for the Liberals, Democrats and Reformers, and had been nominated by the Austrian Government – at the time an SPÖ/ÖVP coalition, with an SPÖ Chancellor and an ÖVP Foreign Minister, the present Chancellor, Dr Wolfgang Schüssel. As required by the Austrian Constitution, I had been unanimously nominated by the coalition government, although the SPO leader of the Austrian delegation in Strasbourg, Peter Schieder (today the Assembly's President), was also Chairman of the Socialist Group, who had chosen the Labour MP, Terry Davis, as their candidate. Had he chosen to give his group's line priority over national solidarity, Peter Schieder's influence within the SPÖ would certainly have allowed him to block my nomination. Since he had not, I was not unduly irritated by the fact that Hanna Suchocka was a member of my own group, and so likely to take votes from me.

Nonetheless, the first ballot left Terry Davis only three votes ahead of me. Hanna Suchocka was a long way behind and withdrew from the next day's second ballot. This took place at the afternoon sitting on 23 June. Voting closed at 7pm, and the count got under way – supervised by the Deputy Clerk of the Assembly, Gian-Paolo Castanetto, and the tellers chosen by lot, Giuseppe Arzilli (from San Marino) and Edeltraud Gatterer (by chance, from Austria). At 7.50 pm, the President of the Assembly, Lord Russell-Johnston, announced the result, so far known only to him and to the tellers:

'Votes cast: 277. Invalid: 3. Valid: 274.' And the President continued: 'Terry Davis: 136, Walter Schwimmer, 138.' A two-vote majority had given me a five-year term as Secretary General of the first and broadest European organisation, the Council of Europe. In the fullest sense, I had made it to Strasbourg. As the Council's Head of Press ushered me straight from the Chamber to my first press conference as Secretary General elect, and I snatched a few moments to ring my wife and my mother on my mobile, I knew: for those five years at least, I would no longer be free – I now belonged to Europe.

NOTES:

1. At the top-level meetings in Rome (7–8 November) and Maastricht (9–10 December).
2. In the 'Declaration on Russia' adopted at the Summit.
3. At the time, Monaco had not applied to join the Council, and was not regarded as a potential member. Since 21 October 1998, it has been on the official list of candidates.

CHAPTER FIVE

2000 – beginning the millennium

Proliferating plans for the common European home

The Hague Congress of 1948 – attended by Winston Churchill, Konrad Adenauer and François Mitterrand, among others – still had a clear vision of a united Europe. Its proposal was equally clear: an assembly of representatives of national parliaments was to be set up to explore the political and legal implications of a European union or federation.

Today, however, no model seems capable of conferring clear contours on the whole of Europe. This may help to explain why so many concepts are used (apart from the somewhat outmoded 'Pan-Europa'): 'supranational Europe', 'à la carte Europe', 'polycentric Europe', 'variable-geometry Europe', 'federation of national states', 'variable-speed Europe', etc. At the back of their minds, quite a few people also cling to Walter Hallstein's old concept of an 'incomplete federal state' and the idea of a European Constitution, which the 'Convention' has revived.

Nearly all of these concepts are tailored to the EU, and seek to make sense of a process of diversification which accompanies deepening integration. But surely there must be a model which applies to the whole of Europe and can still accommodate all these variables? In my view, concentric circles still provide the most helpful paradigm:

The outermost circle is Europe of the Council of Europe, covering almost the whole continent. The next is Europe of the EU/EC. The innermost circle is federal Europe, which is still largely virtual, but has taken embryonic form in the EU's Economic and Currency Union (EECU) – and which can develop further into a 'core Europe' (another catchphrase), whoever may be in it.

Don't forget Greater Europe

People's attention today is so focused on the future of the EU that the 'outermost circle' – the pan-European Council of Europe, with its wide-ranging activities and numerous successes – is often overlooked. This is unfair, since the Council is the place where European standards are developed and implemented on the basis of shared values. It is important for two reasons. First of all, it is working for peace, and its contribution to European cohesion should not be underrated. After 1989–1990, for example, it played a notable part in overcoming the European divide by admitting the new democracies (even those which still had some way to go) to the European community of values.

Secondly, it lays essential foundations for the extension of the EU, with membership conditions which actually anticipated the EU's 'Copenhagen criteria' (1993). In fact, the very same requirements spelled out in those criteria (e.g. abolition of the death penalty) have applied to states wishing to join the Council since the early 1990s. Indeed, it is thanks to the Council that Europe today (Belarus excepted) has no death penalty. Turkey, for example, even before it had abolished it in peacetime, had not enforced it for nearly 20 years – certainly because it had no wish to attract criticism in Strasbourg. Since it joined, the same has applied to Russia.

New Council of Europe members are required, not only to abolish the death penalty, but also – of course – to accept the European Convention on Human Rights and provide guarantees concerning media freedom and respect for the law by the police and in criminal proceedings. Not least, they are also required to accept the 1986 Anti-Torture Convention, and compliance is strictly monitored by a special committee (the CPT). As we have seen, the Council has special monitoring machinery to ensure that new members respect their obligations.

All of this helps to create a pan-European legal area, reflected most clearly in the European Convention on Human Rights (ECHR) and in the European Court of Human Rights, which is fully independent, has jurisdiction in all the member states – and is thus supranational. This is the only institution of its kind in the world, and its protection now extends to 800 million Europeans. The Court is backed by the Council of Europe's Committee of Ministers, which ensures that states comply with its judgments, and take any action required of them.

But the Council of Europe is helping to create a pan-European legal area in many other ways as well: for example through its 200 or so conventions, such as that on the protection of minorities, or special bodies, such as the European Commission against Racism and Intolerance (ECRI). Also important are its 'partial agreements' ('partial' because they do not apply to all its members), which can certainly serve as a pattern for 'enhanced co-operation' within the EU. One of the most important of these is the Venice Commission, which has helped many countries in central, eastern and south-eastern Europe to draft constitutions.

The importance of the outermost circle for the innermost circle is clear from the fact that no state has ever joined the EU/EC without first being a member of the Council of Europe – and this is not going to change. Doing justice to the sheer range of the Council's activities is not always easy, but one thing is clear: seeing it as a mere stepping-stone to the EU is a gross simplification. Some member states will have to wait a long time to enter the innermost circle, but the things they learn about democracy and the rule of law at the Council are essential for admission – whenever it comes.

Many concepts, one Europe

The Council of Europe includes both EU and non-EU states, and the EU/EC itself has long ceased to be a monolith. The Benelux Union was the first example of a special relationship between certain member states, but is now less important than it used to be. This is not true of the Franco-German Treaty of 1963, and particularly of the 1988 Protocol covering co-operation on security and defence – the origin of the Eurocorps, in which Belgium, Luxembourg and Spain are now involved as well.

Since Maastricht (1992), these narrower forms of co-operation have been overshadowed by the EU's Common Foreign and Security Policy (CFSP), and particularly, in recent years, the Common Security and Defence Policy (although this has to allow for the special traditions of Finland, Ireland, Austria and Sweden, and is not wholeheartedly accepted in Denmark). Now that the Western European Union (WEU) – a defence organisation, whose membership does not include all the EU countries – is part of the EU, the picture is even more complex. Increasingly, the EU/EC recalls the polycentric model, or *à la carte Europe*, with everyone free to construct his own menu – an impression strengthened by the Schengen Agreement.

This agreement, covering the removal of passport (and customs) formalities on internal frontiers, was initially concluded outside the EC Treaty. It was signed in 1985 by the Benelux countries, plus France and Germany, and others joined later. In 1997, its provisions were incorporated into the EC Treaty, with exemptions for Britain and Ireland, and special rules for Denmark. It represents a notable surrender of sovereignty, even though it does not apply to the whole Community.

This is also true of the European Economic and Currency Union (EECU), and particularly the euro, which Denmark, Britain and Sweden have yet to accept. This special form of co-operation constitutes the nucleus of a virtual European federation and the innermost circle in our concentric model. Monetary policy is profoundly political, and monetary sovereignty is a 'sacrosanct' aspect of state sovereignty. There is no saying whether – and when – the EU's member states will risk going further and forming a federation. In addition to economic and monetary union, its minimum ingredients will have to include a supranational foreign, security and defence policy, and also a passport union. The present CFSP procedures are ponderous, and essentially intergovernmental, and member states may opt out of joint initiatives at will. It has recently been agreed, however, that the CFSP will also accommodate various forms of 'enhanced' co-operation. The question is: which states are prepared to combine a genuinely supranational CFSP with the EECU, and so lay the foundations of a federation?

This is a mere sketch, and not a full picture of the various forms which European union can take. Between the innermost (EU/EC) and outermost (Council of Europe) circles, there are many different types of *ad hoc* and regional co-operation (free electrons provide a good simile) – and transcontinental co-operation as well. 'Alphabet soup' is the perfect term for the proliferating acronyms. The 'ingredients' include: the European Free Trade Area (EFTA) with Iceland, Liechtenstein, Norway and Switzerland; the European Economic Area (EEA), or the EFTA countries minus Switzerland; the Visegrad Group and the Central European Free Trade Area (CEFTA), which started with Poland, Slovakia, Slovenia, the Czech Republic and Hungary.

The Commonwealth of Independent States (CIS) already extends beyond Europe, since it includes the five former Soviet republics in central Asia. So does a very different institution, the Organisation for Security and Co-operation in Europe (OSCE). In spite of its name, this is not an international organisation, since it is not based on an international founding treaty, but is essentially a standing diplomatic conference. Canada and the USA participate, making it tri-continental. In Europe, it has done particularly useful work on conflict reduction and resolution. Like the Council of Europe, it also sends observers to monitor elections. Its Secretary General, Jan Kubis, and I have secured an agreement to prevent rivalry and duplication between our organisations, and are trying to ensure that their work is complementary.

Genuinely international organisations include the transatlantic NATO, with its 19 member states already, and the Organisation for Economic Co-operation and Development (OECD).

By taking in seven new members (Estonia, Latvia, Lithuania, Slovakia, Slovenia, Bulgaria and Romania) and concluding an agreement, extending beyond the 'partnership for peace', on co-operation with Russia, NATO has finally shaken off its 'west European' bias.

The OECD, which has members in all five continents, is the market-economy industrial countries' main economic organisation, and produces analyses and recommendations to help them co-ordinate their economic policies. The Council of Europe's Parliamentary Assembly acts as its parliamentary forum, forming a bridge between the two organisations, and we also work with the OECD on specific issues, e.g. anti-corruption measures.

Rearranging the rooms in the common home

One might therefore say that Europe's concentric circles are thus surrounded, by a number of sub-continental and transcontinental institutions. This helps to enrich the many blueprints for the common European home, but without obscuring the basic structure – harmonious coexistence of the Council of Europe and the European Union, and salutary co-operation between them (actually one of the factors which will determine our continent's future).

The fact that the European Union, which is still sub-continental, is preparing for 'big bang' enlargement – from 15 to 25 and, three years later, 27 – makes no difference to the basic plan for the European home, but it does mean reshuffling the rooms. From mid-2004, more than half the Council of Europe's member states will be in the EU, and another three are negotiating.

After the failed attempt to reorganise Europe in 1945 and the transition successfully made by the former Soviet peoples in 1989–90, this is the third radical redrawing of the political map of Europe – and the third challenge for the Council of Europe.

The Council itself was founded in response to the first challenge, as an answer to the horrors of the Second World War. And it also rose to the second, when 1989–90 brought sweeping changes, and central and eastern Europeans ('We are the people') declared for democracy and human rights – and the Council moved in to help them.

And now the third challenge is approaching: a Council of Europe in which almost all of Europe is united, and an enlarged, more integrated EU, embarking on a common foreign and security policy, with 'Schengen' frontiers in Finland, the Baltic states, Poland, Slovakia, Hungary and Slovenia. The question is: where do these frontiers leave the dream we dreamed when the Berlin Wall came down – no more walls, no more Iron Curtain, no more dividing lines in Europe?

The Council of Europe is staking everything on a Europe without new dividing lines. I am convinced that the EU, too, cannot – and will not –

reject this goal. Indeed, it is already starting to tackle its responsibilities beyond the old and new Schengen frontiers. Javier Solana's missions in Macedonia, and his attempts to help solve the Yugoslav constitutional problem between Serbia and Montenegro, are a good example. In both cases, Council of Europe experts were also on hand to help. In the whole of south-eastern Europe and recently (in wholly different circumstances) Turkey too, the EU Commission and the Council of Europe have been running joint programmes to promote democracy, justice and media freedom.

Obviously, the EU is also aware of the its 'big bang' enlargement's pan-European dimension. Javier Solana, the High Representative for the CFSP, and Chris Patten, the Commissioner responsible for external relations, have submitted a joint paper on 'new neighbourhood policy' to the EU Council – although this policy can mop up only some of the effects of the latest political adjustments in Europe.

Over 50 years on from the European Congress in The Hague, an EU Convention, comprising government representatives, members of the European Parliament, and representatives of national parliaments in member and applicant countries, is again tackling the big question of Europe's future. In 1948, it was the fault of 'the political situation', not the 'hosts', that nearly all the countries of central, south-eastern and eastern Europe were absent in The Hague. The hosts at today's Convention are less generous, although they do not realise that. True, invitations have gone, not just to the 'old' 15 EU countries, but also to those which will have joined on 1 May 2004, plus three others – Bulgaria, Romania and Turkey. But the fact remains: half of Europe is simply not there when 'the future of Europe' is being discussed.

Will enlargement 'shrink' Europe?

So who will get a say when Europe's future, the future in Europe, is being discussed? One needs a sharp ear for the half-tones here. There is suddenly talk of some people's 'coming back to Europe', being 'ready for Europe' (the implication being that some others are not), of 'rapprochement with Europe' and a 'way to Europe'. Does this mean that the ones still 'outside' (not outside Europe, but outside the EU) must content themselves with dreams for the time being? Instead of making Europe bigger, will enlargement of one of its main institutions paradoxically make it smaller?

I sometimes have the feeling that these anxieties may not be unfounded. When an EU Commissioner, speaking at an official ceremony, welcomes the presence of a delegation from the host town's Russian twin, 'because this underlines the fact that our co-operation extends beyond Europe', when 'Europe' is no longer used as a geographical concept, or to denote a shared cultural heritage and a shared identity based on democracy, the rule of law and human rights, but is equated with a particular integration project (however important) – then pan-Europeans should hear the alarm bells ringing.

The issues are not just theoretical. For the countries joining the EU in the next round (and especially for them), Schengen suddenly means two different things. On the plus side, it will make freedom of movement a reality from Warsaw to Lisbon, from Nicosia through Budapest to the Arctic Circle. On the minus side, however, it will place fresh obstacles in the way of good neighbourly relations and transfrontier contacts, which have taken time and effort to build up, e.g. between Hungary and Romania, or between Poland and Kaliningrad (Russia).

Moreover, the 'Union', which is gearing up for enlargement, is far from being a uniform structure, with institutions (let alone member states), which automatically speak with one voice. At the beginning of 2003, when enlargement had already been decided, significant differences of opinion started to emerge within EU Europe, both on European questions, such as Yugoslavia's joining the Council of Europe, and on world political issues. The result is an even stronger tendency, at least among the bureaucrats, to put on a brave show of unity, while moving fast to neutralise anything which threatens to interfere with decision-making – already increasingly difficult, with (shortly) 25 states, a Presidency, a Council, a Commission and a Parliament. And 'interference' does not even have to be active – simply taking account of certain factors is enough.

When Kofi Annan invited me to represent the Council of Europe and lead its delegation (just one, of course) at a meeting of regional organisations with UN connections, I found myself sharing the table with four different EU delegations: the (then Swedish) Presidency, the Council, the Secretary General of the Council (attending separately) and the High Representative for the CFSP – and the Commission as well. Malice might suggest that simply dealing with one another must leave them little time to deal with anyone else. And indeed their problems of internal co-ordination make it understandable that they should see other European institutions less as an enrichment, than as useless competition, an obstacle, or basically not worth bothering about. Nonetheless the fact remains that, for the EU and its institutions, the forthcoming enlargement will leave the European glass, not just half full, but half empty. And that there is an institution where European unity is becoming a reality, and where the glass is all but full already – the Council of Europe.

To prevent misunderstandings, let me say plainly that the Council of Europe is not jealous of its richer, but (in membership) smaller sister, and that I do not underestimate the importance of deepened integration within the soon-to-be-enlarged EU. On the contrary, it is no exaggeration to say that the European Council's Copenhagen decisions are of historic importance for European unity.

Re-dividing tasks in tomorrow's Europe

I have offered my congratulations to the countries which are resolved to take integration further. Their decision will certainly produce major changes in Europe's political architecture. I am also convinced, however, that clearly defining the Council of Europe's role within this new complex is one of the main challenges we shall find ourselves facing in the next few years. New dividing lines must not be the consequence of EU enlargement. There is just one Europe – the whole continent with its 800 million people. Since 1989, the Council of Europe has been helping to make this 'one Europe', which is based on shared values, a reality. The massive new start which Europe made when the Berlin Wall and the Iron Curtain went must not be sacrificed, 15 years later, to another new start, in itself quite as desirable.

If this is seen clearly, and Europe is not to be just a synonym for the EU, then the EU Convention must give serious thought to the whole question of relations (based on equal rights) between the enlarged EU and European states outside the EU. In my memorandum, '800 million Europeans', I put forward a number of fundamental ideas on the future of Europe as a whole, based on close co-operation between the various institutions, particularly the European Union and the Council of Europe. The Commission's former Luxembourg President, Jacques Santer, submitted this text to the Convention as an official document.

The future, enlarged Union must be built on solid foundations, using the existing legal frameworks and institutions. Laeken, from which the Convention derives, gives us a unique opportunity to establish a uniform complex of European institutions, all working together. This is why – and this was my memorandum's main point – the Convention must decide how the EU, as the central element in the European process, can use existing structures to maximum effect. I also made that point personally to the President of the Convention, the former French President, Valéry Giscard d'Estaing.

The Convention's final report, which Giscard presented at the EU's Saloniki Summit at the end of June 2003, essentially accepted these suggestions, and recommended that the EU accede to the European Convention on Human Rights. The legal personality, which the Constitutional Treaty will (at last) give it, will allow the EU to do this, and also to participate in other Council of Europe conventions and activities concerned with such problems as terrorism, corruption, organised crime, trafficking in human beings, drugs, everyday violence and, last but not least, racism and xenophobia. I have already suggested that the EU should – as an entity *sui generis* which, without being a state, has many of the rights and powers of a state, and frequently acts like a state – become an associate member of the Council of Europe, and this (like membership of other international organisations) will also be possible in principle. The Convention may not have done everything people hoped it might, but if these, and other proposals which the Governmental Conference has still to approve, make the EU more democratic and European, then its efforts will not have been wasted.

EU accession to the European Cultural Convention would be the logical next step. I am convinced that Europe's 800 million people do have a shared culture, or at least a shared cultural heritage. Tolstoy and Shostakovich are quite as European as Shakespeare and Mozart. The third step would be accession to the European Social Charter – acknowledging that Europe rests on social cohesion and solidarity.

Article 303 of the EC Treaty already provides that the Union is to 'establish all appropriate forms of co-operation with the Council of Europe'. This co-operation should extend to all areas of EU responsibility, and particularly the so-called second and third pillars (common foreign and security policy, internal security and justice). The European Commission already has a seat (but not a vote) on the Council of Europe's Committee of Ministers, although it does not always attend and, when it does, almost invariably sends a member of the secretariat. It is certainly useful, in view of the EU's complex power structure, for the Presidency to be represented on the Committee of Ministers by the Foreign Minister or Ambassador of the country currently holding it. However, unless it has a political representative (logically the Commissioner responsible for external relations) as well, the EU is not 'fully' represented. Obviously, the Commission should also be represented on all the Council of Europe's interministerial groups of experts.

EU accession to the Council of Europe itself would certainly have to be looked at more closely, but would, in view of the EU's supranational character, be a logical development – and accession to the European Convention on Human Rights may set the ball rolling. In January 2003, I accordingly suggested that the Parliamentary Assembly start exploring the possibility of associate membership for the EU.

And so the common European home, of which so many people dreamed, has become a reality. The Council of Europe might be seen as the roof, with room beneath it for everyone. As for the rest, we must keep on building – and the Convention gives us a perfect opportunity to do that.

The time has come to take the old structure, which has worked well enough with additions and adjustments, but has never had a uniform plan, and reshape it. With 25 states in the enlarged EU, and 45 in the Council of Europe (46 when Monaco joins – and Belarus will eventually turn democratic and come in as well), unification is still incomplete, but the process is on the right track. Indeed, nearly all of Europe is already united, as a community of values, within the Council. With respect for its values, political stability, economic maturity, the capacity to participate in the Common Market and acceptance of Community law as yardsticks, membership should be open to all the countries of Europe. I am convinced that everyone, ultimately, will want that. There is only one Europe – that for me is an article of faith.

Strength in unity

There is nothing new in looking to military partnerships for security. Coalitions and alliances – some long-term, others short-lived – have always been formed for that purpose. There were also, in the first half of the 20th century and well before that, security systems with thoroughly political aims. Following Napoleon's defeat by a military alliance, one of the aims of the Congress of Vienna in 1815 was to establish just such a system to defend the old order.

This was why, after the horrors of the Second World War, and even before the first move towards European unity, the first step was to conclude defence agreements and try to establish a security system. It was no mere chance that France and Britain led the way in 1947 with the Dunkirk Treaty, which foreshadowed the Western European Union and which the Brussels Pact extended to the three Benelux countries in 1948.

NATO – backbone of the free world

On 4 April 1949, just a month and a day before 10 European foreign ministers met in London to sign the Council of Europe into being, the agreement on founding the North Atlantic Pact, or NATO, was signed in Washington by 10 west European states,[1] the USA and Canada.

> 'The parties to this treaty reaffirm their faith in the purposes and principles of the Charter of the United Nations and their desire to live in peace with all peoples and all governments. They are determined to safeguard the freedom, common heritage and civilisation of their peoples, founded on the principles of democracy, individual liberty and the rule of law. They seek to promote stability and wellbeing in the North Atlantic area. They are resolved to unite their efforts for collective defence and for the preservation of peace and security. They therefore agree to this North Atlantic treaty.'

For a long time, this transatlantic treaty remained the uncontested backbone of the security policy of the western democracies of the 'free world', providing a Euro-Atlantic guarantee of their continuing existence during the Cold War, even though the neutral states of western Europe did not (and still do not) belong to it. The forming of a European army was also considered at a very early stage. Alongside the Coal and Steel Community, René Pleven's plan for a 'European Defence Community' (EDC) was discussed. However, the EDC agreement attracted the concerted opposition of both Gaullists and Communists (among others), and the French National Assembly rejected it in 1954. The 'Western European Union', an alternative successor to the earlier Pact, was founded in 1955, but fell far short of the first ambitious scheme (and was eventually absorbed into the EU).

It should not be forgotten that a 'European Political Community' was projected alongside the EDC, and was allowed to drop with it, being resurrected later in the EU's ambitious plan for a Common Foreign and Security Policy.

Once the end of the East–West conflict had become more or less official in 1990, the search for a new European security system began. Those mainly involved were NATO (particularly the USA) the EC/EU and Russia. It was clear that NATO, which had extended the hand of friendship to the then Soviet Union in 1990, would have to grow into a new role. Bipolar confrontation was a thing of the past, and co-operative structures were needed to replace it.

The CFSP takes shape

(Western) Europe's capacity for action outside NATO was a problem from the start. Neither before nor after the Maastricht Treaty (1992) was 'the consistency of its external activities as a whole in the context of its external relations' (EU Treaty) guaranteed. Of course, the Community countries really knew all the time that joint external trade would not be enough in the long term, and that a concerted foreign policy would be needed as well. But the first moves in this direction, e.g. the 'European Political Co-operation' (EPC), initiated in 1973 as an interstate mechanism outside (!) the Community treaties, remained very modest. It was not until 1986 that the 'Single European Act' made this a Community matter. Against the background of the 1989–90 developments, it was chiefly Helmut Kohl, the German Chancellor, who insisted that the forthcoming governmental conference on economic and monetary union must be accompanied by negotiations on political union. The result was the EU's Common Foreign and Security Policy (CFSP) of 1992.

The EU Treaty declared that the CFSP's general aim was to ensure that the Union's 'combined influence' was 'exerted as effectively as possible by means of concerted and convergent action', and 'as possible' remains the operative phrase. Most decisions still have to be unanimous, and even those taken by qualified majority are subject to a *de facto* veto. A country which abstains does not block a decision, but is not required to implement it either. If too many use their right to opt out too often, how much of this 'common' policy will be left? The Nice Treaty makes that question even more acute. It extends 'enhanced' co-operation to the CFSP, though with numerous provisos. For example, a minimum of eight member states (i.e. more than half at present) must be involved. Enlargement seems likely to make a cohesive foreign policy even harder to attain. Some of the new members have, after all, been in thrall for years, and are revelling in their new freedom – and highly conscious of their own sovereignty! On security issues, above all, they are far more 'transatlantic' in their outlook than some of the existing members.

The CFSP's present dilemma was perfectly illustrated by the EU governments' sharply divided reactions to the second Iraq war, and by US Defence Secretary Rumsfeld's not unsuccessful attempt to split Europeans into 'old' and 'new'. An Austrian newspaper made the point that the disagreements were not simply fuelling a transatlantic quarrel, but could well inflict lasting damage on the European Union as a political project.[2] The same paper carried an editorial, 'Europe without a foreign policy'. Once the war had been concluded (happily sooner than expected), and Britain had gone some way towards accepting the European line on a major role for the UN in post-war Iraq, intra-European discussion again began to focus – thanks, above all, to the diplomatic skills of the EU's Greek Presidency – on other, internal questions, and particularly the EU's future power structures.

Nonetheless, the CFSP has also scored some definite successes, particularly in Europe itself. The Treaty of Nice assigns a number of new tasks to the EU, whose common security and defence policy is now to include 'humanitarian and rescue tasks, peacekeeping tasks and tasks of combat forces in crisis management, including peacekeeping' (the so-called Petersberg tasks). As a result, the EU now has a military component, and is acquiring an operational capacity – a 60,000-strong rapid reaction force. Decisions on deploying it are taken jointly by three bodies: a Political and Security Policy Committee, a Military Committee and a Military Staff. In spite of structures which are not exactly tailored to intensive, trust-filled co-operation, and an in-built conflict of authority between an external relations Commissioner and a Council Secretary

General who is also 'High Representative' for the CFSP, the EU has achieved some spectacular successes, particularly in south-eastern Europe, where it helped to create the State Union of Serbia and Montenegro to replace the crumbling Yugoslavia, and to end the civil war in 'the former Yugoslav Republic of Macedonia'. The fact that Council of Europe experts on constitutional issues and local self-government, whom I had provided, were significantly involved in this, shows how closely our two institutions are linked – and also that co-operation between them is necessary and useful. Since then, the EU has taken over a number of important international tasks from the UN in Bosnia and Herzegovina, and even some military tasks from NATO in 'the former Yugoslav Republic of Macedonia'.

No

Wanted – a new identity

NATO itself was already looking for a new identity, since it was clear that the end of the Cold War would leave it struggling to justify its continued existence as a simple alliance for collective self-defence. With an eye to the new European security system, it raised its sights beyond the old alliance, assumed a key role in overcoming the after-effects of division in Europe, and began to see security management (in the broadest sense) as its essential task.

It has, for example, made stability in south-eastern Europe one of its central concerns. After military intervention in both cases, it has, with SFOR in Bosnia and Herzegovina (since 1996) and KFOR in Kosovo (since 1999), emerged as Europe's most important peacekeeping structure – and its ability to preserve, and when necessary restore, peace in Europe has become the litmus test of its pan-European security function and legitimacy. Europe also knows, at least since 11 September 2001, that it faces global dangers too, and so NATO – against the background of terrorism, but also of conflict and tensions in the Middle East, the Caucasus and central Asia – sees itself as having a global role as well. This appeared most clearly the day after the attacks in New York and Washington when it formally mobilised, without knowing who the organisers or perpetrators had been.

Current efforts to set up a comprehensive political and military system to protect free Europe on a continental scale deserve special attention. New co-operation structures are emerging in various institutions. One of these is the Euro-Atlantic Partnership Council, a kind of OSCE for security policy. It has 46 members (the 19 NATO countries, the rest of Europe minus Andorra, Bosnia and Herzegovina, Yugoslavia, Liechtenstein, Malta, San Marino, Monaco and Cyprus, and the five former Soviet republics in central Asia). It serves as a forum for consultation on peace-keeping issues, and efforts to achieve a joint operational capacity. Considerably smaller is the Partnership for Peace, which was founded in 1994 and has 27 members. It is concerned with new security relations between the partner states, and particularly with joint operations. Some bilateral agreements have also been concluded, e.g. the 1997 'Charter on a Distinctive Partnership' between NATO and Ukraine. This reflects Ukraine's vital geo-strategic position, and provides for regular dialogue and co-operation. A Joint Permanent NATO-Russia Council was also established in 1997 as a platform for dialogue and military co-operation.

Good relations with Russia is one of the new NATO's priorities. What it wants is a relationship of trust, marked by mutual respect and under-standing – hence its efforts to forge ever closer ties between Russia and the West. In May 2002, the original Permanent Council was replaced by the 'NATO-Russia Council', a 19+1 equal-rights body with a comprehensive agenda: action against terrorism, crisis management, non-proliferation of weapons of mass destruction, defence against short-range missiles, arms control, scientific and environmental co-operation, civil defence plan-ning, marine rescue, etc. It is no coincidence that the USA has also agreed a two-thirds reduction in strategic nuclear weapons with Russia. Indeed, everything possible is being done to bind it firmly to the West.

Enlargement Summit in Prague

Obviously, all these initiatives and gestures have to be seen against the background of NATO enlargement, which is still resented, and indeed feared, by many people in Russia. The first new members in the East – Poland, the Czech Republic and Hungary – were admitted in 1999. At its Summit in Prague,[3] NATO then invited the three Baltic states (for decades an enforced part of the Soviet Union), Bulgaria, Romania, Slovakia and Slovenia to open membership negotiations. Most of these states have experienced Soviet rule, and have not forgotten it. For them, NATO represents, in its original role as a collective defence alliance, a form of reinsurance.

Russia, on the other hand, is less than happy to see yesterday's 'enemy' pressing forward to its frontiers. More than once in its history, invaders have penetrated those frontiers, which are geographically open – one of Stalin's reasons for establishing a broad western buffer zone after 1945. Loss of that buffer zone is a source of deep uneasiness, and may well revive old traumas. The West, however, sees NATO enlargement as part of the drive to erase the residual effects of division and create a political and military framework for a free and peaceful Europe. The broadest possible co-operation structures should be established to help relieve Russian anxieties.

These conflicting views and positions are not easily reconciled, particularly as Russia is finding it hard to come to terms with loss of its world-power role. Ideally, it would like Europe's non-aligned countries to stay non-aligned, and its neutrals neutral, which is why talk about Austria joining NATO cannot fail to strike a jarring note. In its residual sphere of influence, or 'periphery', it is forging new military alliances, like those recently concluded with Armenia, Belarus, Kazakhstan, Kyrgyzstan and Tajikistan. It welcomes the US Government's increasing tendency (of which the Iraq war is one example) to bypass NATO at times of crisis and conflict, and establish *ad hoc* coalitions. This threatens NATO's identity and creates a risk of its being remodelled on OECD lines – and it also gives Russia a chance to step forward as a vital partner and reclaim its superpower role.

I am convinced, however, that these 'after-pangs' of the Cold War and Europe's division are themselves a proof that a common external, security and defence policy is essential, and a proof that this policy should ideally cover all Europe – seen not as a land-mass, but as an area of partnership, in which all the partners have equal rights. Such a policy cannot be restricted to the area which the EU happens to cover at any given time. Nor can it simply take the form of bilateral arrangements between the EU and a few outside states. European countries which are not on the waiting list for EU membership are being invited to a 'European Conference', but this – in the loose form envisaged – is little more than a chat-room, a kind of stretched working lunch. However, the fact that the EU includes 25 of our 45 member states means that it has a very firm footing at the Council of Europe, and is also – if unofficially – a decisive part of the 'first comprehensive organisation which, unlike earlier sectoral integration models (economics and defence), is focused on political unification and is thus responsible for all matters of concern to Europe (defence excepted)'.[4] The Council's Committee of Ministers, comprising nearly all of Europe's foreign ministers, and its Parliamentary Assembly, which is 'the' European Assembly, make it the ideal platform for giving the CFSP the broader basis it requires. If the EU had associate membership, with the new CFSP supremo on the Committee of Ministers, and a delegation from the European Parliament in the Parliamentary Assembly, then Europe would indeed be able to speak with one voice.

The same undoubtedly (and particularly) applies to the 'new neighbourhood policy', which is part of the CFSP, since the Council of Europe can make that 'new neighbourhood' coextensive with the Europe it created, with huge effort and limited resources, after the changes of 1989–90 – a Europe without new dividing lines or barriers.

Shattered dream – not everyone loves Europe

On the website of the Convention on the Future of the European Union, I recently found a contribution from a British Liberal MP, which gives a vivid picture of the heated feelings which discussion of Europe's future can provoke: 'Last month, I published a model Constitution for a federal Europe. Since then, my letterbox has been overflowing. Most of my new "pen-pals" are fiercely anti-Europe, and would like to see me hanged for high treason. There are also a few militant federalists, who accuse me of selling out on European parliamentary democracy.'

Obviously, 'you can't please everyone' is as true of the European debate as it is of everything else, but the Europhobes' violent reactions also show that the European dream is not sweet for everyone.

The main target of the sceptics and 'antis' is 'Brussels'. Bureaucracy, centralisation, jargon-ridden texts, threats to national identity: all of this gives them the very ammunition they need – and the demagogues and populists are right behind them.

Money, of course, is the main irritant: 'We pay Brussels too much, and don't get enough back.' The single currency brought variations: 'Now they're even taking our pounds, marks and francs', and 'The euro's going to cost us – it's just giving the bureaucrats in Brussels a chance to devalue the good money we've got'. All of this sounds plausible, but is very hard to verify. It gave me quite a shock when some of my British colleagues – people I had credited with economic sense – turned up in the Assembly with pound symbols pinned on their lapels. And indeed Margaret Thatcher's anguished cry, 'I want my money back', which eventually got Britain a hefty rebate on its EU contributions, still reverberates today.

Eurosceptics everywhere

Euroscepticism and europhobia play a big part in United Kingdom politics. The ostensible targets are alleged plans to turn the EU into a federal state, rob Britain of her sovereignty and impose outside rule. Obviously, 'pound v. euro' features prominently in the discussion – although that discussion ignores the fact that the euro is a Community currency, adopted, as the logical consequence of a common market, by a number of fully independent states.

Within an EU which is working steadily towards uniformity, little Denmark fears the levelling influence of the larger countries. Now that their country is actually 'in', most Danes are unwilling to forgo the benefits of membership – and so the 'antis' are targeting the euro, which they have managed to keep at bay so far. Itself a European power in the Middle

Ages, modern Denmark is squeezed between continental Europe and the rest of Scandinavia (which is why it feels closer to Britain than it does to its immediate neighbours). Its past explains its present anxieties, which should certainly be taken seriously. It also has a tradition of anti-tax, anti-bureaucracy parties, some of them decidedly radical.

Sweden's reservations on the euro are harder to rationalise. It joined the EU at the same time as Finland and Austria, both of them neutral and both of them members of the European Monetary Union, and has no significant tradition, political or public, of being anti-Europe. However, it does seem to have a subliminal fear of losing its identity if integration 'goes too far' – which is why the Social Democrat government is obviously wary of joining the euro-zone without a referendum.

Among the countries I have mentioned, Denmark is the only one where euro-scepticism openly goes hand-in-hand with an anti-immigrant stance – a combination all too common, alas, further south in the EU.

The Netherlands, previously a model of liberalism, gave Europe a shock when a populist party, named after its founder, Pim Fortuyn – a flamboyant academic, millionaire and open homosexual – came from nowhere and captured mass support, largely thanks to Fortuyn's attack on his country's immigration policy. Although he was shot by a political fanatic shortly before the election, his party still scored a phenomenal success. Easy come, easy go: after various party splits and resignations, the Christian Democrat Prime Minister called new elections just three months later, and the remnants of the Fortuyn party were decisively defeated.

Breaking the moulds

Political life in the Netherlands rapidly came back to 'normal', but it was clear that voters could no longer be tidily sorted into the old left/right categories. In the first election, the 'left-wing' Social Democrats lost votes to the 'right-wing' Pim Fortuyn party, only to retrieve them in the second. Results like these suggest that something more than traditional left-wing and right-wing loyalties are at work.

Another startling example. All Europe, and not just France, was shocked when the self-confessed right-wing extremist, Jean-Marie Le Pen, outpolled the Socialist Prime Minister, Lionel Jospin, in the first round of the 2002 presidential elections, coming in just 3% behind the incumbent, Jacques Chirac. The total vote for the two mainstream candidates barely exceeded that for the extremists, right and left. And this was not simply due to the fact that both right and left fielded anti-Europe candidates.

In the second round, democratic France rallied behind Jacques Chirac, whose 82% share of the vote was a clear thumbs-down to extremism. An open champion of European co-operation, he even won the votes of euro-sceptics right and left. Clearly, Le Pen's shock result in the first round was less a success for him than a defeat for his opponents. But it was also a warning that politicians needed to take the voters' concerns more seriously. Jacques Chirac heard that warning – and not only heard it, but made it the basis of convincing successes in the second presidential round and later parliamentary elections. The fact that he stuck to a clear pro-Europe line throughout shows that hard-core anti-Europeans constitute a small minority. The trouble is that demagogues know exactly how to exploit general dissatisfaction with politics, and uncertainty regarding Europe's future, for their own purposes.

Parties like Belgium's Vlaams Blok and Italy's Lega Nord, which build on regional grievances and anxieties, allegations of discrimination, etc, also take occasional pot-shots at Europe or, rather, 'Brussels'.

Parties on the slide are easily tempted to exploit anti-Europe prejudice (usually coupled with xenophobia) in the battle for political survival. Among these I would include the People's Party in Portugal, whose appeal for Christian Democrat voters was eroded by the Social Democrat Party, which has since joined the European People's Party.

The 'special case' of Austria

In Austria, changing attitudes to Europe in Jörg Haider's Freedom Party (FPÖ) make a fascinating study. A look at the various phases through which it passed shows that its thinking on Europe was almost entirely shaped by two (certainly connected) factors, its determination to score over other parties, and its sense of how the public wind was blowing – shows, in other words, that it followed a classic populist line. As long as the SPÖ/ÖVP coalition government had not applied for EU membership, Haider kept pressing it to do so, knowing that this would help to win him disaffected ÖVP voters (who blamed their party for failing to take a firm line with the SPÖ, which had reservations over joining the EU).

Before the country could blink, however, he had changed tack completely. Once the application had been sent, all the things which had moved too slowly were suddenly moving too fast. Suddenly Haider started claiming that Austria was insufficiently prepared, while the EU (which had too much power anyway) was trying to rob it of all the things that made it a good place to live. When a referendum was held on joining the EU, Haider 'warned' Austrians that Brussels would take away their water reserves and put blood in their chocolate and bugs in their yoghurt. The Greens, for their part, fearing that Austria's neutrality would be compromised, adopted the same sceptical attitude to the 'capitalist' EEC as the Socialists earlier, and spread scaremongering rumours that EURATOM would force the country to 'go nuclear'. They, too, were using the debate on Europe as a stalking-horse, since it got their views a hearing. Nonetheless, in 1994, nearly 67% of Austrians voted to join the EU.

In the October 1999 elections, Haider's party beat the ÖVP into third place with a paper-thin lead. When it then went on, in February 2000, to form a coalition government with the ÖVP under Wolfgang Schüssel (a former Foreign Minister with unblemished European credentials) as Chancellor, the 14 other EU states over-reacted by imposing the famous/ notorious sanctions. (In fact, the sanctions had no basis in European law, and were never discussed, let alone decided, by any EU or Council of Europe body. At the Council, I joined the British President of the Parliamentary Assembly, Lord Russell-Johnston, and the then Chairman of the Committee of Ministers, Brian Cowen, Irish Foreign Minister – and thus an official representative of the 14 – in issuing a statement, in which we declared that the Council judged governments by their words, programmes and actions, and would do so in the case of Austria.)

In the preamble to their declaration on taking office, the reviled government (and its two constituent parties) had not only declared their acceptance of Europe's common values, but had also committed themselves to a policy of extending and deepening European integration. Both during and after the 'sanctions' (which were quietly dropped six months later, on the strength of a report by three 'wise persons', nominated by the President of the European Court of Human Rights, and including a former Council of Europe Secretary General and a former member of the European Commission of Human Rights), the Austrian Government and its FPÖ members played an active role within the EU, particularly regarding the enlargement process. The impression made by the FPÖ ministers in the various ministerial councils was by no means negative – any more than that made later by the Italian Lega Nord ministers. When, for domestic political reasons – or, rather, internal party reasons – the FPÖ effectively withdrew its support from its own members of the government, European (and immigration) issues played very little part in this.

'Old' and 'new' Europe

The political landscape also varies greatly in the 10 countries which are due to join the EU shortly – a step favoured not only by most of their politicians, but by a clear majority of their voters. In spite of anxieties beforehand, all the referendums produced a clear 'yes' result. In these states too, the 'antis' include both people with genuine reservations of principle and populists on the make.

Malta, the smallest country, produced the closest result, and also the highest turnout. The fronts in this Mediterranean island, which is one of the cradles of European civilisation, were more clearly drawn than anywhere else. The governing Nationalist Party (Christian Democrat) favoured joining, the Labour Party did not. The latter – certainly still influenced to some slight extent by the ageing former Prime Minister, Dom Mintoff, and his insistence on neutrality – argued that Malta's exposed position made this inadvisable and, during its short time in government from 1996–1998, actually froze the application procedure. Just in time to let Malta sign the Treaty in Athens, over 53% of its electorate voted for accession.

Slovenia (in other respects too, a model candidate) probably had the fewest problems. 60% of the electorate turned out and nearly nine-tenths of the votes – or 89.61% to be precise – were in favour. All the significant political groups backed accession.

Hungary also voted before the Treaty was signed, like Malta on 12 April 2003. Although the 83.76% 'yes' vote was unequivocal, a turnout of just over 45%, and the fact that over half the voters stayed away, showed that there was a fair amount of euroscepticism. It is true that the Social Liberal Government and the Conservative opposition (part of the EPP group at the Council) are basically agreed on the need for European integration, and that only extra-parliamentary right-wing extremists oppose it, but increasing political polarisation makes it harder to project this unity, which is now unusual, onto the voters.

The situation in Lithuania resembled that in Slovenia. The referendum attracted a 63.4% turnout, and the 'yes' vote topped 91%. Obviously, the Lithuanians did not share fears voiced in the two other Baltic states that people who had just escaped one union's yoke might balk at surrendering part of their hard-won sovereignty to another. At most, scepticism and uncertainty may have helped to keep a few of the one-third non-voters away.

The pro-European Slovak Government certainly breathed a sigh of relief when the referendum produced the 'yes' which had never really been in doubt. There had, on the other hand, been very real fears that the necessary 50% turnout might not be achieved. The Christian-Liberal governing alliance, backed by the Coalition of Slovak Hungarians, had made no secret of their strong pro-Europe views. But things were changing on the opposition side, where populism was a definite element in both traditional and newer groupings. It is true that former Premier Meciar, long regarded as a nationalist, had recently been trying to establish his European and also his transatlantic credentials – pro-Europe and pro-NATO – and had proved it by coming to see me in Strasbourg. His party colleagues in the

Slovak delegations to the Parliamentary Assembly and the EU Convention also follow a clear pro-Europe line. After various internal splits, the 'Democratic Left' (Social Democrat) is no longer represented in parliament. The 'SMER' (Direction) party, founded by Robert Fico, a former Social Democrat, is also populistic – but not anti-Europe.

Poland's referendum got a 59% turnout and a 'yes' vote in excess of 75% – both unexpected. Serious anxieties among farmers (agriculture, though structurally weak, remains a powerful force) and the anti-EU line adopted, with strong media backing, by some influential nationalist/Catholic groupings had suggested that the necessary turnout and majority might be hard to achieve. The Polish Pope's unequivocal declaration of support for Europe and EU enlargement undoubtedly tipped the scales decisively, at a time when the pro-Europe left-wing Government was in serious political trouble, having lost its majority in parliament.

The Czechs were the last to vote before the summer. As in all the other candidate countries, their government – a Social Democrat/Christian Democrat/Liberal coalition – was unequivocally for accession. The 'old' Communists (i.e. those who not become Social Democrats) were against, and even they had some prominent, pro-EU exceptions. The conservative ODS party, on the other hand, included both 'antis' and supporters. And, while the former President, Vaclav Havel, actively supported accession, his successor, the former ODS President, Vaclav Klaus, stayed neutral. Nonetheless, the result again was a clear one: a 55%-plus turnout, with a 'yes' vote in excess of 77%.

The nightmares are not over

The history of Europe is, among other things, a history of conflict, war and unspeakable suffering. For centuries, it seemed that Europeans, and above all their rulers, had learned nothing from it. The Thirty Years War, the Turkish wars, the wars of succession, the Napoleonic wars – no part of the continent was spared. The late 19th and early 20th centuries brought various conflicts in the Balkans, and finally the huge, destructive storm of two world wars swept across the whole of Europe.

After the Second World War, and for the first time in our continent's history, it looked as if things might be changing. The sabre-rattling continued, of course, and for a time there was a massive arms race, but the Cold War's 'balance of terror' seemed to be sparing Europeans a repetition of the horrors which the 'shooting wars' had brought them.

We must not forget, however, that the benefits of freedom and growing prosperity were available to only half the continent's people. Millions of central and eastern Europeans were subjected to oppression and political persecution, and deprived of economic and social opportunity. For close on 50 years, to use Pope Jean Paul II's vivid phrase, Europe breathed on one lung. But Europeans east and west shared the dream of a Europe united, peaceful and free – and none of us who were living when the Berlin Wall came down will forget the scenes we witnessed then.

Personally, I will never forget the faces of people from the former GDR as they crossed in their 'Trabis' from Hungary through Austria to 'West' Germany. Or the faces of Czechs on their first-ever day out in Vienna. They seemed, all of them, to be moving in a dream.

Alas, dreams are not the whole story. There are nightmares too, and even the dream of a united, better Europe – which now seems to be coming slowly true – has been marred by war, terror, destruction, killing and rape. All too quickly, the horrors of the past caught up with us again. One reason for this was the unsolved problems, which had gone on simmering underneath the lid which the Communists had clamped on them, and now erupted like volcanoes. We may have 'frozen' the various conflicts in the meantime, but hundreds of thousands of European refugees are still living in wretched conditions, far from their homes. They cannot lead normal lives, let alone dream of prosperity and peace.

War – still part of the European scene?

Even as I write this book, for example, the conflict drags on in Chechnya, where young Russian servicemen are still being killed in terrorist attacks, and Chechen civilians dying when the Russians strike back.

In the southern Caucasus, two Council of Europe member states, Armenia and Azerbaijan, are still officially at war. Even before the Soviet Union had collapsed, they had clashed over Nagorno-Karabakh (an enclave in Azerbaijan, largely populated by Armenians), and war had followed, resulting in the occupation of large tracts of Azerbaijan and endless streams of refugees in both directions. In January 2001, the Council of Europe admitted both countries to membership, in the declared hope that this would help them to settle their differences. So far, alas, nothing has come of this.

In Georgia too, the end of Soviet rule triggered conflicts, due partly to the age-old mix of peoples in the Caucasus, partly to the centralising urge of the modern state. Led by members of the old *Nomenklatura*, who suddenly started posing as national heroes, Abkhazia and South Ossetia sought closer ties with Russia, not a settlement with Tbilisi. The results: fighting, deaths, refugees, etc.

There is another, currently 'frozen', conflict which is linked to the Soviet Union's precipitate demise. Like the other Soviet republics,

Moldavia became independent when the Union collapsed. Like many of them, it had been fought over for centuries by its powerful neighbours. Initially part of the Ottoman Empire, it later passed into Russian, Romanian and finally Soviet hands. In addition to Romanian-speaking Moldavians, it had large ethnic Russian and Ukrainian communities, and a number of minorities, such as the Turkish-speaking (but Orthodox Christian) Gagauz. In Transnistria, east of the Dniester, Slavs – Russians and Ukrainians – were, and certainly still are, in the majority. Also important was the presence in the region of a whole army – the former 14th Soviet Army – with a massive stock of weapons waiting to be used. This again was the stuff of which conflicts are made. The (provisional) result: fighting, innocent victims and a separatist regime (not recognised by the international community), which runs the country like a museum of Leninism/Stalinism, while giving the leadership all the privileges of capitalism.

Unfortunately, that is not all. South-eastern Europe – a persistently troubled part of the continent – is discussed in detail elsewhere. On the other hand, the western Balkans (a geographical misnomer) are today a 'pacified' zone – at least in terms of the situation which existed in the former Yugoslavia from 1991–1995, and in Albania up to 1997. Nonetheless, Europe should keep a watchful eye on 'the former Yugoslav Republic of Macedonia', where relations are strained between the Slav majority and Albanian minority, and where the outbreak of fighting (certainly instigated from Kosovo) took the international community largely by surprise.

On the subject of Kosovo: the fighting, thank God, is a thing of the past – not so the problems. We once had to worry about Kosovo's Albanians; today, it is the Serbs who need watching and protecting. Destroyed orthodox churches, ghost-villages emptied of their Serbian inhabitants – these are two of the depressing images which stick in my own mind. Since NATO intervened in 1999, Kosovo – legally a Yugoslav or, more accurately, Serbian province – has been administered by the UN. It is absolutely clear that a majority of the population will never again submit to Yugoslav administration or control. Ignoring appeals from Belgrade, Strasbourg and New York, most of Kosovo's despairing Serbs stay away from provincial and local elections. So – is this just another frozen conflict?

Finally, there is the 'green line' in Cyprus – for a long time, not the colour of hope, but a symbol of division, flanked on both sides by a drab no-man's-land. Since Turkey invaded in 1974, the island has been divided, while around it Europe has been striving to achieve unity. In fact, it is only half true to say that it has been divided since 1974. There was a dividing line before that, but it followed a zigzag course across the island and between the communities, skirting isolated Turkish-Cypriot enclaves.

UN troops are now stationed along the green line, to prevent the two sides from clashing. In 1974, UN troops could do nothing to stop the invasion, prevent aggression or protect human rights. Some of them – like my friend, Lieutenant Izay, who was serving with the Austrian UN battalion and was killed when a Turkish plane attacked his jeep – actually died in the fighting.

Present conflicts, past roots

The Republic of Cyprus is a member of the Council of Europe, just like the three powers which guaranteed the Cyprus Agreement of 1960: Greece, Turkey and the United Kingdom. Obviously, they are all members of the UN as well. For 30 years, the UN has been trying to mediate, so far without success. Here again, the causes lie more in the past than the present. At one time, Cyprus, which has rarely been self-governing, was part of the Ottoman Empire, which succeeded the Crusaders and the Venetians as rulers of the island. Under British colonial rule, the Greek and Turkish inhabitants were – as so often – not consulted on their wishes. Accustomed to living peacefully together, they nonetheless quarrelled over the island's political future once it became independent. And the slogans, 'Enosis' (union of the whole island with Greece) and 'Taksim' (union of the Turkish part with Turkey) were so powerful that the island remains divided today, and 'normal' Greek and Turkish Cypriots had to meet in London (where Glafcos Clerides and Rauf Denktash, the two community leaders, got on well as young lawyers). Only the 'Greek' Republic of Cyprus is internationally recognised, while the primitively led 'Turkish Republic of Northern Cyprus' owes its existence to Turkish military protection.

War in Chechnya, occupation and a state of war with Armenia in Azerbaijan, separatism in Georgia and Moldova, endless provisional arrangements in Kosovo, division in Cyprus – are our dreams of peace, reconciliation and equal rights just empty visions after all?

I believe and hope they are not. The peace we are working for in Europe is more than just an empty dream. Of course, there are many for whom the new Europe and its new values have come too late. But if Churchill and the others had thought only of past horrors in 1945, they would never have found the strength to dream of a new Europe. The difference between then and now – and I say this plainly – is that the Second World War (obviously to varying degrees) brought suffering to nearly everyone in Europe.

Chechnya's agony, the refugees' misery in Georgia, Armenia and Azerbaijan, the ethnic cleansing in Bosnia – all this took (and is taking) place at a time when hundreds of millions of Europeans were, and are, enjoying new peace and prosperity. The refugees from crisis regions who make it to the 'safe' parts of Europe can count on a sympathetic welcome – provided they come in hundreds only. Once they start coming in thousands, they are treated as a burden or a threat.

Here again, of course, we must not generalise. We hear a great deal about indifference, but there is commitment too. Non-governmental organisations (NGOs) – international associations, privately founded by committed individuals – are working all the time to open people's eyes, highlight problems and mobilise humanitarian aid. Many of these activists risk their lives in doing so. The International Committee of the Red Cross, some of whose workers were recently kidnapped and beheaded by terrorists, is just one NGO which can tell a sad tale of the people it has lost. But personal commitment also exists in the international organisations, whose staff often have to endure discomfort and work in conditions which are anything but safe. Lack of heating or hot water is a mere detail, but the Council of Europe's human rights experts in Chechnya, for example, daily visit places where terrorists or anti-terrorist squads have struck just a few hours before – and that is a very different matter. People need courage to work in conditions like these, and they need to believe in what they are doing. Thank God, there are people like this in the Council – and elsewhere. They help to make sure that these conflicts are not forgotten, and remind those at the top that the only possible solutions are political.

Chechnya – what dreams are still possible in Grozny?

When I was elected Secretary General of the Council of Europe on 23 June 1999, I already knew that Russia, the Council's largest member state, would – with the many problems attending its transition from the Soviet system to pluralist democracy, from the planned to the market economy, from central administration to federal decentralisation – make heavy demands on my attention. But the special part which Chechnya would play in all of this became apparent only slowly.

Since 1996, when the Kasavyurt Agreement was concluded between Yeltsin's special envoy, Alexander Lebed (whom I had met in Moscow in my capacity as Deputy Chairman of the Assembly's Ad Hoc Committee on Chechnya) and Dudayev's successor, Aslan Maskhadov, there had been considerable tensions in the separatist republic. Kidnappings (the victims included foreigners), ransom demands and killings were everyday occurrences.

Early in 1999, Maskhadov, who had been elected President two years before, announced a plan to introduce the Islamic legal code or Sharia;

however, various 'field commanders' had already been enforcing the code, including barbaric punishments and executions, and now called on Maskhadov himself to step down. In March, Moscow's representative in Chechnya, General Gennadi Shpigun, was abducted from the airport in Grozny and murdered. Even then, Moscow remained patient and seemed unwilling to take renewed military action in Chechnya.

During the summer – between my election and my taking office – the situation worsened dramatically. Armed gangs of Chechens tried to invade Dagestan, and bring the 'jihad', or 'holy war' against the infidel, to that largely Muslim country. Maskhadov declared a state of emergency, and the invaders officially withdrew from Dagestan, but turned to guerrilla tactics instead. On 31 August, the day before I took office, a bomb, which Chechen terrorists were suspected of planting, exploded in a Moscow shopping centre. In September, further bombs went off in a military residential district and in several Russian cities. Russian troops re-entered Chechnya, and Russian planes again bombed Grozny, while President Yeltsin and his newly-appointed Prime Minister, Vladimir Putin, proclaimed a nation-wide 'anti-terrorism campaign'.

On 1 October 1999, the Russian army officially took this campaign to Chechnya. Moscow withdrew recognition from Maskhadov and his government, and Russian troops reached the outskirts of Grozny on 18 October. The question for me, as neophyte Secretary General, was not whether to react – but how.

Fight terrorism – but respect certain limits

Russia's right (and not just its right, but its positive duty) to protect its people against terrorism, bomb attacks and armed aggression had never been in doubt. Nor could I condone developments in Chechnya itself: the kidnapping industry, the barbaric Sharia-based punishments and the arrival on the scene of terrorist groups from outside – all in a region which was legally part of a Council of Europe member state. From the start, however, I insisted – often as the only political figure to join the NGOs in doing so – that Russian action must remain proportionate, uphold the rule of law and respect human rights.

After all, the civilian population, who had already suffered grievously in the first Chechen 'war', and at the hands of independent field com-manders, had to be considered. They were Russian citizens, with a right to be protected by their own government. As well as insisting that Russian action must be proportionate and respect basic principles, I called for a political solution, which I saw as a necessary concomitant to military action.

At its Istanbul Summit in November 1999, at which I represented the Council of Europe, the OSCE also recognised that Chechnya was part of Russia and called for a political solution. In the meantime, after engaging fiercely with the rebel Chechen forces, Russian army and police units had reached the gates of Grozny. In the two months since the fighting had begun, over 250,000 people had fled to the neighbouring Russian republic of Ingushetia (the Chechens are closely related to the Ingush). At the end of November, the Council of Europe's Commissioner for Human Rights visited Russia for the first time, and also parts of Chechnya already controlled by the Russians.

Innocent victims

On 6 December, the Russians gave the civilian population of Grozny an ultimatum: anyone who failed to leave the city would be treated as a terrorist. The Russian Minister of Internal Affairs was in Strasbourg on 8 December, and I seized my chance to protest against this threat, which I saw as a flagrant violation of human rights and the rule of law. The EU also became alarmed, and even considered imposing sanctions on Russia. As the ruins in Grozny still show today, the military onslaught was ferocious, but the ultimatum itself produced no further effects. Regardless of who was first to blame, however, the fact remains that the capital city of a Russian republic was relentlessly shelled and bombed with no thought of its remaining civilians.

On 13 December 1999, I decided that it was my duty, as Secretary General, to activate Article 52 of the European Convention on Human Rights (the first time this had been done in its nearly 50-year history) and ask the Russians for details of the action they had taken to comply with the Convention during the military operations in Chechnya.

Foreign Minister Ivanov's answer arrived on 10 January. In the meantime, Yeltsin had resigned on 1 January, and Vladimir Putin had succeeded him as President. Ivanov justified the Russian military intervention in Chechnya, but failed to answer the decisive question – namely, how Russia had satisfied its obligation to protect human rights in the conflict.

At this point, international and parliamentary diplomacy began to play a part too. The Chairman of the Committee of Ministers, Irish Foreign Minister David Andrews, flew to Moscow for talks with his Russian counterpart, and the Parliamentary Assembly despatched a delegation, led by its President, Lord Russell-Johnston, to Dagestan and Chechnya. At a meeting with Lord Russell-Johnston, President Putin agreed to accept an international presence in Ingushetia and Chechnya.

When its delegation returned from Russia, the Assembly voted against expelling Russia from the Council, but called on Moscow, in Foreign Minister Ivanov's presence, to terminate the 'indiscriminate and disproportionate' military operation in Chechnya forthwith. I discussed the situation with Minister Ivanov myself, and repeated my demand for details of the action taken to protect human rights in what was undoubtedly an extreme situation.

It must be said, however, that extreme situations are exactly the ones which highlight the difference between democracy and autocracy, law and lawlessness, human rights and despotism. I hoped I was making it clear to Minister Ivanov that I was not attacking Russia – on the contrary, it was in Russia's own interest to give proof of its new, democratic status and uphold its dignity as a law-governed state.

On 1 February 2000, the last of the rebels withdrew from Grozny, and the Russian troops took over a devastated city, but a city in which people were still living. One day, perhaps, we shall know what happened next – perhaps not. There were no international observers or 'embedded' journalists on the scene, as there were later in Iraq. My own disturbing memories include the man I met some months later in a refugee[5] camp at Znamenskoye. He was looking desperately for his wife, who had gone with their two little daughters, on 5 February, to find out what had happened to their flat in Grozny. She was never seen again.

The new Russian President was also aware that the situation was serious, both nationally and internationally. He reacted by appointing Vladimir Kalamanov, himself a member of a small Caucasian minority, as his human rights envoy in Chechnya. On 24 February, I joined Mary Robinson, United Nations High Commissioner for Human Rights, and Jan Kubis, Secretary General of the OSCE, in calling for international monitoring.

At the end of that month, the Council of Europe's Commissioner for Human Rights, Alvaro Gil-Robles, visited Moscow and Chechnya for the second time. The Anti-Torture Committee also visited the northern Caucasus and Chechnya, and inspected the notorious holding camp at Chernokozovo. This led to immediate improvements. I invited Vladimir Kalamanov to Strasbourg and discussed co-operation with him; our interests, after all, were supposed to be similar.

The Council's mission takes shape

After two days of tough, but fair, negotiation, we agreed that three Council of Europe experts would be despatched to Chechnya, where they would help to set up Kalamanov's office and process complaints from the local population. They would have all the rights of staff of his office, but would take their orders from me, be free to travel anywhere in Chechnya (except when dangerous) and report direct to me. All of this was formally agreed – which meant that the Council team's presence was covered by international treaty.

But not everything went so smoothly. I felt that Ivanov's second answer to my request for information under Article 52 was still unsatisfactory – and told him so. In his answer, the Minister assured me that all the measures taken to restore human rights and the rule of law were justified and lawful, and that the Russian authorities were doing everything possible under Russian law to investigate violations and punish the culprits. Russia also agreed to publication of the Anti-Torture Committee's report.

The Parliamentary Assembly's attitude to Russia's handling of the conflict in Chechnya remained highly critical. It took the view that its January demands had not been met, and not only withdrew the Russian delegation's voting rights, but even requested the Committee of Ministers to take the first steps towards expelling Russia from the Council.

The Russian delegation (apart from three Liberal members) reacted by boycotting the Assembly. But the dialogue continued at government level, and Foreign Minister Ivanov had informal talks (restricted to ministers and secretaries of state) with his colleagues from other Council countries at my residence, on the eve of the Committee of Ministers' full session.

Sending Council of Europe experts to a region in crisis, where conditions were close to those existing in wartime, was something which had to be carefully considered and meticulously planned. Security issues had to be clarified, and local accommodation arranged.

At last, on 22 June, the experts arrived in Znamenskoye, the small district town where the office was located; I followed next day, with Umberto Ranieri, Italian Under-Secretary of State for Foreign Affairs (representing the Italian Chairman of the Committee of Ministers), and Vladimir Kalamanov for the 'official' opening. I shall never forget the people we met in the two nearby refugee camps. Suddenly, all the safety precautions seemed unimportant. The inmates produced photographs of missing relatives, told us about the things they had lost, and showed us their tents and the primitive conditions in which they had to live. Precautions or no precautions, none of us came to any harm.

We also had an instructive meeting with religious leaders from the local Muslim community. The muftis were far from supporting Maskhadov's rebel government, and accused his followers of distorting the traditional teachings of Islam. We also heard complaints of past Russian injustices – from the subjection of the Caucasian people to the discrimination faced by former Stalin deportees. It was clear that an immense amount of work would have to be done on reconciliation before a political solution could be found.

The following day, we joined the newly-arrived Chairman of the Committee of Ministers, Italian Foreign Minister Lamberto Dini, for a long and frank exchange of views with President Putin in the Kremlin. Putin committed himself to future self-government for the Chechen Republic within the Russian Federation – provisional to start with, then fully institutional. He did not deny that Russian forces had committed abuses and human rights violations, but claimed that these were isolated incidents. The Kalamanov Office had been set up to ensure, with the Council experts' help, that they ceased. A National Public Commission (the Krasheninnikov Commission) had also been established to investigate abuses and misconduct.

The truth about Chechnya

Back in Strasbourg, I submitted my report on the visit to Moscow and Chechnya to the Committee of Ministers – and with it an expert opinion, declaring that the information so far received under Article 52 of the Convention on Human Rights was insufficient. I proposed a special monitoring procedure, and the Committee later reacted by instructing me to include information on the situation in Chechnya from other sources in the monthly reports on the Council experts' work.

Over 30 reports have now been submitted. These are issued as public information documents (also posted on the Internet), and are an important source of objective information on developments.

On 29 June 2000, Vladimir Putin sprang a surprise by appointing the former Grand Mufti of Chechnya, Akhmed Kadyrov, who had sided with the separatist government, to head the Republic's provisional administration. By-elections to the Duma were held on 20 August, and Chechnya's one (and only) seat went to Aslanbek Aslakhanov.

The Council of Europe's criticisms of continuing human rights violations in Chechnya were confirmed in mid-September by the Krasheninnikov Commission, which accused Russian troops of 'widespread abuses' in the region. The holding of a public hearing in the Duma, to which the Chairman of the Committee of Ministers and I were invited, as well as a 12-strong delegation from the Parliamentary Assembly, was encouraging. Aslanbek Aslakhanov accused the government and military of failing to protect human rights, and named specific units which were known to have committed violations.

The appointment of eight judges by the Russian Supreme Judicial Council in November was a hopeful sign that things were coming back to normal. Our experts, whose brief had already been extended to tracing missing persons and inspecting prisons, got another new job: to help install an independent, impartial and incorruptible judicial system.

At this stage, the Russian forces appeared to have nearly all of Chechnya (apart from some mountainous regions in the south) under their control, but the situation was still tense. A network of control points, many of them centres of oppression and extortion, covered the country. At night, 'mopping-up units', usually masked and travelling in unmarked military vehicles, attacked villages suspected of harbouring terrorists or their supporters. Arrests and maltreatment were common, and many locals were robbed or forced to ransom themselves or members of their families. The mopping-up operations mainly targeted small villages, but other areas – and particularly Grozny – were ruled at night by the terrorists.

In his annual address to the Federal Assembly on 3 April 2001, President Putin announced that the army had completed its task and would soon be withdrawing from Chechnya. Two years on, and in spite of further developments (some of them positive) the army is still there – and many of the problems are the same.

Normalisation – repeated attempts, but no real successes

In ostensible confirmation of the claim that the situation was returning to normal, the Provisional Administration left its temporary home at Gudermes for Grozny in May. In September 2001, and again in December 2002, its new headquarters in Grozny were the target of serious attacks, leaving many dead and injured in their wake.

Having restored the Russian delegation's voting rights in January 2001, the Parliamentary Assembly set up a joint working party with the Duma to find a political solution. Cautious contacts were also made with individuals and groups close to Maskhadov

In mid-June 2001, after a 30-month absence, the OSCE mission also arrived in Znamenskoye, in the Council experts' immediate vicinity – but its members could do little more than observe. In a further attempt at normalisation, an 'Advisory Committee', comprising the head of the Provisional Administration and 'prominent politicians, academics and religious leaders', was set up.

The Council experts' reports from Znamenskoye remained ambivalent. The Kalamanov Office was 'up and running' – in other words open to receive complaints, serious or otherwise, from the public. Misconduct, extortion, missing relatives, late pension payments: all of this was noted, passed on and, at our experts' insistence, followed up. With the help of the special office established within the Provisional Administration, hundreds of missing persons were traced, some to refugee camps, some to other villages, and some to prisons where they were being wrongfully held.

However, the experts made little headway with the Military Prosecutor's Department, which always managed to find reasons for its failure to investigate reported offences (the units in question had left Chechnya, the culprits could no longer be identified, the references to 'masked men in camouflage' and 'unmarked military vehicles' were too vague, etc).

The Kalamanov Office and the prosecution service (including the Military Prosecutor's Department) set up a joint working group to remedy this situation, and refute allegations that offenders were not being punished (the experts' main complaint in their reports). This was also a question which came up repeatedly at my meetings with politicians, and above all with the Minister of Justice and the Attorney General, in Moscow.

In its spring 2002 report, the Monitoring Committee found that Russia's greatest problem, after six years in the Council, was its failure to settle the Chechen conflict peacefully. The need to investigate all human rights violations and abuses of power, and punish offenders regardless of rank, had still not been satisfied.

Human rights partner

Military Order No. 80, issued by the Commander of the North Caucasus United Army Group, Lieutenant-General Vladimir Moltenskoi, marked a thoroughly honourable attempt to forestall abuses and human rights violations. Among other things, it stipulated that representatives of the civilian authorities and the prosecution service must be present during mopping-up operations. As the General himself noted ruefully, many of his subordinates simply ignored it.

In spite of all the problems, Vladimir Kalamanov, Putin's special envoy, had become, not just a fair partner, but a genuine ally in the fight for human rights – which he saw (like me) as a vital part of a political solution. Violence and abuse of power are no antidote to terrorism – on the contrary, they encourage it. If robbery, extortion and summary arrests are part of the picture when Russian troops raid a village where a couple of terrorists have taken refuge, then the end-result is a hundred rebels more – not two terrorists less.

On 29 May 2002, President Kadyrov of Chechnya and President Zyazikov of Ingushetia concluded an agreement on the voluntary repatriation of all the Chechen refugees. The only problem was that Chechnya, whose official population had again topped one million, was materially unable to absorb the returnees. No one knows, even now, where the millions of roubles, which Russia poured into the country to cover reconstruction, actually went. A simple look at Grozny suggests that they did not find their target.

Since many things still needed to be done to normalise the situation and reach a political settlement, I decided that our experts' mandate would have to be extended. In June 2002, after months of negotiation, we reached agreement with the Russian Foreign Minister on terms and a six-month extension.

The Council experts were now given the extra task of helping the courts and civil authorities to improve their working methods. This covered the training of staff, judges and elected representatives, as well as help with development of the school system and the psychological rehabilitation of women and children. They were also to advise on legislation, and assist the various forums, e.g. the Human Rights Protection Council.

Not everything, however, works the way it should – as the Constitution put to referendum in spring 2003 clearly showed. This had been through at least five drafts, none of them discussed with our experts. It was not until a date had actually been set for a referendum on the final text that the President of the Parliamentary Assembly and I received copies. The Council's Venice Commission, which also saw the text, had criticisms, but did not reject it.

Having left the office vacant for just over a month, President Putin appointed Abdul-Khakim Sultygov, formerly co-ordinator of the joint 'Duma-Parliamentary Assembly Working Group', as his new human rights envoy in Chechnya. To avoid wasting time, I arranged to meet him in Vienna, where I was taking home leave.

The tragedy continues

The summer and early autumn of 2002 brought more trouble. First of all, 118 people (most, but not all, of them servicemen) were killed and another 33 injured when rebels shot down an army helicopter near the main base at Khankala. Secondly, a full-scale crisis started to develop with Georgia, which Russia accused of harbouring Chechen terrorists in the Pankisi Valley – while Georgia accused Russia of mounting air strikes on that region. In fact, a number of Chechens – arrested in possession of arms, while trying to enter Russia from Georgia – protested to the European Court of Human Rights against extradition to Russia. The Court initially ordered suspension of this measure but, on receipt of further information, raised no objections.

But the most serious incident – probably the worst since the fall of Grozny – took place, not in Chechnya, but in Moscow. Some 50 terrorists occupied a Moscow theatre and took 850 hostages, killing some of them and threatening to blow the building up. Three days later, Russian special units stormed the theatre using stun gas, killed the terrorists and freed the hostages (of whom, however, over 160 died, mainly from gas poisoning).

On 12 December 2002, President Putin announced a referendum on a new Chechen Constitution and new laws on elections to the Chechen Parliament and Presidency. On 27 December, a bomb exploded at government headquarters in Grozny, killing 72 people and injuring 150. On 31 December, the OSCE assistance group, whose mandate had not been extended, was obliged to terminate its work officially.

In Strasbourg, the European Court of Human Rights declared that applications brought by six Chechen citizens, alleging human rights violations by the Russian forces in 1999–2000, were admissible. And on 29 January 2003, a stormy debate took place in the Parliamentary Assembly, the main question being whether conditions for the lawful holding of a referendum had been satisfied. Lord Judd, rapporteur and co-Chairman of the Joint Duma-Assembly Working Group, even considered resigning.

A joint Council of Europe/OSCE 'technical assessment mission' to Chechnya concluded that normal monitoring of the referendum by the two organisations was impossible. The referendum itself was held on 23 March 2003. There were no serious incidents. Official sources put the turnout at about 88%, and recorded a 96% vote in favour of the new Constitution.

Much, if not everything, now depends on implementation of the Constitution, and on strict enforcement of earlier texts, such as General Moltenskoi's Order No. 80. The sorely-tried people of Chechnya are now pinning their hopes on normalisation, self-government and withdrawal of the Russian forces.

Yet another sign that Chechnya's troubles were not over came on Easter Monday 2003, when a bomb attack was made on a convoy in which our experts were travelling. Thank God, only a few people were slightly injured – a driver and three members of the 'Spetsnaz' (an elite anti-terrorist unit, taking orders from the Ministry of Justice).

My five years as Secretary General of the Council of Europe have been five years with Chechnya on my daily programme. In the time left to me, I shall have to keep on working hard to ensure that people in Grozny, Gudermes or Znamenskoye can still dream of a shared European future.

Where does the dream end?

With the Federation of Serbia and Montenegro already in, Monaco perhaps arriving shortly, and even Belarus to be hoped for (once the necessary democratic reforms have been effected), it is clear that the Council of

Europe is approaching the end of its natural growth cycle. Having barely got used to that idea, we now have some Mediterranean (and even central Asian) countries knocking on the door. Observer status is the first thing they want, but some are already hoping for full membership of certain partial agreements. One of them, Israel, has actually had observer status in the Parliamentary Assembly since 1956.

The EU is a long way behind. Even when 10 new members were admitted on 1 May 2004, 23 European states will still remain outside[6] – although most have already shown interest of one kind or another.[7] Basing his estimate on 'accession criteria, the EU Treaty and the map',[8] Commission President Prodi speaks of a possible 35 members. At the EU too, some countries which are not geographically European are knocking on the door, while the 'Barcelona Process' is giving it a role in the Mediterranean, and some central Asian countries (even Mongolia) are participating in its support programmes, such as TACIS.

Is Europe bursting its boundaries?

Surely, if outsiders share its dream, Europe can (or could) be 'stretched' as well as 'enlarged'? There is nothing immediately preposterous in this. After all, the Council of Europe and its conventions cover the Asian parts of the Russian Federation and Turkey, and the organisation has already given geography a slight political twist to let Armenia, Azerbaijan and Georgia come in.

It is also true that some European nations have colonial pasts. Memories of this time, when they set out to put their mark on other peoples, may not always be happy, but cultural ties and connections have survived – and help to make Europe, which is largely at peace, and in many places prosperous, a magnet.

So where is Europe heading and where does the European dream stop? In spite of trials and reversals, Europe is pressing inexorably forward on the road it first took when the Council of Europe was founded in 1949, and which is enshrined in its Statute – the road to greater unity between its peoples. Both the institutions committed to that goal, the Council of Europe and the EU, are helping Europeans to stay on that road.

One really cannot say that the two institutions are themselves on different roads, one shorter and faster, one longer and slower – even if the EU sometimes seems to be leading. It is, of course, true that more fortunate historical circumstances, and above all economic strength, have helped the 'old' 15 EU states to move ahead faster on the European path. It is also true that the 10 states which signed the accession treaty in Athens on 16 April 2003 are favoured by proximity to, and historical ties with, the existing members. And the eight which belonged to the 'Eastern bloc' before 1989–90 had not suffered as long as the other former Soviet republics under Communist hegemony. Also, unlike the countries of south-eastern Europe, they had made a peaceful transition to democracy – which eased the path to joining the 15.

The image of two cars, travelling at different speeds, is also misleading. All the countries which are in the EU, or want to join it, are also in the Council of Europe. True, one might think that some of the 15 (I hope this will not be the case with some of the new members too) had forgotten this – they show so little interest in the Council in the ordinary run of political events. Happily, appearances are deceptive. Behind the scenes, in the practical day-to-day work of our steering committees and groups of experts, the EU states, too, are well aware of the benefits they derive from the Council.

Wanted – a uniform plan for the European home

Ultimately, this kind of abstract speculation is futile. The fact is, two institutions with the same vision and dream are at work and already – surprisingly for dreamers – getting very tangible results. The ultimate goal is one they can only reach together. At present, laboriously, they are preparing the one thing the travellers forgot when they set out: a uniform plan for the common European home.

Under its Statute, the Council of Europe is ready to admit any European state which shares the same basic values and aims as other members. Article 49 of the EU Treaty cites almost identical principles, and allows any European state which respects them to seek membership. This being so, no state which complies with these rules must be denied admission to the common home – and the plan must also make room for every state qualified to enter.

This means that, at the end of the road, Europe will consist of: states large and small; peoples of Baltic, Germanic, Celtic, Latin, Slav, central Asian and other origins; people with different beliefs – Catholic, Orthodox and Protestant Christians, Jews, Muslims and others, including agnostics and atheists; some 200 language communities in countries, themelves very different, with ethnic minorities entitled to preserve their identities. In short, even 'one' or 'united' Europe will be a Europe of diversity.

This also means, however, that Europe's constitution cannot, and will not, be that of a strong central state, since an over-powerful central authority (government or parliament) would never be able to cater for all the needs implicit in this diversity. The answer is to decentralise (already an established trend) and aim at a balance of power, while also creating a common area of legal security and internal order, with a solid political armature to shield it from outside threats.

This may sound contradictory, but it actually makes good sense. If this common European area faces the outside world firmly, then potential dangers – not just from 'enemies' in the normal sense of the term, but also from trade restrictions, etc – will steadily decrease. Legal security and harmonisation of law make individual action less dangerous and open the way to a thriving market economy and social cohesion, while decentralisation helps to ensure that creative initiative is not stifled by bureaucratic and unrealistic regulations. And a balance of power prevents an originally democratic central authority from degenerating into despotism and dictatorship. This is why 'successful' dictatorships, once they oust democracies, always start by eliminating the decentralised echelons which preserve a balance of power. The Nazis did this by bringing the regions 'into line', and the Bolsheviks by imposing central control on a system of basically decentralised councils.

I see these trends as inherent elements in European unification. Projecting them onto the two institutions working for that purpose, the EU and the Council of Europe, I get the following picture:

The Council of Europe corresponds – perhaps overmuch – to decentralisation and a balance of power, although the latter applies only between states. With the exception of its basic conventions, and above all its human rights texts, its harmonisation of law is voluntary, and so not really complete. Even the European Social Charter has not been ratified by all its members. The European Cultural Convention, the first genuinely pan-European convention (applying even to states still outside the Council), is primarily focused on co-operation. It remains true, of course, that the Convention on Human Rights and the Anti-Torture Convention have established a supranational area of basic rights and freedoms. Council of Europe instruments aimed at combating terrorism, organised crime and corruption already cover much of the continent as well.

The EU has been most successful in harmonising law in the fields of economics and competition – but is open to the charge of introducing unrealistic and bureaucratic regulations. Aiming at freedom of competition, it sets central economic priorities over decentralised priorities of another kind, e.g. cultural priorities. Though still not universally applied, other initiatives, such as the Schengen Agreement or monetary union, serve to promote, not only liberties, but also harmonisation of law and legal security.

The EU's greatest contribution has probably been to external influence and security. At the same time, the 'Common Foreign and Security Policy'

(CFSP) still remains its weakest point. With 15 members today, and 25 tomorrow, the Union cannot be ignored – provided it speaks with one voice. It was speaking with one voice which allowed it to bring peace to 'the former Yugoslav Republic of Macedonia', and federate Serbia and Montenegro, thus promoting stability in a troubled region.

Often enough, however, its external political power depends on money, which may or may not be available. Also, when it comes to the EU's speaking with one voice, and so acquiring political weight in the world outside, the CFSP remains mere theory. Nothing could have made that plainer than the Iraq war. Small wonder that proposals on appointing an EU President, or on various combinations of Vice-President, External Affairs Commissioner, Foreign Minister, etc, have been hotly discussed, both inside and outside the Convention. A permanent EU seat on the UN Security Council is another admirable suggestion – but the fact that France and the UK would then be unable to keep their own seats makes it seem a lost hope. Should it ever join the EU, the same would apply to Russia.

Which path to take?

A mixture of the Council of Europe and the EU, with an upgraded common foreign policy, would certainly be the best structure for 'one Europe'.

This 'one Europe' should be uniform in terms of democracy, legal policy (above all on basic rights and freedoms) and internal security. It should also be decentralised, preserving a balance between local, regional, national and European government, and should present a strong, united front – speaking out for freedom and stability. This is a Europe in which we can be Muscovites, Russians and Europeans, just as we can be Innsbruckers, Tyrolers, Austrians and Europeans.

Who can and should belong to this Europe? All those who rejoice at being able to share their cultural heritage and values with others. All those who want to be good and peace-loving neighbours. All those who are not content simply to give their own identities a 'European tinge'. In short, all those who really accept the shared European identity as their own, and who see a shared cultural heritage, shared values, and also geographical proximity, as a solid basis for the 'one Europe' which millions of people have been dreaming of for centuries.

NOTES:

1. Both NATO and the Council of Europe had 10 European founder-members, but these were not the same: Belgium, Denmark, France, Italy, Luxembourg, the Netherlands, Norway and the United Kingdom were in both from the start; NATO had Iceland and Portugal as well, and the Council Ireland and Sweden.
2. *Der Standard*, 8 February 2003.
3. 20–21 November 2002.
4. Description in *Europarecht, Recht der EU/EG, des Europarates und der wichtigsten anderen europäischen Organisationen*, Fischer/Köck/Karollus, Linde Verlag , p. 29.
5. The international term would be IDP = 'internally displaced person'.
6. Albania, Andorra, Armenia, Azerbaijan, Belarus, Bosnia and Herzegovina, Bulgaria, Georgia, Iceland, Croatia, Liechtenstein, the 'Former Yugoslav Republic of Macedonia', Moldova Monaco, Norway, Romania, the Russian Federation, San Marino, Serbia and Montenegro, Turkey, Ukraine, and – outside the circle of potential Council of Europe member states – the Vatican.
7. Bulgaria, Romania and Turkey are already recognised candidates, and Croatia has applied.
8. In *Europa leidenschaftlich gesucht*, published by the Alfred Herrhausen Gesellschaft für internationalen Dialog, Piper Verlag, Munich, 2003.

CHAPTER SIX

The challenge for us

Greater Europe without new dividing lines

In April 1999, Georgia became the first of the three south-Caucasian republics to join the Council of Europe. The President of this far from placid country, former Soviet Foreign Minister Edward Shevardnadze, came straight from a NATO meeting in New York for the accession ceremony in Strasbourg.

This left only six potential members outside:

(1) The tiny Principality of Monaco – independent for centuries, but obliged to make concessions to its powerful neighbour, France, in the 20th century. Its sovereignty was seriously curtailed in consequence, and its status as a parliamentary democracy was also flawed. Its application for membership is still being processed: realistically, it can expect to join in 2004.

(2) Bosnia and Herzegovina, still suffering the effects of the terrible war between its three communities, and a *de facto* international protectorate. However, it made great efforts under a non-nationalist government, and won admission to the Council in April 2002.

(3) The post-Communist and nationalistic Federal Republic of Yugoslavia, still ruled by Slobodan Milosevic, whose brutal treatment of the Albanians triggered the Kosovo conflict in spring 1999. NATO forced him to retreat, UN administrators took over in Kosovo, and a multinational force, the KFOR, was installed to keep the peace.

Montenegro – with Serbia, the last Yugoslav Republic still within the Federation – distanced itself increasingly from Belgrade's policies and effectively went its own way. Blatant doctoring of election results, after Montenegro's rejection of an amendment to the Yugoslav Constitution, provoked public outcry even in Belgrade, and Milosevic was finally toppled. Vojislav Koštunica, the real election victor, became President and installed a democratic government with strong civil society connections.

In spite of many problems (e.g. a split in the democratic camp which had rallied against Milosevic, failure to hand over war criminals – like the Bosnian Serb butcher of Srebenica, General Ratko Mladic – and Monte-negro's strivings for independence) the democratic and legal reforms needed for admission to the European family were completed. Once a Constitutional Charter for a State Union of Serbia and Montenegro had been accepted, the former Yugoslavia became history at last, and the way to Council membership was basically open.

However, the old regime showed its brutal face once more, when the Serbian Prime Minister, Zoran Djindjic, one of the leaders of the demo-cratic revolution, was murdered by the commander of a special police unit. Far from obstructing the path to Europe, this actually hastened the process. On 4 April 2003, I was able to greet Serbia and Montenegro, the Council's 45th member state, with the words: 'Dobrodosli kuci', welcome home!

In spite of some serious misgivings, Armenia and Azerbaijan, former Soviet republics in the South Caucasus, which were still officially at war, were admitted in 2001, although hopes that their joining at the same time would produce an early settlement of the Nagorno-Karabakh conflict remained unfulfilled to start with.

Finally, there was (and is) Belarus, whose admission procedure (and spe-cial guest status with the Assembly) was suspended, and eventually 'frozen' early in 1997. This became inevitable, once Lukashenko had substituted a 'selected' parliament for the elected one, and democratic and human rights shortcomings became patent. Belarus remains outside the Council to this day, although contacts have never been totally severed. It plays a full part in activities covered by the European Cultural Convention, has a representa-tive in Strasbourg, and is watched by both the Parliamentary Assembly and the Committee of Ministers. There are still contacts, too, with civil society, non-state media and the democratic opposition.

All of these were potential member states. Without them, the organisa-tion's statutory goal of 'greater unity', i.e. a Europe without dividing lines or barriers, could – and can – never be achieved. The Council is pursuing a new-style expansionist policy, a policy untainted by aggression, and its aim is to bring all these countries together in an area where democratic security, the rule of law, and human rights are the norm. Five years earli-er, with the three South Caucasian republics, the Parliamentary Assembly had already drawn the geographical, cultural and political boundaries.

Central Asia and the Mediterranean

The OSCE, the Organisation for Security and Co-operation in Europe, had extended its reach when the Soviet Union collapsed. From the start, it had not been limited to Europe, since both the USA and Canada were members. To that extent, therefore, admitting the former Soviet Republics in central Asia was no innovation. Under Italy's chairmanship,[1] our Committee of Ministers also discussed special status for these countries at the Council. However, for various reasons (and because hopes of progress on democracy and human rights were not over-sanguine), the matter was taken no further.

Kazakhstan (whose few sparsely settled territories west of the Ural River form the basis of its claim to be a 'European' country) was the only state in the region to show any real interest in closer contacts – observer status with the Assembly, for example. At present, however, a life-time presidency and other symptoms of authoritarian government suggest that it lacks the basic democratic, rule-of-law and human rights credentials needed to join the European club. At the same time, its large Russian (and considerably smaller Volga-German) minorities do form a cultural bridge to Europe, and neither this, nor its interest in minimum European standards should, perhaps, be ignored in the long term.

The south-eastern Mediterranean countries also have long-standing ties of various kinds with Europe. The Romans called the Mediterranean 'mare nostrum' ('our sea'), and rated its North African and European shores as equally important. The rise of Islam brought a certain parting of the ways, but neither cultural nor political – let alone economic – ties were ever totally severed. For centuries, Moorish Spain ('Al Andalus') gave North African civilisation a bridgehead in Europe. In the 19th century, European colonial expansion again brought closer contacts (not always voluntary), and these survived the colonial era's demise.

Finally, UN approval of Israeli independence in 1948 led to the founding of a Europe-inspired state in the eastern Mediterranean – but also created a new flashpoint. As I have already noted, Israel's Knesset was given observer status with the Parliamentary Assembly in 1956. Later, when the now sadly lamed peace process began, the Assembly led the way in seeking closer contacts with the Palestinians – contacts which had already been sporadically and cautiously cultivated. As a member of the Assembly's Sub-Committee on the Middle East, I myself met official representatives of the Palestinian National Council in Amman as long ago as 1993. The Council also sent observers to monitor the first elections to the Palestinian Authority and, when the second *intifada* began, came forward – in an effort to save and restart the peace process – with offers of help on confidence-building measures. On an official visit to Israel and the Palestinian territories in summer 2001 (when I met, among others, President Katzav, Knesset President Avraham Burg and Foreign Minister Shimon Peres on the Israeli side, and Chairman Arafat, but also Tansim leader Marwan Barguti on the

Palestinian side), I offered to organise human rights training for the security forces on both sides (ideally together) and to help examine history textbooks, with a view to removing anything that might strengthen prejudice and incite to hatred. Both sides agreed, but escalation and the steady, appalling growth of violence have so far blocked any move in this direction. But the offer stands, and I am confident that it will – one day – be accepted and implemented.

There was one scheme, however, which – in spite (or because) of a terrible cycle of killings and reprisals – I was not prepared to shelve. In April 2003, I invited a number of young Israelis and Palestinians, Greek and Turkish Cypriots, and Armenians and Azerbaijanis to come together at the Council and discuss ways of settling the supposedly insoluble conflicts between their peoples. No group started with its 'own' problem, but joined its 'conflict partner' in tackling someone else's. Israelis and Palestinians thus discussed the Cyprus conflict – and not only discussed it, but 'agreed' on a settlement. In the same way, Greek and Turkish Cypriots devised a sound basis for negotiations between Armenia and Azerbaijan on Nagorno-Karabakh, while Armenians and Azeris worked out constructive proposals for a lasting peace in the Middle East.

Two of the conflicts the young people discussed are home-grown in Europe – even though the states involved are, in both cases, members of the Council of Europe. This may prompt readers to wonder how the two things can go together, and whether the Council is not undermining its own values by admitting two countries – Armenia and Azerbaijan – which are still officially at war. In the case of Cyprus, they may also wonder why, in the last 40 years, the Council has failed to stop two communities on a small island from drifting apart. Have we sold out on our values there too?

The Council of Europe: human rights watchdog?

My answer to this is a resounding 'no'. The Council is not just a human rights watchdog – barking, and biting if necessary, whenever democracy and human rights are threatened. It wants to go further, and to plant and nurture those values in places where they are still unknown or imperfectly realised. If we must have an image from the animal kingdom, the best is that of the patient, steady packhorse, carrying a precious load over sometimes stony terrain. The last remaining tract of stony terrain outside the Council today is Belarus. Some day, democratic and legal reform will also allow this former Soviet republic to become part of 'one Europe'.

But patches of stony terrain still exist within the Council itself, and extension also needs to be consolidated. The main key to this is having a lived democracy, in which opposition rights are respected in parliament and outside, governments untainted by corruption uphold the rule of law, police and security forces respect human rights, people are free to speak their minds, the media are responsible and independent, and minimum standards of social protection are guaranteed. Only when this work of consolidation has been completed throughout the continent will we really have a Europe without dividing lines.

Fortress Europe or open doors and solidarity?

A small Luxembourg village, not far from the Belgian frontier (long since erased by the Benelux), has given its name to a treaty which rouses very mixed feelings in Europe: Schengen. In fact, there are two sides to this treaty. On the one hand, it allows land, sea and air travellers from Helsinki to Lisbon, from Oslo to Athens, to realise the dream of a Europe without frontiers, visas or – but for the terrorist threat – passports. On the other, it has given fortress Europe (accessible only to 'Schengen visa' holders) a name. And, when the EU expands in 2004, the fortress will grow with it: the present ramparts will be levelled, and new and stronger ones constructed further out.

To be fair, the fault is not all on one side. My own passport is full of visas for Council member states outside the Schengen area, some of them valid for one visit only. For example, my diplomatic visa for the USA will outlast my passport, but my visa for Russia needs renewing every six months. I have already mentioned Haris Silajdzic's grandfather who, under the Dual Monarchy in 1900, could travel the length and breadth of Europe without a passport. Silajdzic himself knows what freedom of movement means. At the time of the fighting in Bosnia, he had to crawl through a culvert under the motorway to reach the airport outside Sarajevo and, even today, he can barely get further than Zagreb without a visa – hence his plaintive question: 'What kind of Europe are we living in anyway?' Surely the answer to that question should be the same for him as it is for the French and German youngsters who can start a disco evening in Strasbourg and finish it in Kehl?

No new dividing lines

After the Second World War, the former East Prussian city of Königsberg passed to the Soviets and, as Kaliningrad, became a region within the Soviet Republic of Russia. Recently, the Baltic states' recovery of their independence has turned it into an enclave squeezed between Poland and Lithuania, and separated from Russia by Belarus. So far, however, Kaliningraders have succeeded in coping with the situation. They have relatively easy transit links with Russia, are well integrated in their surroundings, and have offset the economic drawbacks of their peripheral position by cultivating trade relations – partly on the grey and black markets. However, when Poland and Lithuania join the EU and enter the Schengen area in 2004, Kaliningrad will be encircled by the EU's external frontier. This prospect has set the alarm bells ringing for Vladimir Putin (whose wife comes from Kaliningrad) and he has appointed Dimitri Rogozin, leader of the Russian delegation to the Parliamentary Assembly – certainly not a random choice – as his special envoy for free movement of persons to and from the city. Part of the problem (but only part of it) has been solved by the agreement concluded between the EU and Russia in Brussels on 11 November 2002. The EU is to introduce a 'Facilitated Transit Document' for Russian citizens, while Russia – interestingly – undertakes in return to speed up the issuing of passports to its nationals. Both these elements are important for the future. Indeed, greater unity of the kind foreseen in the Council of Europe's 1949 Statute cannot be achieved outside the EU unless all Europeans have greater freedom to travel! This was why the EU–Russian Summit, held in May 2003 to mark the 300th anniversary of the founding of St Petersburg, also called for a 'Europe without new dividing lines'.

The main obstacle here remains the richer countries' fear of uncontrolled immigration, with its attendant risks of higher unemployment and greater insecurity. Populists exploit these anxieties, and actually stoke them by highlighting cultural and religious differences, which – they claim – are unbridgeable.

The first thing to be said is that all of Europe's past history (among other things, a history of migration, integration, cross-fertilisation of cultures and religious diversity) disproves this. The second is that most of the immigrants have arrived already. There is no denying that numerous problems have arisen, partly because the reactions of many politicians – not least (and here the vicious circle closes) in deference to the populists – have been purely defensive. In recent years, immigration into Europe has reached an all-time high. The 1990s, in particular, were marked by a wave of immigration from central and eastern Europe, including some of the CIS states, while the Balkan wars, oppression of minorities, discrimination, etc, brought a very steep increase in the number of refugees. Specifically, a sudden influx of refugees from the war in the former Yugoslavia brought immigration to its highest level since the end of the Second World War, peaking in 1992–1993.

The peak has passed

Of course, Europe has always been a magnet for immigrants, but the statistical trend has been downward for some time – the one exception being the period covered by the Balkan wars. Estimates in 1999–2000 put Europe's total foreign population at approximately 21.16 million – in other words, foreigners account for some 2.6% of average population. Most of these foreigners live in western Europe, where the UK and Germany have the highest proportions. As I have said, the high point came in 1992, when immigrants totalled about 700,000. This fell to 261,000 in 1996, rising again to 480,000 in 1999 (a direct result of events in Kosovo), with a slight decrease, to approximately 467,000, in 2001. Generally, there is a steady flow of skilled workers to western Europe. These are an undoubted loss to their home countries – prompting one to ask who the winners and losers really are.

At present, one hears three main arguments when immigration policy is discussed in Europe.

The first is that immigration will do much to arrest or offset falling birth rates and ageing of the population in western Europe – and may even help to reverse the trend. Most of the scenarios used to back this argument focus on immigrant numbers, but tend to forget that it is not just immigrants, but *skilled* immigrants, who are needed.

The second (counter-)argument is that population figures are falling so sharply that it is far from certain that immigration can compensate effectively for natural growth. Nor is it certain that immigration can actually meet host countries' labour market requirements, in terms of either numbers or skills. Clearly, supply does not always match demand – Germany's 'green card' for IT specialists gave recent proof of that. On the positive side, one aspect (increasingly discussed at the Council of Europe) is the part which immigrants play in promoting the economic growth and prosperity of host countries. As workers and taxpayers, they contribute significantly to economic development – in short, provide the human basis of economic success.

Again in support of immigration, a third argument relies on the direct part which the new arrivals play (as consumers and taxpayers) in the life of host communities. Their positive contribution to GDP can be usefully highlighted here. This line suggests that immigration will, in the medium term, cost developed countries nothing or indeed leave them richer. Greece was acting on this assumption in 2000–2001, when it regularised the situation of many illegal immigrants.

Regularisation pays

The Greek example shows that bringing clandestine workers out of the shadows makes good economic and social sense, and undoubtedly contributes to the host country's stability and development. So far, most

European countries have handled the problems raised by integration and naturalisation of immigrants reasonably well, although there is plenty of room for improvement. However, the fact that things have gone well in the past is no guarantee for the future – and this makes it doubly important to monitor governments' immigration policies, and public perceptions of those policies. There is an increasing need for policies which make it possible to 'manage' immigration. Governments must remember that the nature and quality of immigration are changing, that the needs of the western democracies and industrial states are changing too, and that considerations of supply and demand will lead to immigration's being seen, not as a burden, but a benefit. These arguments are gaining ground steadily.

As long ago as 1998, the Council of Europe outlined a strategy for immigration. Basically, this comprises four main elements. First of all, immigration must proceed on orderly lines, i.e. must be regulated to optimise the individual immigrant's abilities and opportunities. Secondly, immigration countries must be helped to form a clearer picture of the processes involved. Thirdly, every effort must be made to put a stop to illegal immigration and trafficking in human beings, and remove their many harmful side-effects. Fourthly, host countries must protect immigrants, helping new arrivals to integrate and ensuring that marginal groups are not maltreated or exploited.

Immigration – a process based on partnership

Immigrants must be helped to integrate, and an appropriate naturalisation policy introduced in the long term – in other words, the basic conditions for full integration must be created. These conditions can be worked out effectively only on the basis of permanent dialogue and co-operation between home, transit and host countries – the countries on the receiving end of immigration. Making immigration work is a two-way process. People in host countries must learn to see immigrants as an asset, economic and social, and immigrants must familiarise themselves with the rules applying in host countries and accept them. One cause of the problems so far has been the politicians' preference for piecemeal over global solutions. In other words, economic issues, asylum, illegal immigration, naturalisation and deportation have all been tackled in isolation. Fragmented responsibilities and disconnected policies are the reason why there has never been any consistent, long-term planning in this area.

Managing migration – the Council has ideas

This is where the Council of Europe can help, as a continental organisation, to knit all these aspects together and establish a time-scale, leading from short-term observation, through medium-term strategy, to long-term integration. This new approach to managing migration is the only one likely to prove effective. Home, transit and host countries need to work on it together, since this holds the only key to creating a context in which individuals can fulfil themselves. Europe's neighbours, particularly those south of the Mediterranean, will certainly have to be involved as well.

If Europe (or part of it) stops behaving like a fortress, then attempts to pierce its defences will automatically diminish. After all, the Hungarians, Slovaks and Poles who work (and are needed) in Austria or Germany arrived well ahead of EU enlargement. Once EU membership creates new optimism and prosperity in their own countries, some of them will certainly be tempted to go home – like Spaniards, Portuguese and Greeks in the past. Of course, many stayed on then, and many will now. But so what?

Think of Beethoven, an 'Austrian' composer from Bonn, or Chopin(ski), a 'Frenchman' from Poland. What would Europe or its culture be without its migrants? France has a Minister of Internal Affairs called Sarkozy, who brings a dash of Hungary to Paris, just as Austria has a Regional Governor called van Staa, who brings a breath of Holland to the Tyrolean mountains.

And here I am myself – an Austrian in the capital of Alsace, with a name which comes from the southernmost corner of that region. My ancestral home was the Sundgau, my home city is Vienna and my homeland is Austria. My wider home, however, is Europe, where so many things connect me with so many places: my love of Shakespeare with England, my awe at its megalithic temples with Malta, my ancestors with Slovakia, France, the South Tyrol and Bohemia, my passion for history with Athens and Rome, my musical tastes with Russia, and (I confess) a kind of overarching Habsburg nationality with all the peoples of the old Dual Monarchy. I am at home in Europe, and so are 800 million other Europeans, even those to whom it has never occurred that one can leave one's own country, and still be at home – in Europe.

That is why we should all have the right to go where we want – to admire other people's buildings, listen to their music and hunt for bargains in their flea markets. People from the richer countries may well take all of this for granted (visas are no problem for full wallets), but some Europeans are still admitted to other countries 'by invitation only' – and may even have to show that their living and medical expenses will be covered. People should be free to study in the places where they feel they can learn most. European culture and European science were shaped – not least – by students who travelled freely between universities. And it was the sharing of skills and knowledge which gave Europe its cultural identity.

And people should also be free to work – legally, securely and contentedly – wherever there are jobs they want to do.

Europe must, in other words, be a home for everyone – a home where people can live, learn, work and enjoy themselves. Fortresses – even the strongest – always fall in the end. But homes endure, because homes are anchored in the heart.

Balkan problems

The daily TV pictures from the world's trouble spots – wrecked homes, mutilated corpses, despairing survivors and streams of refugees – shock us when we see them, but the next disaster or bomb attack soon drives them from our minds. We rarely lose sleep over these horrors, lulled by the thought that they are all happening – thank God! – a long way from us. Even when the pictures come from Tel Aviv, Ramallah, Algeria or Chechnya, most of us still forget that these places are really 'next door', just two or three hours away by plane.

We all take it for granted that none of this could happen in Europe. Even in the final stages of the Cold War, we were already sure of it: Berlin in 1953, Budapest in 1956, Prague in 1968 – it was all in the past. And surely, when the Berlin Wall and the Iron Curtain went in 1989, the chapter was finally closed? It all (or almost all) seemed to have gone remarkably peacefully. Even Ceaucescu's ghost in Romania had been rapidly laid. Now, things could only get better.

And then suddenly, in the summer of 1991, we started seeing pictures from the martyred city of Vukovar in the Croatian province of Eastern Slavonia, burned and devastated by the army of the Socialist Federal Republic of Yugoslavia.

Yugoslavia: from harmony to horror

Yugoslavia seemed to have started its transition comparatively early. Tito had kept it out of the Cold War and, under Communist single-party rule, apparently turned it into a model federal republic, comprising national and multinational republics and autonomous provinces, all with equal rights. The many Yugoslav guest workers in western Europe also helped to forge ties, and institutional links with the Council of Europe dated back to 1987, when Yugoslavia had signed the European Cultural Convention. For all of these reasons, everyone assumed that it would find its feet in the new, democratic and wider Europe faster and more easily than many other countries.

Instead, expectations of trouble focused on Albania – probably the most absurd dictatorship ever seen in Europe – where Enver Hoxha had imposed an idiosyncratic mix of Maoism, Marxism and Leninism. Rigid atheism and total isolation were the hallmarks of his rule, and his political and military paranoia (by no means rare in dictators) produced some strange effects, like those mini-bunkers, which helped to drain the country's already depleted resources. I still have the model the Europa Hotel gave me as a souvenir on my first visit to Tirana in the early 1990s. I do not put it on show, but I keep it as a reminder of the things that have been possible in Europe in my own lifetime.

Basically, the outside world had little idea what was really happening in the Balkans. Internal processes in Yugoslavia and developments under Hoxha and his acolytes received scant and superficial attention. The memorandum on alleged oppression of the Serbs in Kosovo, signed by 112 Serbian intellectuals and issued by the Belgrade Academy of Sciences on 21 January 1986, was barely noticed, let alone taken seriously. Eighteen months later, when the Central Committee of the Serbian Communist Alliance approved Slobodan Milosevic's nationalist line, the rest of Europe again took little notice – although this was a direct prelude to the catastrophe which would engulf the western Balkans just a few years later. In fact, economic reverses, rising unemployment and a parallel battle for resources were bringing unsolved national problems, which even Tito's Constitution had not managed to smooth over, to the surface. The new elites looked to democratic western Europe for guidance, and challenged the artificially harmonious 'Federal State of Yugoslavia' which was Tito's legacy. The old elites pinned their hopes on a new combination of Communism and nationalism. This not only put pressure on a multi-ethnic structure with little experience of democracy, but also – of course – massively impeded the progressives' efforts at reform. Western leaders simply took it for granted that Tito's Yugoslavia – a federal structure, with an economy supposedly self-managing on democratic principles (but often, in fact, at the mercy of corrupt party officials in managerial positions) – would evolve naturally into a free democracy, where human rights were respected. Behind the scenes, however, revolutionary changes were brewing. Slovenia was the only one of the six republics in which these changes led to a rapid, briefly disrupted (by a clash with the Yugoslav federal army in the early summer of 1991), but otherwise peaceful and total transition to European standards.

Disaster overtook all the other republics, shocking the rest of Europe from its slumbers. In 1988–1989, outsiders were still willing to see only the positive developments, e.g. the economic reforms and the – at least theoretical – reduction in the Communist Party's influence on state and economy. In 1988, neither the massive demonstrations by Kosovo's

Albanians against Serbian policy, nor the massive demonstrations by Serbian nationalists against the autonomous government in the multi-national province of Vojvodina registered as warning signs.

There was something almost fated about the course of events from then on. In March 1989, a new Serbian Constitution largely abolished the autonomy of both the Vojvodina and Kosovo. Two months later, the 'spiritual father' of these measures, Slobodan Milosevic, became President. The rest of Europe, however, saw only the election of a liberal Croatian economic expert, Ante Markovic, as Yugoslav Prime Minister, and failed to realise that rising Serbian nationalism was undermining the power of the federal authorities. At the same time, the Yugoslav Communist Alliance found itself competing in the republics with other parties, such as the 'Croatian Democratic Community' (HDZ), led by Tito's former comrade-in-arms and partisan leader, and later Croatian nationalist dissident, Franjo Tudjman.

Looking back at all of this is not just a matter of piecing together a sequence of events, but of trying to grasp what the basic issues were – and still are. What are the challenges for Europe in this region, and why are we unable to find satisfactory – and, above all, lasting – solutions to the problems which still need them? For example, the Serbian province of Kosovo, mainly inhabited by Albanians and currently administered by the UN, exemplifies the need to find a formula which will allow a mosaic of different ethnic and religious communities to live peacefully together.

What inconceivable horrors have war, concentration camps, targeted expulsion and even systematic rape and genocide brought back to Europe, just a few hundred kilometres from Athens, Rome and Vienna – indeed at the very point where circles radiating from those centres of European civilisation intersect? During the war in Bosnia, I often had to remind other Austrians that Mount Igman – repeatedly mentioned in the papers as the scene of fighting near Sarajevo – is barely further from Vienna than the ski-slopes on the Arlberg, and that Sarajevo is far closer than Zurich. The news from the 'former Yugoslavia' came as a special shock to Western Europe, content in its own prosperity and confidently believing in ever-lasting peace after the fall of the Berlin Wall. As Paul Garde, the French expert on Yugoslavia, put it: 'Because of the tragic events in the former Yugoslavia, "clash of civilisations" has replaced "end of history" as the dominant mood.'[2]

International law – or might as right?

Europe also had to make up its mind on a major point of international law. Did the principle of the right to self-determination apply to territories (the 'republics' and 'autonomous provinces' which had made up the former Yugoslavia) or peoples? The old Yugoslavia had been a state of many peoples; Slovenia apart, its constituent entities were mainly multi-ethnic. Serbs, for example, had been living in Croatia (or, more specifically, the Krajina and Baranja) since the Habsburgs first settled them on the 'military frontier' as a bulwark against the Ottomans. Conversely, Croatians, as well as Slav Muslims and Albanians, had been living in Serbia for centuries. The Vojvodina was a real ethnic jigsaw, with Hungarians, Croatians, Slovaks, even Ukrainians and, of course, Serbs. Parts of Macedonia and Montenegro were inhabited by Slav Muslims and Albanians; Macedonia and Kosovo had Turks as well. Bosnia and Herzegovina were 'classically' Yugoslav, with Bosnians (Slav Muslims), Serbs and Croatians.

The two Germanys had just been reunited in the Federal Republic, while the Soviet Union was fragmenting, and Slovak nationalists were preparing to split Czechoslovakia. In these circumstances, Europe's answer to the Croatians and Slovenes was bound to have broader international implications.

The Slovenes, Croatians, Macedonians and Bosnians were hopelessly at odds with the Serbs who, ignoring the administrative boundaries of the old Yugoslavia, were aiming at a greater Serbia. The international community, and also the European institutions, decided to champion the principle of 'inviolability of frontiers' (including internal frontiers in former federal states), while supporting the rights of minorities – which did not include the right to secede.

There was another question, a question still open today, which gets a separate answer in each case, usually after much soul-searching and delay: to what extent should the international community and the European institutions intervene when international humanitarian law has been seriously breached? In the early years of the conflict, Europeans were torn between two principles: respect for sovereignty (particularly when 'external aggression' appeared to be absent), and justified intervention to prevent or put a stop to human rights violations.

These questions were far from abstract. At the EU, first of the 12 and later the 15, they had a direct bearing on the decision to recognise (or not) the independence of Slovenia and Croatia. At NATO, and particularly between NATO and Russia, they later had a direct bearing on the decision to intervene (or not) in Bosnia, and mount air strikes on Yugoslavia during the Kosovan crisis. They provoked fundamental disagreements, and no one can claim that this was good for Europe, the Balkan peoples or indeed the cause of peace. Ultimately, it encouraged the 'if in doubt, use force' parties, and ensured that no uniform pressure could be applied in favour of peaceful solutions – and above all solutions which respected human rights.

The whole of Europe might (like Germany and Austria) have recognised Croatia and Slovenia, or it might have tried to keep Yugoslavia intact. Either way, there would have been a clear, concerted message to all the parties, and above all Belgrade: don't attack – negotiate. It is also probable, of course, that united action would have shown that Belgrade – or, more accurately, Milosevic and his allies (including non-Communist nationalists) – were not interested in preserving Yugoslavia, but were bent on creating greater Serbia. However, disunity and procrastination are always misread by those who believe that might (and/or determination) put them in the right.

The course of events was far more disastrous in Bosnia and Herzegovina than it had been in Slovenia (where there had simply been a few skirmishes between the federal Yugoslav and Slovene forces). An incredible free-for-all, in which each of the parties – Bosnians, Croatians and Serbs – was against all the others, led to appalling atrocities, barbaric destruction and frenzied, but also systematic killing. All the warring parties had their heroes and war criminals (often enough, they coincided). The Croatians and Serbs founded their own mini-states, Herzeg Bosna and Republika Srpska. Only the Bosniaks (Slav Muslims) stayed officially loyal to the joint state, although some of their leaders – partly propelled by events, partly tempted by the other communities' absence – did try to carve out a purely Bosnian state. On its own, this would have been quite as unworkable as the other two (although these were backed by Croatia and Serbia, their mother or kin states, and indeed took orders from them). History, and above all the conclusions of the Hague-based International Criminal Tribunal for the former Yugoslavia, will show us how evenly or unevenly guilt was divided between the various ethnic groups.

A painful new beginning

The former Yugoslav countries have come through in different ways and to differing extents. Slovenia, furthest to the north-west and also most prosperous, has obviously done the best. It was not affected by greater Serbian, greater Croatian or greater Albanian ambitions, had small, respected minorities, was in action only briefly against the federal army, and is now on the point of joining the EU. Croatia has repaired, or is repairing, most of the material damage – although the intangible damage is still a part of the post-Tudjman scene. Many of the Serbs who fled from Croatia to what remained of the former Yugoslavia have yet to return, and many of the Croatians who fled to Croatia from Bosnia are still in the country. Nonetheless, definite progress has been made, including progress on minorities. Croatia has now applied to join the EU, and stands a fair chance of being admitted with Bulgaria and Romania in 2007. For a long time, it looked as if Macedonia had escaped the Balkan maelstrom. Its main problems were with Greece, and concerned its name and flag, but the international community found the tongue-twisting title, 'former Yugoslav Republic of Macedonia', to save the day provisionally. In autumn 2001, however, fighting broke out between Albanian guerrillas and the mainly Slav republic.

Many critical observers in Bosnia and Herzegovina were pleased that the Dayton Agreement had put an end to the actual fighting, but also felt that it cynically underwrote the war gains and the ethnic cleansing. Gradually, however, people started to relearn the habits of peaceful co-existence, agreeing to let refugees vote in their home places, seeing the multi-ethnic authorities as something more than mere *ad hoc* bodies for the sharing out of (slender) resources, accepting the High Representative's dismissal of hard-line nationalists from public posts, and even going along with the Constitutional Court's ruling that all the country's three peoples were 'constituent' communities, not just of the state, but of its federated entities, the Bosnian-Croatian Federation and the Republika Srpska (even this has had a multi-ethnic government since early 2003). Minuses include the fact that (at least when this book was written) neither Radovan Karadzic nor Ratko Mladic, who bear the main guilt for most of the atrocities, have been brought before the Hague Tribunal. Karadzic is frequently sighted in the Republika Srpska, and is rumoured to have visited Montenegro repeatedly. SFOR is clearly unwilling to risk an arrest which is certain to be resisted violently (or do some of its people not want an arrest?). There are reports that Mladic, too, is frequently seen in Yugoslavia, and I was told, on a visit to The Hague, that he and other former Bosnian-Serb commanders, wanted on war-crime charges, are still drawing their Yugoslav army pensions.

Yugoslavia – or, more accurately, the remnants of this once mighty successor to the kingdom of the Serbs, Croats and Slovenes, founded in 1918 – was the slowest to improve. People took a long time to look past Milosevic's marshalling of nationalist forces in support of his greater Serbian dream and against supposed threats to the sacred soil of Serbia, and recognise his glaring failures. He had not been able to win either Krajina or Eastern Slavonia for Serbia. On the contrary, hundreds of thousands of Serbs had fled in panic from territories they had occupied for centuries. Nor had he been able to divide Bosnia with Croatia. The economy, too, had steadily declined, driving thousands of well-trained young people to leave. Even when he over-estimated the democracies' patience and applied a radical solution in Kosovo – the killing and expulsion of Albanians – the NATO bombings seemed to rally the people behind him. But 11 years after the Berlin Wall, his bastions fell when the people stormed them – first, by voting bravely against him, and then, when he tried to falsify the results, by taking to the streets in Belgrade.

In my office I have a framed letter, which the Yugoslav Consul General in Strasbourg was ordered to send me on 4 October 2000, protesting at my 'interference in the domestic affairs of Yugoslavia' (I had called for recognition of the true election results, and thus of Koštunica's victory). Milosevic resigned the following evening and, two days after that, Vojislav Koštunica was President! The process, of course, was far from finished. True, under its new democratic leadership, Yugoslavia returned rapidly to the UN and the OSCE. Similarly, in President Koštunica's presence, Foreign Minister Svilanovic handed me its application for Council of Europe membership on 8 November. But the real, hard work of democratisation was only beginning. Most of the other east European countries had an 11-year lead, and Belgrade now had to catch up. The necessary reforms were also impeded by the fact that the victorious DOS (Democratic Opposition of Serbia) was a rainbow coalition of small and tiny parties (essentially, indeed, citizen action groups), and needed to find a political identity, over and above opposition to Milosevic.

Another problem was the Federation's second republic, Monte-negro, which had already started to go its own way, and effectively cold-shouldered the new regime in Belgrade. President Djukanovic's reason for this was that Belgrade's institutions were formally based on Milosevic's amended constitution, which he had rejected. Moreover, President Koštunica and Prime Minister Djindjic were obliged to form a coalition with Milosevic's former allies (and Djukanovic's opponents) in Montenegro, since this was the only way of securing a workable government and parliament. The abortive presidential elections held in both Serbia and Montenegro at the end of 2002 showed that many democratic lessons had still to be learned. Only the future will show whether the founding of the State Union of Serbia and Montenegro early in 2003 has put an end to the uncertainty. The tragic murder of Zoran Djindjic in March 2003 was a sign that democracy and the rule of law are still threatened by organised crime and adherents of the old regime.

Ultimately, Yugoslavia's admission to the Council of Europe on 3 April 2003 was longer in coming than expected. The Parliamentary Assembly had given its green light at the end of September 2002, provided that the Serbian and Montenegrin parliaments approved the Constitutional

Charter of the new State Union – which they did only at the beginning of February 2003. The commitments which they had accepted – still as the Federal Republic of Yugoslavia – included 'continued, unlimited co-operation' with the International Criminal Tribunal for the former Yugoslavia in The Hague. Slobodan Milosevic had already been handed over, and the former Serbian President Milutinovic had appeared voluntarily before the tribunal in January 2003. The political leadership felt that this was sufficient proof of goodwill – particularly in view of the prominence of the accused. At the same time, the army's reluctance to surrender its 'own people' was clear from the fact that Mladic, the 'Vukovar three' and other military personnel had not been handed over. It hardly needs to be said, however, that one essential feature of a functioning democracy is total subjection of the armed forces to democratic, civilian control!

After the dramatic events of spring 1997, Albania, which came later to democracy than most of the other ex-Communist countries, did not hit the headlines again until 1999, when hundreds of thousands of refugees streamed over the border from Kosovo.

Even though there had been no major crises in the meantime, Albania remained a persistent cause of concern to the international community, and especially to Europe. Mismanagement, corruption and Mafia influence were all threats to the fragile plant of its democracy, as was the irreconcilable hostility between the political camps (typified by the endless, bitter contest between Fatos Nano and Sali Berisha), who thought in black/white terms, and for whom compromise seemed to be, not just a foreign word, but a wholly unknown concept. When the pyramid funds collapsed in 1997, the country teetered on the brink of chaos, and the Kalashnikov carried by every adult and even adolescent male seemed well on the way to replacing the mini-bunker as the national emblem. Even in 'quieter' times, however, reciprocal accusations of electoral fraud, corruption, and links with the Mafia were constantly flying back and forth. Another problem was the fact that the country's 'new' leaders – apart from a very few people, who had spent the Hoxha years in prison or re-education camps, e.g. Pjeter Arbnori, former parliamentary Speaker – had held senior positions or been otherwise privileged under the old regime, or were the children of people who had. A minister from a small conservative party, serving in a coalition government led by the Socialists (former Communists), felt obliged to warn me against an opposition politician from the Democratic Party. He told me that the man's father had been a high-ranking Communist and director of the Institute for the History of Marxism-Leninism. When I asked him how he knew, he explained that he knew because that same father had pushed him out of the job.

After Bosnia, the second great crisis in south-eastern Europe came in Kosovo. After Milosevic had taken away the region's autonomy in 1989, an Albanian shadow administration, with underground schools and a parallel health system, had emerged under a separately elected president, Ibrahim Rugova. For nearly a decade, the official Serbian administration and Rugova's shadow regime co-existed almost harmoniously. Increasingly, however, Rugova's patient, pacifist and democratic generation was challenged by a new one – aggressive, less patient and also more intolerant. Under the name UCK, or Kosovo Liberation Army, they not only felt able to take on the Serb occupying forces (as they saw them), but actively sought confrontation. In Milosevic and his special units, military and paramilitary, they found partners only too willing to join them in this ugly game. Starting in late 1997/early 1998, attacks and clashes increased, and the Serbs responded brutally, wiping out whole villages and clans. Eventually, 'helped' by Serbian massacres and atrocities, the conflict led to the expulsion of about one million people – half the province's population – and NATO's attacks on Yugoslavia and on Serbian-Yugoslav forces in Kosovo.

The UCK's warlike – and Rugova's peaceful – dream of an independent Kosovo was not to be realised. The Serbian yoke was indeed shaken off, but the province was taken over by UN administrators, who organised local and regional elections, set up provisional institutions of self-government, and gave those elected a part to play in running them. Having previously feared for the Albanian minority's welfare, the international community now has to try – often against considerable odds – to protect the remaining Serbs and their enclaves. In fact, hundreds of thousands of Serbs (also settled in Kosovo for centuries) fled to Serbia, Montenegro and Bosnia to escape the expected revenge of the Kosovan Albanians. Again, the international community finds itself facing the insoluble problem of reconciling opposites: the right to self-determination, and the Albanian majority's clear demand for independence, with the principle of territorial integrity and inviolability of frontiers. In short, south-eastern Europe remains a problem region.

Future prospects

This explains the presence in that region of all the institutions which are working for co-operation in Europe. One of them, of course, is the Council of Europe, which has had a liaison and programme office in Pristina, the capital, since August 1999. It also has a long-term presence in Sarajevo, Tirana and – since early 2001 – Belgrade. The OSCE, which plays a 'firefighting' role at times of crisis, is widely represented in the field: in eastern Slavonia, Bosnia, Macedonia, Albania, Kosovo before (a 'verification mission') and after the conflict, as well as southern Serbia and Belgrade itself. The UN is in Kosovo and, apart from the 'High Representative', was running projects of its own in Bosnia and Herzegovina until the end of 2002. The EU, too, has become increasingly involved, not only with economic and humanitarian aid programmes, but also via its Common Foreign and Security Policy (Solana's successful mediation missions in Macedonia and between Belgrade and Podgorica) and, above all, the 'Stability Pact for South-Eastern Europe'. The Pact, administered from 1999 by Bodo Hombach, former Minister in the German Chancellor's office, and since 2001 by Erhard Busek, former Austrian Vice-Chancellor, is intended to play an active role in promoting democracy, human rights, economic development and internal security. The Council of Europe is actively involved in the Pact and works with it on certain projects in the region.

The failures of the international and, above all, European communities, and also their undeniable successes, are nowhere more closely juxta-posed than they are in south-eastern Europe. This also applies to the Council of Europe, which has always been careful to tailor its ambitions to its actual capacities.

But the Council may also have been too starry-eyed in its dealings with Milosevic and his henchmen, when it initiated the procedure for admission of the Federal Socialist Republic of Yugoslavia in February 1990, regardless of inroads on the autonomy of Kosovo and the Vojvodina, and thus on minority rights. The picture which Yugoslavia presented at that time was admittedly very contradictory. However, the moment it was clear that the progressives and democrats (people like Milan Kučan in Slovenia and Stjepan Mesič in Croatia, who were later to play leading roles in the independent republics) were not going to win through, and that Serbia (with Montenegro still in tow) was totally in thrall to Milosevic and his wife, Mira Markovic, the Committee of Ministers suspended all co-operation with the Yugoslav authorities in October 1991, and the Parliamentary Assembly withdrew the Yugoslav Parliament's special guest status a month later. In September of the following year, the Committee of Ministers issued a statement, declaring that the Federal Socialist Republic of Yugoslavia had ceased to exist.

In retrospect, this all sounds logical. In reality, Europe found it very hard to reach any concerted decision on recognising Yugoslavia's independent successor states, or on reacting to the use of force in violation of international law and human rights. I could not, and cannot, avoid the impression that some states were so utterly surprised by the things that were happening in south-eastern Europe in 1991 that they simply put their clocks back to 1914 and 1918, and tried to start again at the very point where European policy had already gone wrong then. This lack of unity and direction also stopped the Council of Europe from playing a more active part. Apart from the Parliamentary Assembly, which was soon using very plain language indeed, the Council was forced back, by its own member states (or, more accurately, some of them) to the minimum role which its dedicated Secretariat refused to let anyone take from them: helping all the international agencies involved to work out new constitutional arrangements and, above all, promoting and encouraging civil society, and indeed enabling it to survive dictatorship. Particularly in the case of Yugoslavia, we reaped the benefits of keeping in touch with civil society and backing it actively, from October 2000 on, when we suddenly found our old NGO partners in leading political and ministerial positions.

It was not until NATO got involved, and the Dayton Agreement was signed, that the Council was given, at least partly, the job which its statutory role and expertise fitted it to do in Bosnia and Herzegovina. Long before that country joined the Council, it was using the European Convention on Human Rights as a yardstick, both for itself and for institutions like its Human Rights Chamber, Ombudsperson and Human Rights Commission. The Council helped to train judges, draft important laws and reform the school system, and it also took part in the conference on implementing the peace.

From the start, the Council and – again in the run-up to membership – its Parliamentary Assembly exerted a more powerful moral and practical influence on the progress of Slovenia, Croatia and the FYRO Macedonia[3] towards pluralist democracy, the rule of law and human rights. Later, membership of the Council, denoting compliance with rule of law and human rights standards, and symbolising admission to the European democratic family, made these countries receptive, like other members, to guidance, help and (when necessary) criticism from Strasbourg, and qualified them to co-operate in monitoring compliance with their own commitments.

Whenever the international community, or the institutions it works through, 'forget' the Council of Europe, the ill-effects are usually felt quickly. It was certainly a mistake, for example, that UN Security Council Resolution 1244 on Kosovo did not, like the Dayton Agreement, refer to the Human Rights Convention or involve the Council directly. Nonetheless, it worked from the start with the UNMIK administration in Kosovo and was given a number of special jobs to do by both Bernard Kouchner[4] and Michael Steiner.[5] A difficult one at present is working out a decentralisation plan for Kosovo.

Javier Solana, the EU High Representative for the Common Foreign and Security Policy, turned to the Council of Europe and its Venice

Commission ('Democracy through law') both in the FYRO Macedonia, where drafting and implementing the Ohrid framework agreement was the problem, and during the negotiations with Serbia and Montenegro on setting up a State Union of the two republics. Finally, the Council is also actively involved in the Stability Pact for South-Eastern Europe.

Faced with the prospect of 'never-ending conflicts', which were possible or latent in Kosovo, Macedonia and other parts of the region, the international community, chiefly under pressure from the EU, managed to come up in 1999 with this ambitious Stability Pact for South-Eastern Europe. This provides a framework for three linked 'working tables' which (following the Helsinki Final Act pattern) are to deal with democratisation, economics and security. Probably, the Helsinki link also explains why the Pact was placed 'under OSCE auspices', although this has no practical consequences. The Pact's first three years were a time of great hopes – and disappointments. Although relatively few of the promises made at starting have been kept, the Pact may have made south-eastern Europe more cohesive and helped it to realise the truth of the old saying: help yourself, and others will help you (perhaps). Today's buzzword is 'regional ownership' – let us hope that all the people who use it will actually do something about it.

South-eastern Europe, including the 'western Balkans', has a European future. Now that Serbia and Montenegro have joined, the whole region is formally within the Council of Europe, and its people are part of the 800 million-strong family gathered in its member states. With its 'stabilisation and association process', the EU has also reached out to them, and they are certainly anxious to follow their northern neighbours, Slovenia and Hungary, in joining. Indeed, Croatia applied for EU membership in February 2003.

When I said that the region was 'formally' within the Council of Europe, I used that term because of the unsolved problem of Kosovo, which is still excluded *de facto* – and will remain so unless Serbia and Montenegro's insistence on sovereignty and the Kosovan Albanians' desire for independence can be reconciled. This problem, like the problems of flawed reconciliation in Bosnia, co-existence in the FYRO Macedonia, and the need to consolidate democracy in Albania and the new State Union of Serbia and Montenegro may no longer be robbing us of sleep, but we cannot afford to relax until we are sure that, here too, there will be no turning back on the path to Europe.

Europe and the dream of democratic security

The Council of Europe's first Summit (Vienna, 1993), which I already saw from the sidelines, hammered out the concept of 'democratic security':

'The end of the division of Europe offers an historic opportunity to consolidate peace and stability on the continent. All our countries are committed to pluralist and parliamentary democracy, the indivisibility and universality of human rights, the rule of law and a common cultural heritage enriched by its diversity. Europe can thus become a vast area of democratic security.'[6] Following the end of ideological, political and economic division, 'democratic security' formed part of the effort to establish a new system of peace, security and stability in Europe. Various existing institutions have a part to play in sustaining this new system, which means that they must adjust to new tasks and support one another's efforts. The result will be a new, multidimensional European structure, covering not just the military, but also the human, economic, ecological, social, cultural, ethnic and political aspects of security. This structure will embrace the UN, NATO, the OSCE and the EU, as well as the Council of Europe. Democratic security itself is the Council of Europe's special responsibility, since it fully corresponds to its basic mission – to prevent armed conflicts by implementing its principles of pluralist democracy, the rule of law and human rights.

As it was in the Council's early days, 'democratic security' remains a vital part of any comprehensive approach to security. On the political plane, it complements military and economic security – although it actually determines all the other security and stability factors. In saying this, I am not claiming primacy for the Council of Europe, but merely stating a fact. World political developments since the end of the Second World War have confirmed the truth of this. The free world has learned that dictatorships, or rather dictators, are the least constant and reliable of partners.

The concept of democratic security applies both to security in inter-state relations, and to people's need for security within their own communities. It thus acknowledges a link between the destabilising effect of tensions within societies and traditional threats to inter-state security.

Partners only

The distinctive feature of a security system based on an area of democratic security is that it contains no foes, only partners. This is the great opportunity, and also the great challenge, which such a system offers. With the Second World War 59 years behind us, we western Europeans have had plenty of time to stop thinking in terms of 'enemies', but there are places in eastern and south-eastern Europe where the scars are still fresh. Armenia and Azerbaijan joined the Council of Europe together early in 2001 – the first new arrivals since I had taken over as Secretary General. As I have said earlier, they were still officially at war, and we hoped that membership would give them a new sense of partnership – and a basis for settling their dispute over Nagorno-Karabakh. Bosnia and Herzegovina was not allowed to join until 2002, i.e. until the Parliamentary Assembly and the Committee of Ministers were both satisfied that its three 'constituent' peoples were really prepared to work together. Similarly, democratic, post-Milosevic Yugoslavia's relations with its neighbours were an important factor in deciding whether it was ready for membership. For me personally, one little incident, which is not recorded in any official report on Yugoslavia or the western Balkans, was far more encouraging than a string of official declarations.

In April 2002, UNESCO had joined the Council of Europe in organising a conference on education in south-eastern Europe. Its Director General, Koïchiro Matsuura, had invited the delegates to lunch in the organisation's rooftop restaurant. It was a fine spring day, and aperitifs were served on the terrace, which gave us a superb view over the city to the Eiffel Tower and Montmartre. Three of the participants were standing together, chatting away happily in their own language and clearly getting on well: the Foreign Minister of Yugoslavia and the Deputy Foreign Ministers of Bosnia and Croatia.

In New York, Istanbul and Strasbourg I also had several opportunities to observe the personal friendship and real understanding which existed between the Greek Foreign Minister, George Papandreou, and his Turkish colleague, Ismael Sem. Nonetheless, the Cyprus conflict remains unresolved, 40 years after it started (in 1963, the Turkish representatives walked out of the island's joint institutions, when President Makarios curtailed the rights of the Turkish community) and 30 years after the Turkish invasion. Now at least, the representatives of the two communities are again talking face-to-face. The Presidents of Armenia and Azerbaijan meet too – and (as we recently heard) not just to discuss Nagorno-Karabakh. Opponents still, perhaps, but no longer enemies and already partners in many Council of Europe activities; this is how an idea begins to work, and how a dream of security gradually becomes an area of security.

These changes do not simply happen. A number of basic conditions must be satisfied first. In political terms, the basic condition of democratic security is that countries everywhere should commit themselves to implementing the principles of democracy, human rights and the rule of law. At the Council, this commitment is the subject of a guarantee based on reciprocity and institutionalised at European level. It gives every member state a say in monitoring the others' compliance with their commitments. And it gives each and every one of their people legal protection, based on supervision and control machinery. If the principles are violated, reparation must be made. The backbone of this system of guarantees is, alongside the Council of Europe's Statute, the European Convention on Human Rights.

But democratic security is also a process, involving a constant effort to make things better and rise to new challenges. A few basic aspects deserve highlighting here. First of all, democratic security creates trust between governments and peoples, and this becomes ever more important, as European co-operation intensifies and national frontiers are dismantled. Democratic security also guarantees individuals comparable political, social and economic conditions throughout the area it covers, and opens the way to fruitful transfrontier co-operation. It makes political processes and social change transparent, helping countries to react rapidly to negative trends and the tensions they generate. Civilian control of the military is another basic requirement. This was why the Council of Europe clearly could not accept the seizure of power in Greece by the colonels in 1967, and in Turkey by the army, in 1960 and again in 1980. The colonels only saved Greece from expulsion by withdrawing from the Council first, and Turkey – not least because of pressure exerted by the Strasbourg procedure – made a relatively rapid return to parliamentary democracy.

But citizens rightly expect democratic security to do more than 'simply' guarantee the basic conditions needed for democratic decision-making. It also provides a basis and framework for joint efforts to combat organised crime. Key factors here are vigilance, confidence that the measures and sanctions imposed are appropriate, mutual support and, last but not least, agreement on what terrorism – which must not be confused with the struggle for freedom – is, and on what should be done to prevent it. Long before 11 September 2001, the Council of Europe had provided the necessary instruments: the European Convention on the Suppression of Terrorism and various agreements on mutual aid in criminal proceedings.

Rule-of-law standards, and independence and efficiency of the courts, protect the interests of natives and foreigners equally, as well as their acquired rights and investments, i.e. their contribution to prosperity.

Quite as important, however, are joint efforts and co-operation to protect the community, to combat social exclusion and to promote social integration.

An open civil society – the best guarantee of democracy and human rights

However, the main lesson we learned around and after 1989–90 was that cultivating an open civil society at national and European level is vital. Politicians and the state cannot do everything unaided. At that time, it was the countries where civil society was strongest which made the transition from autocracy to democracy with least trouble – and where that transition will be hardest to reverse.

Finally, something must be said about the duty of solidarity, without which democratic security cannot function. For democracy, human rights and the rule of law to develop and be strengthened – particularly, but not solely, at times of transition and change – it is necessary that all the members of a like-minded international community should attend to the needs, problems and differences of others. This is why co-operation and support play an important part in keeping the system running properly. Both at the Council of Europe and, with the EU's Common Foreign and Security Policy, at 'inner European' level, this solidarity has become a reality in Europe today. It covers the 'Friends of Albania', just as it covers rebuilding aid for Bosnia, the numerous OSCE missions, the mainly Europe-backed international structures in Kosovo or Macedonia, etc. The Council of Europe has contributed comprehensively in all the reform states and conflict regions – and is still doing so.

Its co-operation and assistance programmes for the states of central and eastern Europe were set up in 1990, the aim being to back the open-door policy with practical measures. They are based on its principles, values and past work, and help the beneficiaries to integrate within European structures.

In countries on the waiting list for Council membership, the aim of the programmes is to develop democratic security. The first step here is to strengthen the democratic reforms which are essential for membership and for active participation in the European integration process. The emphasis lies on various aspects of the workings of a pluralist parliamentary democracy, which respects human rights and the rule of law.

The following points are covered: law-making, information and training in connection with democratic institutions at local, regional and national level; regulations and machinery to protect human rights; an operational legal system, guaranteeing fair, effective and independent justice; a strong and dynamic civil society, including NGOs and associations; plural, free and independent media; and an education and training system designed to produce enlightened and tolerant citizens, who know and respect their rights and duties as members of a democratic society.

Once states join the Council of Europe, attention focuses on consolidating democratic security, and helping them to fulfil their statutory duties. Increasingly, this involves consulting, and learning from, the countries which joined in the early 1990s.

We can be proud that these programmes have already been successfully concluded in numerous countries; as I noted earlier, 10 of them have now applied to join the EU – and have been able to do this because Council membership and the Council's assistance programmes have helped them to satisfy the 'Copenhagen criteria': democracy, the rule of law and respect for human rights.

Increasingly, the Council of Europe and the EU – natural partners on the path to European unity – are pooling their efforts to promote democratic security. They run joint programmes for Russia (on justice and federalism), for the three south Caucasian states and the Russian north Caucasus, for Ukraine and Moldova and, under the Stability Pact, south-eastern Europe too. They dovetail particularly well in cases where the EU's political weight and the Council's legal expertise need to be combined. Thus Council experts helped Javier Solana, Secretary General of the European Council, to implement the Framework Agreement on peace in Macedonia and also to draft the agreement between Serbia and Montenegro.

Human rights are central

Protecting human rights is, and will remain, the central element in democratic security. The Council of Europe's greatest achievement is undoubtedly the European Convention on Human Rights, and enlargement has added to its lustre, since it now applies to 800 million people. Never before have nationals and residents in 45 states been able to turn, when their basic rights are violated – even by their own authorities – to a supranational court, whose judgments are binding. The Convention also provides criteria for assessing democratic security, and Article 52 gives the Secretary General of the Council a powerful instrument in cases where he finds that application of the Convention (and thus democratic security) is endangered in a specific country. That article allows him or her to require any member state to make a statement on its application of the Convention. To my surprise, before I took office, no country had ever been asked to do that. When doubts arose concerning the proportionality of Russia's military action against the separatist regime in Chechnya, I not only protested (successfully) against an inhuman ultimatum served on the people of Grozny by the Russian army, but also called on the Russian Government to make an official statement under Article 52. This statement (twice improved at my demand) was the basis for the sending of Council of Europe human rights experts to Chechnya. I again used Article 52 against Moldova when, in the run-up to local elections, a parliamentary party was given a one-month 'suspension' for organising peaceful mass demonstrations, and threatened with a total ban. The suspension was annulled, but the statement was also forthcoming, and we used it to work out an assistance package.

Democratic security plays a special part in finding solutions to the problem of protecting national minorities. The reason for this is that action taken to promote it automatically helps to generate trust between different groups in the community and with the authorities. One of the negative developments immediately after 1989–90 was undoubtedly the eruption of nationality conflicts, previously denied by the Communists, which now began to threaten internal stability and also good neighbourly relations. Two Council of Europe instruments which originated at the Vienna Summit – the Framework Convention for the Protection of National Minorities and the European Charter of Regional or Minority Languages – have done much to defuse potential conflicts, and so promote democratic security. The Framework Convention (1995) has now been ratified by 35 member states, and signed by a further seven. Even before they joined the Council, Armenia, Azerbaijan, Bosnia and Herzegovina, and Yugoslavia had already accepted it. It is the first legal instrument in this field, and special machinery monitors its application.

Realising democratic security depends, above all, on the willingness and ability of Council of Europe member states to join in applying the principles of pluralist and parliamentary democracy, indivisibility and universality of human rights, and the rule of law, and refusing to tolerate violations. The Council itself has several forums and instruments for that very purpose.

Bringing all the states which have opted for democracy into the European area of democratic security is the key element in the action taken to extend it since the end of the East-West conflict. The Council's chief instrument in promoting respect for its principles is co-operation and political dialogue – between governments within the Committee of Ministers, its decision-making body, and between elected representatives within the Parliamentary Assembly and the Congress of Local and Regional Authorities of Europe, its two consultative bodies. Convention-based activities are the backbone of co-operation between governments, and the co-operation and assistance programmes were set up to help new member states to integrate within the European structures.

Member states' compliance with their commitments is monitored by supervisory machinery set up under the Statute and various European agreements (particularly the European Convention on Human Rights), and is also subject to political monitoring by the Committee of Ministers and the Parliamentary Assembly.

In the time which has passed since the Cold War ended and Hungary joined in 1990, the Council has largely completed its extension process, and is now the only pan-European political organisation, in which large countries like Russia and small ones like Liechtenstein both find places. Extension itself has done much to help create a large area of democratic security, since all member states are required to bring their institutions and laws into line with the principles of democracy, human rights and the rule of law.

Accession is prepared by political dialogue in the Committee of Ministers, and public debate in the Parliamentary Assembly, with high-ranking representatives of the candidate country. The Council's co-operation programmes serve the same purpose. Similarly, special guest status allows parliamentary delegations from candidate countries to play an active part in the Assembly's work even before their countries join.

Admission to the Council thus depends on progress with reform and is a step towards consolidating democratic security in the country concerned.

International co-operation at the Council is wide-ranging, and covers numerous legal, cultural, economic and social areas with a decisive bearing on democratic security. The nearly 200 European conventions and agreements which it has adopted, and the countless recommendations which it has issued, constitute an impressive body of harmonised norms, and legal and administrative procedures.

Some of its international, co-operative activities are particularly relevant to law-based democratic security. This obviously applies to its multilateral agreements on co-operation in preventing and punishing crime (deportation, mutual assistance, transfer of proceedings, execution of judgments, money laundering, etc) and – something which has recently acquired a new importance – action to ensure that anti-terrorist measures respect human rights.

Activities aimed at curbing racism, xenophobia, anti-Semitism and intolerance also help to consolidate democratic security. The European Commission against Racism and Intolerance monitors member states in this area and makes policy recommendations.

The European Committee for the Prevention of Torture and Inhuman or Degrading Treatment or Punishment has extensive powers to inspect prisons and police stations. For example, it visited Abdullah Öcalan on the island of Imrali after his arrest, and inspected the Russian internment camp for Chechen rebels at Chernokozovo as early as February 2000.

As well as updating its anti-terrorism convention and bringing in the world's first guidelines on protecting human rights in combating terrorism, the Council reacted to 11 September by intensifying its efforts to promote inter-religious and intercultural dialogue in co-operation with its partner organisations.

Monitoring compliance

Monitoring was introduced by the Parliamentary Assembly in 1993 as a way of verifying that new member states were respecting their statutory and specific obligations, and was extended in 1995 to all member states, old and new. The Monitoring Committee reports direct to the Assembly, which can make recommendations and proposals on improvements. It can punish defaulting countries by refusing to recognise their delegations' credentials or suspending their voting rights (as it did with Russia in 2000, because of events in Chechnya). If non-compliance persists, it may recommend that the Committee of Ministers expel the offender from the Council.

In addition to its monitoring procedure, the Assembly has a flexible range of measures it can take when democratic security in a member state is threatened. For example, on the day when it voted to admit Russia, it also decided – again because of the conflict in Chechnya – to set up an *ad hoc* committee (chaired by myself) to review the situation in that region.

In November 1994, the Committee of Ministers decided to set up its own political monitoring procedure, the aim again being to ensure that all the member states honour their statutory democratic, human rights and rule-of-law obligations. This procedure is based on constructive, confidential dialogue, and on intensified co-operation. While the Assembly's procedure targets selected countries, the Committee of Ministers picks out certain Council principles, and then verifies compliance in all the member states (which may, of course, involve looking more closely at some than others).

Much of the Council's work plays a significant part in creating and improving mutual understanding, tolerance and respect between different groups and cultures.

The increasing importance of minority problems (above all in central and eastern Europe, and in the Caucasus) has shown that traditional interstate co-operation is not enough in this area, and that targeted civil society initiatives, based on close co-operation with the communities concerned, are needed as well. This is the rationale for the programme of confidence-building measures, which the Council launched in 1993. This programme supports practical, grass-roots projects, involving people from different communities – which help to break down barriers, promote understanding and defuse tensions which might otherwise erupt in violent conflict. Media, education, youth affairs, local democracy and transfrontier co-operation are among the areas covered, and projects may take the form of radio or TV programmes, youth camps, information seminars, etc.

Since the mid-1990s, the Council has been running a special programme for democratic youth leaders. The main aim here is to transmit democratic know-how and skills in the fields of media, youth work, administration, politics and civil society. Many of the training seminars include modules on settling conflicts by political and peaceful means. The seminars themselves, and a network of former participants, help to consolidate democratic culture and security even in regions which are still a prey to conflict.

Most Europeans may not be aware of it, but the Council of Europe is actually playing a special part in helping to make 21st-century Europe secure. In fact, democratic security can be seen as a way of fire-proofing the common European home, and ensuring that all its materials are non-combustible. This does not mean, of course, that fires are completely impossible. In spite of the fact that democracies do not make war on one another, not all the Council's member states have found political solutions for conflicts smouldering internally or on the border with neighbouring countries.

Nonetheless, the Council of Europe does give governments, parliaments, local and regional authorities, civil society, and thus Europeans in general, a forum which they can use, first to prevent existing conflicts escalating, next to overcome them, and after that to meet new challenges.

The Council now has 45 member states with over 800 million inhabitants (only Belarus still chooses to remain outside the family). Since 1989, and since the Council opened its doors to central and eastern Europe and the Caucasus, its mission has become truly pan-European. The dream of everlasting peace in a united Europe has still to be fully realised, but the 'area of democratic security' has taken on a definite shape.[7]

And still I dream ...

On 1 April 2003 – truly a day of historic significance – I found myself standing, at the invitation of George Papandreou, Greek Foreign Minister and Chairman of the EU Council of Ministers, in the Stoa of Attalos, beside the agora in Athens, to witness the signing of the enlargement treaty, bringing ten new members into the EU. When they join in May 2004, over half the 47 nations in Europe will belong to the European Union, that special form of integration – that entity *sui generis*, between common internal market and political union.

After the Copenhagen Summit, I had already congratulated the states which had decided to go a step further on the path to integration – and so radically alter our continent's political architecture. The Council of Europe has given the 10 new members decisive assistance and, more particularly, has helped the eight new central and eastern European democracies to satisfy the EU's admission criteria. But does this mean that the 'European dream' has been dreamed to the end? That is a question which Europeans everywhere – and particularly Europeans like myself, who have taken on political responsibilities in Europe – should ask themselves.

I may make no friends in Brussels by saying this – but the 25-member Union is still 'incomplete'. Not just as a federal state (if it ever comes to deserve that title), but in almost every respect. Even if all the remaining candidates join, Europe will still remain larger than the EU. It is true that the microstates bordering on the EU, or embedded in EU member states (like Andorra, Liechtenstein, Monaco and San Marino, but also the Vatican), have links with it via the European Economic Area or customs and monetary unions, but they do not wish to join it.

Not everyone can join the EU – or wants to

Switzerland has decided by referendum not even to join the European Economic Area (EEA), and two referendums in Norway have already gone against the EU. There is no assuming, in other words, that everyone is queuing to get in. Indeed, people in some countries have not even been asked. But countries unable or unwilling to join are still part of Europe – and entitled to dream of 'one Europe'. There is nothing contradictory in this.

This is why I am convinced that deciding how the various elements in Europe – countries and institutions – are to fit together is the biggest challenge which the next few years will bring us (defining the Council of Europe's role within the new Europe will be part of it). In 1999, I had already chosen 'For a Europe of Partners' as my campaign slogan for the Secretary Generalship. Particularly at a time when the EU is growing, I believe we must not forget that Europe is indeed a Europe of partners – all of equal value and all with equal rights. What I do not want in Europe is the kind of situation that exists in the Americas, where one great power ultimately determines everything. We want no more superpowers in Europe. Even when they are nominally working together, superpowers never really trust, and are always trying – at least 'for safety's sake' – to outdo and outwit one another. We have been through all of that already – with terrible results for the people of Europe. It is a dream we have rejected for good.

Of course, people fall repeatedly for nationalist propaganda, being only too ready to think themselves 'better' than others. Somehow, however, history never allows them to enjoy their supposed superiority for long. On the contrary, the price of gullibility is usually extinction in the conflict which invariably follows.

This is why my great hope, my European dream, is that we may succeed in really getting all of Europe to work together towards goals which are those of its 800 million people – from the Azores in the Atlantic to Vladivostok on the Pacific, from Akureyi on the north coast of Iceland to Limassol on the south coast of Cyprus. But not under one government. I do not believe that power on this scale should be concentrated – or that it would last if it were. Here again, history teaches us that massive centralised power generates huge centrifugal forces – and that these inevitably find release in violence.

Where does the Council of Europe stand in an enlarged Europe?

No, 'one Europe' must stand together voluntarily, be open to compromise and defend those values which constitute its identity: democracy, the rule of law, human rights, cultural diversity based on shared heritage, social cohesion and solidarity with the weak. Without questioning the importance of economic co-operation (which undoubtedly contributes much to those goals), this brings us to the question of what the Council of Europe's role in 'one Europe' should be.

European society faces major challenges. The EU is enlarging to 25 states. More will join later. Others, as we have seen, do not want to. Others again will probably be unable to join in the next 10 to 20 years. And so there are many European states which will, for the time being, remain outside the EU.

New dividing lines must not be the result. There is only one Europe: a continent with over 800 million inhabitants, based on shared values – the Council of Europe's values. As soon as the EU Convention started work under Valéry Giscard d'Estaing, I suggested that the EU should make full use of the Council of Europe's instruments and institutions. I side with those members of the Convention who are thinking of the future, not just of the EU, but of Europe as a whole. Indeed, the texts adopted by the Convention are an invaluable intellectual and political source for people who think in those terms.

All of these considerations fed significantly into the report which Giscard submitted to the Copenhagen European Council in December 2002, and which spoke of a growing trend in favour of the EU's acceding to the European Convention on Human Rights. In fact, such accession is a vital necessity, which is why Giscard's final report for the Saloniki European Council at the end of June 2003 expressly recommended it.

I have already suggested that the EU, having taken over the Council of Europe's flag and anthem, should also take over the most basic of all its conventions. Having shared the symbols, it should also share the commitments. And I have suggested two further logical steps after that – EU accession to the European Cultural Convention and to the European Social Charter.

No need to invent – the Council exists

A major topic at the moment is the EU's policy on European states which are not entitled to membership, or do not want it at present. I would like to say clearly to all those involved: use the things that are there, the things that have proved themselves already! Devising new structures for co-operation and consultation would be a waste of time and effort. All the states of 'one Europe' are in the Council of Europe. Its Parliamentary Assembly and Committee of Ministers offer natural forums for political dialogue and co-operation – and, for over 50 years, have been proving their effectiveness.

New ideas are needed, however, on shaping our relations – which is why I suggested, in January 2003, that the Parliamentary Assembly should start exploring ways of granting the EU associate Council membership. The EU, of course, is not a state, and not an international organisation, but it is something more than a federation of states. Hallstein's phrase, 'incomplete federal state', is certainly not perfect, but it does contain a grain of truth, insofar as the EU has assumed rights and powers which otherwise belong to states alone. And however flawed the Common Foreign and Security Policy may be, it does exist, and plays at least a certain role in Europe, and even the world.

In these circumstances, international co-operation at the Council of Europe would itself be incomplete if it covered states only, and not the EU. The Council's Parliamentary Assembly and the EU's European Parliament, as well as the Council's Congress of Local and Regional Authorities of Europe and the EU's Committee of the Regions, have already paved the way by holding joint sessions and engaging in various forms of co-operation.

Another point to remember is that many of the problems we shall have to solve in future – international crime, terrorism, migration, bioethics, etc – cannot possibly be tackled by the enlarged EU, working on its own. All Europe, 'one Europe', must be involved. Indeed, there are many cases where our only hope of finding solutions will lie in co-operating with our friends outside Europe.

At global level too, and above all at the UN, the voice of all Europe needs to be heard. I spoke in the UN General Assembly in autumn 2000 and, in December 2002, it adopted – with an overwhelming majority – its third resolution on co-operation with the Council of Europe. Preceded by several weeks of discussion, this vote was clear proof of the importance which the international community attaches to our work. In particular, the Council's contribution to abolition of the death penalty and to the establishment of an international criminal tribunal was supported by all the European states without exception (and by Canada and Mexico, which have observer status in Strasbourg). Again thanks to the Council, a pan-European voice was also heard at the UN Summits on racism (Durban) and sustainable development (Johannesburg).

'One Europe' is facing a host of new challenges today. For one thing, the tragic events of 11 September 2001 have forced us, too, not just to confront security risks we had failed to see or had underestimated before, but to take a fresh look at a whole series of questions which our society still needs to answer.

Going for essentials

To meet the new challenges, the Council of Europe must focus on a number of priority areas in the years ahead. It cannot do everything. But it should do the things it can as well as possible.

Just before Christmas 2002 (the timing was certainly deliberate), we heard alarming reports that a cloned human being had been born. It makes no difference whether these were just a headline-grabbing stunt or all too appallingly true: the fact remains that there are insane 'Doctor Strangeloves' who are busily attempting to tamper with our human nature and dignity. It is up to Europe to decide how scientific progress and basic human values can be reconciled. Many more states must ratify the Council of Europe's Convention on Biomedicine and its Protocol, which bans cloning. This is the only instrument of its kind in the world – but it has to be used!

Today, we are all constantly at risk from renewed and savage acts of random terrorism. The Council has shown that these threats can be countered – without violating basic rights. The success of its guidelines for action against terrorism – known as the 'little brown book' at the UN – is proof yet again that Strasbourg can take the lead in meeting new needs.

Clandestine migration and associated problems, such as trafficking in human beings and people-smuggling, must be tackled. Trafficking in human beings is the modern form of slavery, and an affront to all the values for which the Council stands. We intend to conclude an agreement on action against this scourge of the 21st century, with the full support of our European partner organisations, such as the EU and the OSCE, and the relevant UN agencies in Europe.

The Council must work faster – and even better

In the early 1990s, after the fall of the Berlin Wall, the Council of Europe successfully reorganised its work to meet the new challenges. Today, at the opening of a new millennium, it again stands at the crossroads. It has the necessary know-how. It is meeting many of the new challenges already. But we need to work faster, and we need to get more tangible results.

We need more vision, more political leadership, more motivation 'at the top'. Our heads of state and government will have to think deeply about Europe's future – and the future of its oldest and only pan-European organisation.

If anyone still doubts that the Council has a future, my answer is a clear one: its future is 'one Europe', united, under the blue flag with its 12 gold stars, by freedom, pluralist democracy and the rule of law – a Europe of human rights and social cohesion, with a shared cultural and natural heritage, which we must transmit intact to future generations.

My European dream is pragmatic – and visionary too. Neither empty slogans nor institutional bureaucracy must sap Europe's vitality. The Europe I dream of is:

- an undivided Europe with shared values and a shared cultural heritage;
- a Europe free of coercion and tutelage;
- a Europe of willing co-operation;
- a Europe of partners, where the problems of one are the problems of all;
- a Europe of social solidarity; and
- a Europe of democratic security.

NOTES:

1. From May to November 2000.
2. Francis Fukuyama's *The End of History* celebrates the definitive triumph of 'western' values after the fall of the Berlin Wall and the end of the Cold War. Samuel P. Huntington's *The Clash of Civilisations* sees most contemporary conflicts as conflicts between different cultures and religions.
3. I find the country's internationally 'correct' name equally objectionable in English ('The Former Yugoslav Republic of Macedonia') and German ('Die Frühere Jugoslawische Republik Mazedonien'). 'FYROM', which many people use to avoid the longer form, is both ugly and wrong. That is why I have taken to abbreviating the first part, while pronouncing the name of the country in full.
4. First Special Representative of the UN Secretary General in Kosovo, 1999–2001, founder of Médecins sans Frontières and former French Minister of Health
5. Special Representative of the UN Secretary General since 2002, former diplomatic adviser to the Federal German Chancellor, Gerhard Schröder.
6. Vienna Declaration, Council of Europe Summit, Vienna, 9 October 1993.
7. This section is largely based on 'The Concept of Democratic Security and its Implementation by the Council of Europe' by Hans-Peter Furrer and Jutta Gutzkow, which appeared in the *Romanian Journal of International Affairs*, Vol. II, No. 3/1996, special issue.